GW01424377

THE WHITE ABORIGINE

by Gerald K Walshe

CHAPTER ONE.

August of 1926 was a bad time for southerly busters. These are the fierce icy winds which whip straight off the Antarctic snow fields and travel northward without any impediment. Arriving immediately after winter in the Southern Hemisphere, these weather phenomena bring cold, miserable conditions to all who don't have adequate protection and shelter.

In Melbourne of that year, the southerlies came with all their traditional ferocity and chill and, into this atmosphere, I was born to a woman who was not married to my natural father.

On top of this factor, my mother's family, being very strict and self-righteous Roman Catholic believers, shunned their own daughter and thus condemned me to a life without the warmth and love of normal family relationships. This ostracism was something that I would have to deal with throughout my entire life.

Along the way however, I would meet and be cared for by others who were not blood relations but, thankfully, who felt my pain and took steps to lessen that pain and show me the love that was not forthcoming from my own kin.

The fact of my illegitimate birth also had a profound effect upon other members of the family, some of whom I was unfairly accused of harming but, at every stage, I was to be treated as the 'poor relation'. The fact of my birth was, to these family members, a situation which was totally unacceptable to the stiff-necked, upright and dogmatic people who lived a faultless and strict moral and virtuous life as deemed correct by the teachings of the Catholic Church.

These teachings were strictly followed by my mother's family although my mother, Verna had created a situation which ran contra to the puritanical beliefs of the family. She had breached the family code

1

of behaviour, she had crossed the line and, by committing adultery had, in the eyes of the Church, committed a mortal sin. The Church forbad any woman from giving birth to a child out of wedlock. Not that abortion was an option either.

The teachings of the Church may be so but, there is no reference to this in the Bible.

As a result of being the product of the lustful act of my mother, I was to suffer the consequences all my life. I was never accepted as part of the family and was made to feel unwanted by all. This I was to discover some seven years later when my mother and I returned to Melbourne after the death of my 'father' away on the plains of north-western New South Wales. Even at this tender age I had lived a full life from the age of about four months with the Lieillwan people, an aboriginal clan at Pokataroo on the banks of the Barwon River near Collarenebri.

I had experienced what it was like to be on the lowest rung of the ladder in white society and always felt that this was the way that white folk treated black people; this was their normal relationship to each other and just a way of life.

Although Verna had been married at the time, she was not married to my natural father. Her husband had walked out on her family over twelve months prior and left her with three other children, a boy and two girls. When she realised her position, she was devastated. Having nobody else to turn to for advice, she went to the only person she thought could help her — her own mother — seeking some sound advice.

What her mother said at this point when asked for help really shocked Verna. They were words she hardly expected to hear from her own mother who said," I have been watching you and your marriage for some time, my girl and the many men you have associated with over the years. I knew it was just a matter of time before your marriage failed. Well, now that it's happened, I have to say I'm surprised it lasted this long. Your husband has been very tolerant but, with that said, of course I will help you.

"You are, after all my daughter but, I must warn you, what I am about to say, you will not like at all. However, I feel that you will accept my proposal as you don't have much choice and, you cannot continue without support.

"As I see it, the only way forward for you and your family is to accept this advice."

The old lady strutted to the far side of the small room and glared at Verna.

2

"Regarding your son, David, I am quite prepared to take him and raise him as my own son. There is, however, a catch; before this can happen, you must sign a legal paper to that effect, that he is no longer your son and, from this day forward you will have no further contact with him. I will bring him up in my family as a brother to Thelma, my daughter and your step-sister.

"Do you agree to this arrangement?"

As my mother realised she had no choice, she nodded agreement.

"What about the girls?" Verna asked, tears welling in her grey-blue eyes.

My grandmother's mood changed immediately.

"I'm afraid they will have to go to the Catholic Orphanage in Geelong."

"No! Not that!" cried Verna.

"Don't be silly!" scolded the old lady. "It's already been arranged with the local parish priest. He can organise to have them taken into the Convent Orphanage for ten years. You should be grateful that there are people who will help you in time of need."

Verna sobbed convulsively, not for the future of her two girls but for the fact of the result of her promiscuity. She cried for the disclosure of her sins and the impotence she felt in her present position. Not having much choice, she signed the papers which meant that the girls would spend the next ten years being housed and schooled at Geelong Convent Orphanage.

Later at home, my grandmother told my mother that she was now free and could continue with her life.

"You are only twenty-one years old, you are beautiful so you should make the most of what you have."

Thereafter, my mother and a very kind fellow named Ken lived together for some three months but were very lonely. Verna's family would not have anything to do with them and Ken's family were far away in Queensland where he had grown up on the land. They both decided to leave Melbourne and move closer to his family in southern Queensland. To start a new life where nobody knew them.

They read the 'jobs vacant' ads every week until they found what they were looking for — a sheep station on the Barwon River at Pokataroo named "Trelawney" wanted a cook cum housekeeper and a boundary rider. As my 'father', Ken Carr had worked in the area before going to Melbourne and was known in the district, they applied for the positions and were accepted.

Thus, at the tender age of three months I was to begin a new life on the harsh, hot, black soil plains of north-western New South Wales. This would last more than five years and. although very different from circumstances prior, turned out to be the happiest years of my childhood as I had so many 'aunties and uncles and cousins' to look after me and play with. It was indeed a very large family and the only family I was to know at that very early age.

It all came to a sudden end when, years later, I was taken from them back to my mother and father who, to me, were complete strangers.

When we arrived at Trelawney Station, Verna was very impressed for two reasons; this new place was to be the start of a new life and, she was finally away from the family who had disowned her for the indiscretion of my birth.

She liked the squatter and his wife and their two children. Best of all she loved the big beautiful homestead with its giant gum trees that sheltered it from the hot sun and kept it cool. Inside the house the kitchen was very big with cupboards filled to capacity with provisions.

This was, indeed, a cook's kitchen and to help her run the house, Verna had the assistance of four young Aboriginal girls — two domestic servants and two kitchen hands.

For the first two weeks, all went well. Verna had been accepted as the housekeeper and cook. Ken worked as a jackaroo however, my mother had one other job and that was to look after me as I had to be with her all the time. Feeding times were regular and she seemed to handle this alright until one morning after breakfast, the lady of the house summoned Verna to the parlour.

This was a beautiful, cool room in the centre of the house and was only used by the squatter's family. My mother wondered what could be wrong.

The squatter's wife began," Last night I was looking through your application for this position and discovered that you failed to mention anything about your new-born baby. You only mentioned that you were married. Regarding this position, I feel myself that a hot kitchen is no place for a new-born baby day after day. There is also the question of hygiene being a problem.

"I hasten to add that I am very satisfied with you in the position you hold and would be very sad if anything was to alter the situation. I will leave this for you to solve and ask you to report back to me within one week's time to discuss what you have done about the matter.

"You may return to your duties, thank you."

My mother returned to the kitchen very upset and not knowing what to do. She sat very quietly trying to think of a remedy but could not see any way out. The two girls in the kitchen noticed how quiet my mother was and thought that what had been said at the meeting must have concerned them. This worried them both and they asked Verna if they had done something wrong to upset her.

"No," she answered. "You have both been very good. It is something I have done and I have to find a way out of this mess which I think will be very difficult mainly because I have nobody close that I can discuss it with. My husband is not here and I have to give my answer in a few days to the 'Missus'."

The girls asked if they could help. My mother decided to confide in them so she told them all that was said at the meeting. The girls listened intently and offered their sympathy but said no more and went back to work.

Later, they started to talk very seriously to each other and, after their conversation ended, went to my mother and said they thought they could help.

"We will talk to the elders of our clan when we return to the river tonight and let you know in the morning if we can help or not."

Verna thanked them politely. "I sincerely hope you can,"she said.

My mother did not sleep that night, thinking about the serious problem she faced and wondering if an answer could be found. Losing her position and having to return to Melbourne to the same life she'd left a few weeks prior frightened her. The only hope she had was that the Aboriginal girls could find a solution. She prayed that they would have good news for her in the morning as this would be her last chance.

In the kitchen next morning she was very anxious as she prepared breakfast for the squatter's family. She watched out for the return of the two girls who arrived looking very excited but didn't say anything until breakfast was over and the dishes cleared away.

After what seemed like hours had passed, Verna and the girls sat down to talk. The girls said they always thought that the people of the river would help if they could. When they returned to the river camp that night they had asked to speak to the Council of Elders on a very important matter.

The Council of Elders gathered and called the girls to explain what the very important matter was. They listened with interest to the girls then they spoke among themselves.

"Please bring Yurana to us."

Yurana was a mission girl of the Lieillwan tribe and had been educated at the Aboriginal Inland Mission. She spoke perfect English and, at 19 years, she had recently given birth to a baby girl whom she was breast feeding.

The Elders asked Yurana if she would be willing to look after another child.

"Which child?" she asked.

"A white child, a little boy of four months. You will be required to pick him up in the mornings and return him to the house in the evenings."

She considered the proposition a moment only.

"For how long will I have this responsibility?" she asked.

The Council of Elders fell silent then,"Maybe for a long time. Before you answer, you should think seriously about how you will breast feed two babies as both are only a few months old. Do you have enough milk in your maneroos for both?"

Almost without hesitation Yurana replied," Yes, I will take the baby boy and, yes, I do have enough milk in my maneroos for both babies."

With this answer the Council turned to the girls from the homestead and said, "You have heard the answer. This arrangement is acceptable to us but, two things must be done before it can begin. Firstly, a payment of provisions each month must be agreed to. A list will be given to the girls for delivery and, secondly, a piece of paper must be signed by the boy's mother giving permission for the baby to be fed by Yurana while in her care.

"When both these conditions are fulfilled and papers signed by the Council of Elders, the baby boy can be brought here to the river camp by Yurana."

When my mother heard this news she couldn't believe her luck. She was most grateful to the Aboriginal people, the clan who lived down by the Barwon River. This was the answer to all her prayers. She could now get rid of me — the child she never wanted, an embarassing mistake in her otherwise enjoyable life. She would now be free with no restrictions during the day. Her job was now secure and her new life here at Pokataroo would not be threatened with the prospect of having to return to Victoria.

With that life now behind her she could look forward to a rosy future. She then remarked to the girls that this was the best thing that could have happened to her and she would be grateful to them forever for their help.

Verna agreed to the demands of the Council of Elders and made out the two sets of papers to deal with the situation, signed them and handed them back to the girls to return to the Council of Elders at the river. She reminded them that the baby would be ready to be picked up in the morning.

After this was done, my mother went to see the squatter's wife and told her what had been decided. She asked that provisions which were demanded for payment could be taken out of her wages. The lady of the house said that this could be arranged.

"However," she went on,"Do you honestly think this is the right thing to do? You know nothing about these people or how they live. They are natives of this land and not like us at all. You must also consider how your baby will feel when he is old enough to realise where, and by whom he was raised."

Verna answered,"I'm sure I have done the right thing for my son. As regards myself, this is the only way for me to go forward. I had to sacrifice something otherwise I could not have stayed here. I can only hope that he will understand when he is older."

The squatter's wife's face went quite solemn.

"Well, there's also another thing to consider. As he will be away from you all day every day, how is he going to be fed?'

My mother replied," There's a native girl called Yurana who's currently nursing a baby girl of two months and has agreed to feed my Gerald as well."

The squatter's wife was taken aback. "You mean to say that this Aboriginal woman will give her milk to your child?"

"Yes." Verna replied simply.

The other woman stopped and gave my mother a strange look. "You mean to say that this native woman is going to feed your own son?"

"Yes. You see, I don't have any choice, really." Verna felt weak.

"Well," said the squatter's wife indignantly, "That sort of arrangement would never suit me."

"Unfortunately, this is the only way that I can remain at 'Trelawney' station, otherwise I would have to take my baby and leave. I couldn't do that."

"Well, since this is your own choice, I will say no more. I can only hope that in future you will have no regrets about your decision. But, may I add, I am delighted that you are staying and, I know you will handle the busy time that is coming up with ease. You haven't been here during the shearing season so you're in for a bit of a surprise. It's really something to behold."

CHAPTER TWO

The following morning the two aboriginal girls arrived at the homestead early. They were very happy and Yurana was with them. Of course, I was ready in my pram outside the door of the kitchen. Verna came out to meet the girl who was to look after and feed me. She took Yurana to one side and spoke to her for quite some time then returned to the pram and said to Yurana, "Well, there is my baby. He is now your baby. I hope you get on well together."

Yurana picked me up from the pram, a wide grin on her face.

"I will love him as my own, Missus. You'll see."

Then, still carrying me and pushing the empty pram, she walked away toward the river. At the time I was not old enough to remember the event nor how this moment would affect the rest of my life however, much later I did realise that although I desperately wanted to be part of Yurana, this could never be. I could never be of her flesh or her blood but, because of the circumstances we were both in at the time, I will always carry within my heart a part of her and will, forever, be bonded to her and the Aboriginal people.

On the second day in Yurana's care, we were returning to the homestead in the afternoon. My mother met us at the kitchen door looking grim. She had been told that a few things were going to change around here and I was to be returned, not to the grand homestead where Verna and Ken had accommodation in the guest suite but to the original, old house. This was to be my mother's new dwelling which was a long way from the homestead.

The squatter's wife had mentioned when we first arrived that the guest quarters were needed for friends and relatives so our accommodation was only temporary there. It was thought that the old house would be better than the shearers' quarters

When Verna first set eyes on the old house she wondered how long it would take her to clean it up. It hadn't been lived in for a long time and, although it was quite solid and dry outside, it needed a lot of attention inside. She couldn't believe the squatter's wife could do this to her. It seemed to have been a very quick decision to make — overnight in fact.

The thought did occur to her that the Squatter's wife might actually be frightened about having half the tribe from the river walk back to the house every afternoon when I was brought back. This would never do! What would people think, having Aborigines around the lovely homestead every day? They were on the lowest rung of society here in the bush while the squatter sat on the highest!

After thinking about this, Verna decided to accept what was offered since she again had no choice. So she went back to the old place for a closer inspection. The outside needed a rake and a good sweep with a broom to clean it up. The gutters were full of leaves but the roof looked alright. Inside was a different story.

She couldn't believe the house had dirt floors — no floorboards at all! Well, she thought, this was to be expected as she had been told the house was built in 1880. She was also told to expect the beds to be high off the floor on wooden logs. The reason for this was that snakes were known to enter the building at night and lie on the cool floor. By morning they were gone! Mother was not very impressed.

There was a door you could see through and there were windows but, no running water. There was a half-size tank outside the kitchen door and a wood-burning stove in the kitchen. This was only a small cooker but in very good condition. Mother went round the house looking at the tall gum trees. At least they would shade the house from the sun and keep the place cool during the day.

My mother and father resolved to tidy up the house before moving in. Verna insisted that all doors and windows etc should be sealed against the entry of snakes at night. After the first night, everything that Ken had done to prevent snakes from entering the house had proved successful. My mother was now quite happy to stay in the old place.

The boss's wife visited them and was impressed with what they had done to the house and mostly that they had accepted the situation they were in and made the best of it. The very next morning after Ken had left for work, the squatter's wife asked Verna if she would be interested in becoming her companion. This was something of a promotion and she would be known as housekeeper/companion. It also meant that she would accompany the lady to social events round the district and in town and become part of the social set.

In time she would become well known in the area and, being a very pretty woman, was very popular with the district squatters' sons. This suited her fine; she could again be the centre of attention.

By the end of the second week in this old house there was one other item that needed sorting and which came to all concerned as a complete shock. Verna decided that it would be better for me to stay with Yurana full-time. No reason was given; she simply asked Yurana to convey the news to the Council of Elders and request their advice but with the sweetener that she would increase the amount of provisions to the clan each month to cover the extra time.

The next morning Yurana brought back the answer from the Council of Elders. They had accepted Verna's proposal and the list of extra provisions was given to my mother. Thus, without even knowing it, I became a full-time resident of the Pokataroo (wide river) clan, living in their bark and shingle huts on the banks of the river. This was to be my home for quite some time.

Verna and Ken did visit me from time to time over the next few months but, at my age then, I do not remember them doing so. Besides which I thought of Yurana as my mother and those who surrounded me at the river camp were my family. This was my home and the only home I would remember of my childhood at Pokataroo.

One day, when Ken had been away at the far side of the property for three days, he returned to find a note to say that Verna would not be home as she had gone with the squatter's wife to a meeting of the Country Women's Association. He was far from being impressed, in fact he was quite angry. The note also went on -"I am to be accepted as a member and, as you can see, this meeting is very important to me."

Ken realised two things about my mother; she only ever thought of herself and she was a liar. He'd caught her out many times and, as she loved men, what happened in town that night would remain her secret. He knew that what he would be told in the morning would not be true but, without proof, he would have to accept this lie.

She was very good at lying.

"I will stay in town tonight and return in the morning." she wrote.

After reading this my father decided that he must get a job closer to the homestead so he could keep a closer eye on her. As the shearing season was about to start, he decided to approach the boss for a job shearing. The boss could hardly refuse him as Ken was known as a 'gun shearer'.

My father was born into a family of shearers. His grandfather and his father were 'gun shearers' in their time. Ken had begun working in sheds as a tar boy back in his youth. He had a pot of tar and a stick. When a shearer nicked a sheep and made it bleed Ken would dab some tar on the cut to stop it from bleeding. He graduated to roustabout which entails picking up everything and do anything required around the shed.

From this humble beginning he went on to become a 'gun shearer' in southern Queensland and was experienced on all types of sheep such as big Australian Peppin merino. Peppin wethers being large framed and densely fleeced left the strongest men exhausted. Then there were the American Vermonts with their wrinkled skin — the most commonly found sheep on outback stations. They were extremely difficult to shear.

After presenting his qualifications to the boss, he got his job shearing.

CHAPTER THREE.

While all this was going on at the homestead I was growing up with Yurana. I was now at an age when I could understand what was going on around me. Yurana told me many stories about Aboriginal people — some cruel and some sad stories but some were happy.

One day I asked her,"Do all Aboriginal people live like us?"

"No," she said,"Most are not so lucky to live by a fast-running river. They live in what is known as Yumbas or fringe camps on the outskirts of white townships. Aboriginal folk build housing from whatever materials they can find and dig their own pit toilets."

Due to the way in which these people were forced to live, the mortality rate of new-born babies was very high. Many babies died from malnutrition due to neglect. The squalor in these camps was well known among Aboriginal clans.

Yurana told me about her people and that the basis of all Aboriginal life was belief in the Dreaming Time. It was believed that during this time, great spiritual beings formed the landscape and, for all tribes, established the origins for the emergence and production of humans, plants and animals. They also laid down the way of life that Aboriginal people were to follow and adhere to for the rest of their lives, a very sacred system.

The Dreaming Time spirits stated and decreed that the blood of each tribe must remain pure; it cannot be mixed so that all people within a tribe must marry particular relatives. To marry people of another tribe would not be acceptable. All children produced by these people would have to be born on the land belonging to the tribe. This would ensure they had an inheritance and they would follow the culture and laws laid down by the spirits. Then they would be responsible as all tribes are expected to follow these laws and the passing-on of their inheritance of the land to future generations.

Aboriginal people have been instructed — and they firmly believe — that they are the custodians of the land they live on and of all things that are in that land. They believe their ancestor spirits have been transformed into everything they see around them — animals, birds, reptiles, frogs, stones, trees, rivers, mountains, hills and any other forms on the land.

This belief also applies to the sky, the stars and other celestial bodies that can be seen with the naked eye.

The Aboriginal people knew that this land was their land and that laws which applied to the land were and always would be Aboriginal laws under which the land was not for sale and could not be bought by anyone.

'We, the Aborigines, have been appointed by the Spirits to be custodians of the land forever and white occupation is unacceptable under our law.'

The Aboriginal people who were forced to live miserable and uncertain lives on the fringes of white settlements continued to resist the encroachment of their land. They resisted mixing with whites because of the contracting of diseases that decimated their numbers, hastening de-tribalisation.

This practice was actually encouraged by the Government of the day. Having children of mixed blood caused many problems within tribes as this went against the laws of the Spirit People. 'Only babies of full blood Aborigines born on the land to which the parents belonged could be accepted into the tribe.' Co-habitation with white folk or members of other tribes which then produced children of mixed blood, whether tribal or not, would not be accepted into the tribe.

As a result, such children would be cast out of the tribe.

The people of the Lieillwan tribe of Yurana (my Aboriginal mother) had three words to cover the mixed blood problem — "Do Wanna Nanarabi" This translated as 'You are not of my meat!' so you can never be accepted as a member of this tribe.

As this applied to me there were many things I was not allowed to do under the strict laws of the tribes. We were never let forget that the mixing of blood was forbidden; clan heritage is followed through the male line.

I could never belong to a local descent group having white blood; I had no affiliations with the clan and therefore had no rights to forage on the land. I was restricted from use of fighting sticks or digging sticks which were used extensively to dig for subterranean roots and tubers or digging out the burrows of rodents and reptiles. These sticks were also used to remove bark from trees for shelters or making other wooden utensils and preparing ground ovens for cooking as well as opening termite mounds or prising open bee hives to collect wild honey and knock down fruit from trees. Wooden dishes, large and small, were also used for digging.

Yurana told me other interesting stories about Ballanda, the Dreaming Time before man was created and the spirit people when Nyalod the Rainbow Serpent travelled across the land and formed all the rivers. To do this he became a rainbow to get from place to place easily.

She told of Baiame the Dreaming Time creator and the many stories he told when he and the other spirits created the land after which they all blended back into the landscape where they all are today.

Another story which caught my attention was the story about a duck called Gayga and a water rat named Bigoon. The water rat took the duck by force to be his wife and kept her in his hole on the river bank. As time passed all the other mother ducks on the river had little baby ducks; Gayga also had two babies.

When the other mother ducks saw Gayga's babies they made a terrible fuss and called out "You devil! They are so ugly."

The babies had the bill of a duck and the webbed feet of a duck but, not just two feet like a duck but four feet like a rat. Their bodies were not covered in feathers but in beautiful silver-grey fur. Gayga loved her babies and rightly so because she and Bigoon had created the first platypus.

We were also told by Yurana about the favorite foods of Aboriginal people and what they had eaten in the early days. The menu included lizards, small marsupials, rodents, kangaroos, wallabies, magpie geese, birds, yabbies, mussels from the rivers, bogong moths (Agrotis infusa), witchetty grubs (Cossi daisp), green ants (Oecophylla smaragoina), honey ants (Melophoruspy) and the many by-products of insects such as honey sugar-bag and bloodwood apples or tree gall.

Animals would be cooked in the hot ashes of a fire. The distribution of the meat was then a most important part of the meal ceremony and was determined by the elders and hunters of the tribe. Generally, specific parts went to elders, initiates, pregnant women and children.

Grass seeds were gathered and ground up to make damper. Some plant groups contain seeds that are toxic although they contain abundant hydrocarbons but had to be prepared in a specific manner to avoid the poisons.

Two methods were used by the women. The first method was to grind the seeds then place the flour in a natural bag in running water for several days to leach the poisons from the mixture. The second method involved placing the ground seeds in a bag in still waters for about a month or two allowing the mix to ferment. Both methods depended on the availability of running water to the tribe.

CHAPTER FOUR.

Early each morning all the young Jarjums or children would go to the track with the older kids to wait for the bus from the Aboriginal Inland Mission to take them to school. Black children, of course, could not attend the white school. Strictly not allowed.

After they had gone, we all returned to the cool sand by the river where the dubays or women would watch us play. My tita or sister, Adori was with me all the time; also my friends Mura and Tjaka. My life at this age, about 2 or 3 years, was a very happy one. I had all the people I loved around me.

To say that we were playing is not exactly true as we were learning to survive in this harsh land. For instance we were taught which parts of a kangaroo or wallaby we could eat and which parts we could not; the liver is poisonous and can kill if eaten.

We learned how to track animals, rodents, lizards, birds etc by the marks they left on the ground. We had instruction in finding edible fruit from bushes and trees and to avoid the ones we could not eat. We also learned how to use various native plants for medical purposes such as native pennyroyal, caustic bush, pituri, caustic creeper, flowering dysentry bush, fruit salad plant and many other flora and fauna concerning survival. All these things had to be taught to Aboriginal children at an early age.

In the afternoon when the children came home from school, we would meet them at the bus on the track. Then all the boys would go and find some bait for fishing. We would dig for mulli-grubs and worms. The bigger boys would get out their fishing lines and we all would go down to the edge of the river where the big red-river gums stood, their roots sticking out of the water like a giant spider standing up on its legs.

Everyone would sit down on the roots and let down the lines into the water between the roots. This place was known as the Orana — the home of the perch. These fish would hide in the shadows created by the roots of the tree, we were told, because it was cool and quiet and safe, but, not safe enough it seems as we caught lots of fish at this time. In this way we fed many families as was the custom of the Aboriginal people — everything must be shared and, by doing so, it made many folk happy including those who caught the fish.

One day I was moved to ask some questions of Yurana. This came about because the previous night when we were all sitting round the campfire, I decided to sit next to Nyathung, the Grandfather, who was a tribal elder. He pushed me away saying "Do wana nanarabi" meaning "You are not of my meat."

At the time I didn't understand what he said and, in the morning I had to ask Yurana what he meant. She answered with a question; "Do you remember the day we went out in the bush on the other side of Colly (Collarenebri) to visit an old Aboriginal woman who was not of my colour but white just like you?"

"Yes," I answered. "But she had pink eyes."

"That's right," said Yurana. "That type of person is called an albino, a throw-back from the dreaming time and a mistake of nature. Her being white is a mistake but, she is as Aboriginal as me or Nyathung. Now you, on the other hand, are different and, although I have reared you from a baby, you are not Aboriginal and can never be one of us.

"You are a white boy, you have a white mother and she will one day come and collect you from me. What my father said to you was quite true. He spoke in his tongue but said "You are not of my meat!"

"This means that you can never belong to his tribe and some day you must return from where you came."

After Yurana told me what Nyathung's words meant, I did not understand a lot of what she said. I only understood that I could never belong to her tribe. I accepted that and let things go back to an uneasy normality.

Then one night we had a visit from both the girls who worked at the big homestead kitchen with Verna, my white mother. They wanted to talk to Yurana.

She met them outside the hut and they talked for quite some time. When they left, Yurana came back into the hut, her face had a worried look. She came to the bed I shared with my Aboriginal 'sister' Adori and tenderly tucked us into bed, kissed us both good-night, but said nothing.

17

We both sensed that something was wrong.

Not long after this event, my whole world changed. One morning Yurana said to me and Adori to get dressed and washed as we were going on a long 'walkabout' — all the way up to the big house to see someone very special.

When we three were ready, we started walking from the river camp along the track toward the homestead. I remember the euroka — the sun — was shining brightly and the day was very hot. There were many gilgais — deep holes — along the track and we had to walk carefully.

After walking for some time we saw the jum — smoke — coming from the chimney of the homestead. As we passed along the track we had to stop briefly to allow a bunning — an echidna — waddle slowly across the path. He seemed to be feeling the heat of the day as we were. My nyrang tita — little sister — Adori had to be picked up by Yurana because she was too tired to continue walking.

By now the homestead was clearly visible. When we finally arrived, we walked past the big house and continued toward a smaller, older house. It was further along the same road.

There were lots of gubbas — white folks — standing around and just looking at us but we kept on walking. By this time I was getting quite thirsty and I asked Yurana if I could have some nattai — water — to drink.

"Soon you can, Nabby." She looked down smiling sadly.

We were now close to the smaller house and could see two people standing on the grass in front; one a dubay — woman — and a bagel — man. They both seemed very interested in us. Yurana did not seem at all happy. As we got closer the man began to walk toward us. He was a tall, thin fellow with a big hat and was very tanned as if he spent a lot of time in the sun.

Behind him came the woman. He walked up to me smiling, shook my hand and said "Hello." Then I looked at the woman. She was very dandaloo — pretty. She stooped down and picked me up, hugged me and kissed me on the cheek. Then she spoke very softly.

"Hello Gerald," she said.

I looked at her and said,"That's not my name! Ask Yurana. I am Narbethong. That is MY name... but they call me Nab for short."

"Oh, sorry..." the woman said and put me back on the ground. Then she turned to Yurana, nodded her head and they both walked into the house.

The tall, sun-tanned man then took Adori and me to the shade of a big gum-tree and gave us a drink of water. I had no idea at the time but, I had just met my real mother and father for the first time. I had no recollection of them as I was only five and a half years old. They may even have visited us at the river camp but I have no memory of such an event.

Yurana eventually came out of the house followed by Verna and called me to her.

"I have to explain something to you, Nab. This is very serious. Do you remember not so long ago when Nyathung pushed you away with the words — You are not of my meat! -? He also said that you could never belong to my tribe as you will always belong to another tribe. Do you remember that?"

Solemnly I answered, "Yes."

She went on. "Well, these two people here are your tribe; they are your real mother and father and they want you to come back to live with them in the white man's world. They know that you've been away from them a long time but they love you very much and will try to make you happy. They know that, in time, you will grow to love them too as much as you love Adori and me.

"Now, I want you to remember that I will always be there for you. If ever you need me, you know where to find me and Adori and Mura and Tjaka and all your friends. And most of all, the Aboriginal clan on the banks of the Barwon River at Pokataroo.

"And always remember the wonderful, happy times you spent with us."

I noticed she brushed away a tear with the back of her hand. My head was spinning. What was going on here?

"In those five years when I raised you from being a small baby, don't ever forget what I taught you. Remember that, in future years your long stay with us Aboriginal people has given you a greater understanding of our way of life. With this knowledge, you may even be able to teach white folk about us so that they will have a better understanding of our culture."

When Yurana finished she picked me up. I noticed she had tears running freely down her cheeks. She was trying to say 'Goodbye' but no words came. Looking at her lovely face I felt so sad.

Then I started to cry. We hugged and kissed and our tears flowed together for some time mingling in salty, sweet farewell. She put me down again and Adori came to me. With arms around each other it started all over again. Through convulsive sobs I turned to my Yurana and asked,"Do I really have to go? I love you so much."

Yurana answered simply,"Yes, my Nab, you must go back to them."

She then turned toward the woman who claimed to be my mother with a lingering, sad look. She took Adori's hand and said "We must go now. Good bye."

Yurana and Adori walked slowly away, out of my life. I watched her go through tearful eyes and with a heavy heart until they were well out of sight. I had no way of knowing then but, that was the last time I would ever see my Aboriginal mother and sister. That life had now ended.

CHAPTER FIVE.

And now began my introduction into the white man's world. I had no idea what to expect and I was very frightened of this strange new world and the people in it.

For the first few days after Yurana left me I was very lonely and scared and every night I cried myself to sleep in a large room in a bed all by myself. I had been used to sleeping in a small room with many others and with my own 'little sister' in the bed beside me. Without her I felt fearful in the dark room by myself.

We had always been told by Yurana that we should never go outside at night because the evil spirits came out at night — the Jung-Moggi or bad ghost and the Moggi — the child stealer.

But the one phantom to be most afraid of was the Kadaitcha man, the Jung-Moggi. This man was most evil. He walked about with special slippers on his feet made of bird feathers to cover his tracks and make him silent in his approach. These were the stories in my head and when I opened my eyes in the dark, I imagined I could see these people in my room. After the first night I told my 'new' mother what I thought I saw. She seemed to be too busy to listen to what I said or she didn't understand what I disclosed to her.

All she could say was to hurry up and get dressed as she had to go to work. She seemed not to care and gave me the impression that I was not wanted here and that she only got me back to please my 'father'.

When Ken came home at the weekend she changed from the way she behaved during the week when I was treated like a stranger and she didn't want to have anything to do with me. When my father was home, it was all different.

My life had changed forever.

At my young age of five years or so I knew that I had to adjust. It would be difficult but although I was frightened, I had been brought up the hard way and I was determined to cope. I did, however, miss going down to the cool sands on the bend of the river and playing with the other kids. Here, every morning I had to go with my mother to the big house and stay out of her way in the kitchen.

However, outside the kitchen door was a large expanse of lawn with green grass under a big gumtree. This was a special place for me where I waited each morning to meet the two Aboriginal girls who worked in the kitchen.

The squatter's missus didn't like any Aboriginal names or, for that matter, any Aborigines — including me. Thus, in keeping with working in the 'white area', she gave them gui or white person's names such as Elizabeth and Mary.

Funny... these names didn't suit them at all. Very strange, that.

I walked all around the outside of the big homestead but I never went any further inside the house than the kitchen. It gave me a bad feeling. I resented this segregation. Why should these people have all this when the clan down by the river had virtually nothing?

This I could not answer but I thought — This must be what they call the White Man's World where these folk have everything.

One day when I was sitting in the kitchen with nothing much to do I had a most upsetting experience. I noticed a door on the far side of the kitchen which I had not seen before so I went over and opened it. I went through and found myself standing in a big room with a wooden floor covered in soft, red mats. I had never seen such a big room before and I just stood there taking in the sights — coloured paintings on the walls, beautiful curtains and glass lights. I was amazed to see such glorious things.

Suddenly, another door on the far side of the room opened and the squatter's wife stepped into the room. As soon as she saw me she shouted at the top of her voice.

"Who are you? What are you doing in my house?"

Although I was shaking in fright I managed to admit that I was Verna's boy.

"Oh," she said flatly. "So, you're finally back after all this time."

"Yes." I mumbled, gazing at the floor.

"Hrmmpf." she snorted. "I suppose you have all the stealing ways of the people you lived with. Well, I want you to get out of here right now and never let me see you in here again. You are to stay in the kitchen — always. Do I make myself clear?"

"Yes, Missus." I replied, totally crestfallen.

"I don't want your type ever in my house. Aborigines are not welcome here. This is a white man's house and the only Aborigines allowed inside this house are servants; people who have been approved by me.

"And another thing; I don't want you to come anywhere near my children, ever. You will have no contact with them at all."

"Why not?" I asked innocently.

"Because I, as their mother, do not want them to be contaminated by what you have learned living with those blacks down by the river. Now, get out of my sight and go back to the kitchen where you belong." She stamped her foot at me.

I turned and left the way I had come. I now felt that I didn't belong anywhere. My own mother, Verna, seemed to be like this woman at times. She seemed distant and didn't want to talk to me but, above all, she couldn't be bothered to listen to what I wanted.

The next morning I was sitting under the big gumtree and, for no particular reason, I began to think about the Spirit People. I thought about Nyalod the rainbow serpent and his ground drawing — three circles together and another one by itself with six bent legs. I then went to a patch of bare ground and drew this in the dirt.

Then I thought of Wandjina, the hero people and something popped into my head that Yurana had said to me. She said "If ever you get lonely, sit down quietly and talk to Baiame, the Supreme Being. You will know if he has heard you as you will feel a calmness fill your body."

Remembering this, I spoke to Baiame. My body was filled with a calmness and serenity and the lonliness I felt previously left me. I never felt lonely again.

I knew that I had been cured.

CHAPTER SIX.

Something must have been said by the squatter's missus to my mother regarding catching me in the parlour of the big house. She was very angry with me for 'taking such a liberty, invading the big house'.

These were Verna's own words to me however, after this, I did notice that she seemed to be at home more at night now whereas, previously she would sometimes stay at the big house for quite some time before coming back to our small house.

I could think of one person who would be pleased with this change in habits; that would be Ken as he always objected to her staying out. My father returned from working three days on the fences to the north of the property in the heat and the dust and flies. He was very tired and needed a bath before eating tea. We sat down at the table for our meal but Verna started to tell him about what had happened around here since he'd been away and in particular, what the squatter's wife had said to me.

Ken was furious.

"Who does she think she is — the Queen of England? Or maybe she's God and able to pass judgement on these people. They are just human beings like the rest of us. The only thing that I see as being different is, they are dirt-poor... and black. And, because of this, they are placed on the lowest rung of the social ladder according to her. And, because my son has lived with these poor black people through no fault of his own, he is graded likewise.

"The fault is ours. We sent him away to live with the river clan and, because of this, he too is placed at the bottom of the social ladder according to her. Well, Verna, it seems that from now on around this station, our boy will be known by one and all as the 'white aborigine'. It seems that it's going to affect his life and it would have been kinder to leave him with Yurana rather than to bring him back here.

"A young boy like him doesn't understand how it is different from what he's been used to. I feel that drastic action is needed to solve the problem. What do you think, Verna?"

He placed his knife and fork down with a loud clatter on the plate.

She regarded my father a moment in silence then nodded slowly.

"I have to agree with you, Ken. I cannot see any other solution to the problem but, I must ask you, where will we go?"

My father stroked his stubbly chin thoughtfully, a far-away look in his eyes. "That's not a problem. I have a lot of friends in town and, I've been thinking a long time about going back to what I really love to do; working with horses.

"You see, before I went to Victoria, I worked for this buck-jump show as a rough rider. I used to ride the 'outlaw' buckjump horses and, the last time I was in town here, I met up with one of the brothers who own the show. He offered me a job. He said if I wanted to join him to let him know."

He smiled at me and then went on.

"Now, regarding your second request of when to leave..., I thought we should wait until after the shearing season is finished. Then we will be cashed-up and ready to roll. We can pick up the show in one of the towns further north from here. We can then give young Gerald a new start in life in a place where nobody has to know his past and also give him a chance to make new little friends around his own age. This way he can find out for himself what the white man's world is all about.

"You never know, he may even get to like it but, I have to admit, I don't think he'll ever be as happy as he was in the past — with the river people."

He was right, of course.

Both Verna and Ken began preparing to leave the property they had called home for the past six and a half years. I knew in their hearts they were going to miss it. Just as I would miss the people who raised me down by the Barwon River for nearly five years.

Most of all, I was going to miss my 'other mother', Yurana. I knew I would love her forever. The unfortunate fact was that Verna would never take the place in my heart that Yurana has. She, alone, would always be my real mother.

CHAPTER SEVEN.

The shearing season finished and there was much excitement packing up our stuff on the last night we were to spend in the small house. Parked around the back of the house was Ken's truck loaded with all their worldly possessions. The next day we would be off.

Early the following morning we drove away, never to return. I was very sad to be leaving this place as it held so many lovely memories of the people I grew up with. I was leaving behind the best part of my life so far.

As the sun was just rising we drove past the river camp. The sky was a beautiful palette of colours and I looked out to see if I could see any of my other family. I could make out some dark figures in the distance but couldn't recognise anyone in particular. That hurt me inside.

After driving for some time we reached the town of Collarenebri — place of many flowers. Ken stopped in front of a hotel where he went inside to find out where the buck-jump show had gone to. We had to know the name of the next town so that we had an idea of how long it would take to get there.

While we were waiting there for my father I noticed the swimming pool close by. I turned to Verna and asked her," Mum, why are we not allowed to go in there and swim?"

"Gerald, you can go in there and swim any time you like. Why would you ask me such a question?"

I was quite puzzled but I continued," Well, I came to town one day with Yurana and my friends from the river camp but they wouldn't let us in. They said we were not allowed to swim in this pool."

"Oh," said my mother looking very uncomfortable. "You see, you were with Aborigines so you were looked on as one of them and under the law, they are not allowed to swim in the same pool as white people."

"But I am white and the black people let me swim with them in the river." I desperately wanted a lucid explanation.

After a while, Verna sighed and answered,"Oh, I don't know why, Gerald. Now sit there and be quiet."

My father returned to the truck. Verna looked at him and said tersely, "You are as weak as water. You can't even go into a pub for a quick conversation without having a few drinks. You didn't even think about us sitting out here in this stinking hot truck. Did you think we might have liked to have a cool drink too?

"Anyway, what happened in there? Where abouts is the show?"

Ken cleared his throat and said," It's up at Texas. That will take us a couple of days to get there and that means sleeping in the truck."

"Alright," replied Verna, "In that case, let's get going or we'll never get there."

So we started off to commence my new life in a new world that I knew nothing of and had no idea what to expect. As the day progressed, the temperature inside the cabin of the truck became terribly hot. I asked my father if I could have a drink of water. He stopped the truck and I got out, went to the front of the vehicle and took a drink from the canvas waterbag hanging on the bumper bar.

This happened a couple of times during the trip. The road we travelled seemed not to have an end; it just kept on going until it disappeared over the next hill. We seemed to be following a river as I could see tall red river gums lining both sides of the river course. I felt comforted knowing I could relate to the river although everything else was strange to me. The country was so big I wondered if we would ever get to where we were going.

Late that afternoon we came into a big town but my father drove straight through and down to the banks of a river where we set up camp in a tent beside the truck. Early next morning we packed up again and were on our way. Ken said that if all went well, we should be at the buck-jump show that afternoon.

He was right. We finally came to a strange camp where there were lots of tents in the middle of a clearing and then some coloured huts-on-wheels as well. My father went into one of these huts and spoke to the boss. When he came out again he drove the truck and stopped beside one of the huts-on-wheels. We all went inside and Ken told us that this was to be our home from now on.

As we had been travelling all day in the truck and were hot and tired, it was decided we would go straight to bed and leave it to morning to have a look around. Ken told us he would show us what a buck-jump show was all about then. I was awake early as I wanted to see what a white tribe looked like up close. I went outside and looked at the coloured huts-on-wheels. I decided that this tribe was quite different from Aboriginal tribes as they did not all dwell together; they all lived separate lives in the coloured huts-on-wheels and didn't share with each other.

I didn't think I could live like this as this was so different from the life I had known and the people were so different from my people.

Ken called to me from the door of our hut and, with Verna, walked over to me.

"Now, come with me and I will show you all around the place."

We started at the yards where the horses were held. He told us that these horses were what's known as 'Walers or stock horses with an evil reputation and the station hands couldn't tame or break them in.

To me this place was a Yarramalong — place of wild horses.

My father also told us that a lot of these horses became legendary buck jumpers that have defied the skills of stockmen to ride them. Some have even been immortalised in bush ballads and, while the names of those who tried to tame them have long been forgotten, the animals' names have not. Names such as Dargan's grey, Whipstick, Aristocrat, Curio, Rocky Ned, Mandrake; these were once household names among young men who liked to take the challenge of trying to tame an outlaw horse.

Ken said that he remembered one of the horses as he had ridden and been thrown by him. The horse was 'Aristocrat' and the balladeer Tex Morton had written a song about the beast. He sang part of the song for me;

"He's thrown them in the east
He's thrown them in the west,
He's thrown them in the north
Where the riders are the best.
I've seen him throw them high
I've seen him lay them flat;
I've yet to see a fellow
Who can ride Aristocrat!"

Ken said that this was when he gained his love of horses and when he found out how independent and strong horses can be. "They are a match for any man."

As we continued our walk we could see that the people had left their caravans as this was a working day and they were busy preparing

28

for another busy day at the buck-jump show. There seemed to be more than just buck-jumping going on here because out in front were two tents; one large and one small. The first tent had boards advertising a troupe of boxers, the other was advertising a ballad singer and a whip-crack expert. It seemed that Scuthorp's was a travelling show as well as a buck-jump show.

Later that afternoon my father returned to the caravan after work to have a rest before going back to the evening session. I asked him how did this buck-jump show begin. He said that it began when a group of young men decided to take the challenge of trying to tame an outlaw horse.

Early feats of horsemanship took place in station yards enclosed with railing fences. The station hands would all sit atop the rails and cheer the rider on and shout advice. If the rider felt confident he could handle the beast he yelled for the gate to open and the combination of horse and rider burst out of the pen — the rider determined to take the ginger and fire out of the animal. It rarely ended with the rider taking a brisk canter around the flat ground.

With all this travelling, I was getting used to the new life. I fell in love with the horses and all the other animals and, as they were now my friends, I had an extended family besides my mother and father. Verna seemed to be a lot happier and I know my father loved his job. He had graduated from 'pick-up man' to a demonstrator buck-jump rider.

In no time at all we had travelled all over north-western New South Wales and southern Queensland to places like Surat, Esk, Laidley, Toobeah, Rosemore, Dayboro and soon we found ourselves in the town of St. George.

When we had settled in, after tea we all sat outside in the cool evening air and Ken decided to talk about his past.

"I have decided to tell you both something I have never told you before. You never knew that I was in the Army during the Great War. I served with the Australian Light Horse troops in Egypt — 4th Regiment. The reason I'm telling you this is that, previously I had said that some of these horses had an evil reputation and cannot be broken. Well, that is not exactly true. In the Army, all horses have to be broken — regardless."

He took a long pull on a cigarette and blew the smoke skyward before continuing.

"Three other fellows and I had this job at Liverpool where we were camped before going overseas and, I can tell you, we broke every horse that came our way. So, you see, the show boss here knew about that and it was he who gave me the job. I had no way to prove to all the other folk here what sort of horseman I am but, I just wanted you both to know so you will understand why I was changed from pick-up man to rider."

What Ken had told my mother and me was extra interesting as, only a few days prior, our school teacher, Mr Brown had told the class about the war in Egypt and how the Light Horsemen had fought their way across the desert and finished the tale with the legendary charge at the Turkish gun emplacements at a spot called Beersheba. It was here that the Australian Light Horse conducted the last great cavalry charge in history that became world famous.

I told my father what Mr Brown had told us in school and asked if he had been there too.

"Well, yes, Gerald. I was there with the 4th, 11th and 12th Regiments but we don't talk much about it because it's too painful. And, I would ask you if you would not tell anyone about my being there, please. If I think about those times I get very upset."

I stood up and hugged the man and said,"Alright, Dad. I won't say a word at all but, you can't stop me from being proud of you forever more."

The very next day I went to school as usual in the tent in the camping ground feeling that I was really somebody now. However, a promise is a promise and I could never let down my father — the hero of my life. I really thought that someone would notice the size of my chest as I was bursting with pride but, nobody even noticed.

Possibly the reason was that the show had been advertising the newest big attraction for tomorrow's show was a horse that everyone called 'Satan'. He was unbroken and he was black. Everyone was hoping he would attract a big crowd and also get in the eager, young 'devil-may-care' fellows in town to show off a bit and let off some steam as it were. Those chaps looked upon such events as good entertainment and always turned up to watch.

My father was to be the first to ride this beast since it was not ready for release to the general public to try. It was classed as dangerous, unbroken.

The day dawned when my father would try to break Satan. Everyone in the show was excited, hoping for a huge crowd to watch the struggle between man and the rebel black horse. They were not to be disappointed as folk started arriving in the late morning for the

30

afternoon session.

I didn't see Ken until he came back to our caravan for lunch. While we ate we talked and I asked him if he was frightened at all of the horse called 'Satan'?

He looked at me a moment then went back to his plate, scooping up a forkful of food.

"Well, Gerald, not really scared. Looking back, I think I may have ridden wilder horses than this one but, that's not to say I won't be careful. You see, I've learned over the years that every horse has his own special trick to perform — just before you get to his breaking point. They don't reveal it until the very last minute in desperation.

"When you feel the horse getting really tired, you must stay alert for that something special to happen and hope you can counter it in time before the horse gets the better of you. If you are too slow to act — you are in deep trouble. But, don't worry Gerald, I will break this horse in as I have done countless times before and then be home for tea. All I want you to do, my son, is to cheer the loudest and I will hear you. That will help me a lot."

He then said got up from the table and kissed Verna goodbye and ruffled my hair. "See you both later."

He walked out the door of the caravan and over to the yards where the horses were kept to prepare for his ride.

At the appointed time my mother and I walked over to the stand with many others from the camp and took our seats overlooking the buck-jump ring. There were a few young fellows there, eager to have a chance to show-off their horsemanship and win a prize or cheer the riders they knew. The stands were full and everyone was waiting expectantly for the main event to commence.

The black horse, Satan, was in the holding pen and behaving badly. Ken was sitting patiently on the top rail waiting for the animal to calm down enough to sit astride his back.

At last I watched my father slide into the saddle and take up the reins, his back straight as a ramrod. The pen gate was opened and the horse bounded out into the arena, 'pig-rooting' as it went and trying to unseat the rider. He went round the fence-line snorting and twisting but Ken stayed right there on his back, glued to the saddle. I remember there was a lot of cheering and 'yahoo-ing' from the crowd as they were enjoying the spectacle of the battle between the beast and man. It was something wonderful to behold.

Then, as if to signal it's finale, the horse lowered its head and did something very strange. With it's head almost touching the ground, Satan did a quick flick to the right, landed on his right side with a loud thud and rolled over. The next thing I saw was the horse standing on all its legs but no sign of my Dad. A loud moan rose from the crowd as they sensed something was awry. I wondered where Ken was. Then I saw his form, lying on the ground, quite still, covered in dirt and sawdust.

The pick-up men ran toward him with another fellow and the first-aid men. Verna rose from her seat, her hand to her mouth. She turned to me and said "Stay right there, Gerald."

She rushed down to the ring to be by his side leaving me with Mrs Wilson who was sitting next to us. By this time Ken had been picked up and taken away.

The crowd went awfully silent and the people looked grim. Nobody moved. Mrs Wilson took me back to our caravan and stayed with me for quite some time — maybe hours but I cannot recall. She made some tea for me and I sat outside for a long time waiting for Verna and Ken to come back. It was getting dark and I was worried. "Where are they?" I thought.

Mrs Wilson came over to me and said that I should come inside out of the cold. She had made up my bed. She said that something must have happened to delay them coming home but that I would be alright that night with her.

"You can see them both bright and early in the morning Gerald," she chirped hopefully.

I was still concerned but I took her advice and went into the caravan and got into bed. I tossed and turned a bit, recalling vision of the horse crashing onto Ken but, eventually I drifted off to sleep.

CHAPTER EIGHT.

Early the next morning I rose from the bed in Mrs Wilson's van and went outside. The sun was just rising and all the glorious colours of sunrise lit up the eastern sky. I recall there was a heavy overnight dew on the grass making everything wet. This was to be a morning I would long remember.

I walked over to our own caravan and stepped inside. Verna was lying on top of the bed, still fully dressed from yesterday and her face was wet from crying. The pillow was also drenched.

"Mum, where have you been? And where is my Dad?" I asked quite innocently. She did not answer. Instead she burst into tears.

"Leave me alone...leave me alone!"

I walked outside and sat on the caravan step. Some moments passed until Verna came outside and sat beside me, placing her arm around my shoulder. She now seemed to be a bit calmer but very sad.

Between sobs she said,"Ohh, Gerald... Ken died yesterday in the ring when that damned horse rolled on top of him."

She had followed Ken to the hospital and waited for him but, as the doctors had explained, there was nothing they could have done to save his life being crushed the way he was. After waiting so long and then to be told of his death, Verna had decided to walk back to the caravan in the early hours.

I sat there listening to what my mother told me but I could not feel anything for the loss of my father. I was very proud of this man but I had only got to know him over the past 12 months — not all my life and there is a huge difference.

Besides this, I had been taught by Yurana and the river people that death is only the beginning of the next life with the spirit people. Then, Baiame looks after them and it's a happy time not a sad time. I then began to consider the 'white culture' and how different it was from the

Aboriginal culture which was the only culture I had known up until this time.

Although it was very difficult for me being only about seven years old at the time, I kept trying to understand these white people and their strange ways. A continuous stream of people kept appearing at the caravan to see Verna. They kissed her, they hugged her and they said how sorry they were for the loss of Ken. It seemed to go on for hours. They paid me no heed at all but my main concern was for my mother with all these folk arriving. It actually seemed to improve her outlook. For this, I was glad as she would need to be strong when we attended Ken's funeral.

That would be a very sad day for us, I was sure.

That night, when all the visitors had left and we were alone I decided to go to bed and to be up early next day and prepare for the funeral and help my Mum. I was surprised to see she was all dressed up when she came to tuck me in.

"Gerald, honey, you'll be OK here for a while, won't you." she purred into my ear. "I have to go out for a bit to visit a friend. You don't know him but, don't worry. I won't be too late home. I'll lock the door as I leave."

I lay in my bed wondering why she would be going out to visit another man on the night before my father's funeral. I eventually fell asleep with that thought foremost in mind.

In the morning, there was Verna asleep in her bed — alone.

I lay there in bed, wide awake thinking what the day would bring. I had never been to a funeral before and I had no idea what went on or what they do at a funeral. I began to think back to Ken and how much he had done for me in the short time we had known each other; the talks we'd had and the stories he'd told me about the decisions he'd made for me.

I finally realised for the first time that Ken had been trying to help me adjust to this new life and that he, alone, understood the problems I was experiencing at my tender age trying to cope with a culture of which I had no knowledge, no path to follow and no idea where to begin.

Ken had been the only person I could talk to seriously. He was so kind and he listened to what I was saying. On the other hand, Verna would not listen to me and was not interested in anything that concerned me. It was then that I felt sorry for myself having lost my very best friend.

I didn't feel sorry for Ken as he had told me once that if anything happened to him while riding horses in the buck-jump show I should not worry as he was doing what he loved to do.

"I realise the risks I'm taking." he had told me."I have been there before the war and I'm not afraid of dying. A lot of my friends have passed from this life before me."

With that thought in mind, I got out of bed and got dressed. Mother followed and we had breakfast together. We then sat outside to await the car which would take us to the ceremony.

Driving into town our car fell into line behind another vehicle which had lots of glass windows in the back. Verna said that it was a hearse and the box I could see in the back contained Ken's body. We were on our way to the church and I looked out the back window to see many other cars following. When we stopped at the church my father's coffin was draped in an Australian flag and a soldier's slouch hat placed on top with a row of shining medals. Some men placed some red poppies on the hat as this was something that soldiers did when one had died.

An old fellow in long robes stood up in the church and spoke a lot of words which I didn't understand. Six men picked up my father's coffin and carried it out of the church to the yard where a hole had been dug. The coffin was lowered into the hole while the man in long robes said some more words I didn't understand. The flag was picked up with the soldier's hat and the medals and taken away and then everyone went home.

I would have liked to stay and talk to Ken but my mother said that he was now in Heaven with God and that he was not on earth any longer. This I did not understand as Yurana had taught me that when a person died, his spirit stays around for three days so I knew that my father was still present.

I hadn't heard of Heaven. I knew nothing of God and I'm sure I will never ever fully comprehend this white man's world. It is so very strange to me.

CHAPTER NINE.

We were driven back to the caravan from the churchyard and left at the door. Verna commenced crying again as there soon was a stream of well-wishing folk coming in and saying how sorry they were.

I sat down and watched somewhat dispassionately at all this going on, not being noticed once more as, to them, I was not there. Then I heard something that sparked my interest in the conversation. A man said they had shot the horse that killed my Dad.

Apparently, this is the rule with buck-jump shows that they cannot go on using a 'killer horse'. This news gave me mixed feelings; sad to hear that Satan was dead yet happy to know that he was now with my father and this would make Ken very happy.

This also reminded me of a story my father had told me some weeks earlier about the horses he'd been associated with in his lifetime. It happened on a day he decided to walk into town and he asked Verna if she wanted to go to which she replied 'No!' so he asked me and I said 'Yes!' so, off we went.

It was a very hot day and, by the time we arrived in town, we were looking for a cool spot to rest. We found a seat under a tree in the park in the middle of town. Then, for some reason, Ken began to talk about the war which was something he would never do at home as Verna was not at all interested.

"Gerald," he began,"I would like to tell you about the horses I had and lost during the War in the Sinai Desert. This story is something you should know as it concerns me and what I believe.

"It really began about 2 years before I joined up in the Light Horse Regiment. I had saved some money and I decided to buy my own horse so I asked my father if he would take me to the horse sales at Warwick. He agreed to do this and, when we arrived, we started looking over the animals in the yards. Then I saw the most beautiful chestnut filly

— about 12 hands high — and I instantly fell in love with her.

"I pointed her out to my Dad as the one I really wanted to buy so we kept our eyes on her until she came up for auction. When the bidding started I joined in and the price reached ten pounds but that was all the money I had. It went on to eleven pounds. I told my father and he said he would lend me another two pounds so I bid twelve pounds hoping nobody would bid any higher. They fell away and I bought her."

He'd looked down at me with a proud and romantic far-away look in his eyes as he remembered the day so vividly. He slapped me lightly on the shoulder and went on.

"Thus I owned my very first horse. As the months went by I found out how kind and loving this horse was while I travelled around Queensland working on cattle stations as a drover.

"This horse and I grew very close as we worked together. I gave her the name of 'Bess' which had been my mother's name. She was a very kind and loving person but she died when I was very young."

He sighed and looked away into the distance for a moment, then slapped his knee and contiued.

"Anyway, it was on one of these droving trips interstate that a group of us young blokes decided to join the Light Horse troops. We left the cattle at the railhead but we didn't fancy the long trip back to the cattle station to pick up the next lot so, after being paid off, we headed for the nearest Army recruitment post which was at Dubbo. We filed into the office and fronted up to this Sergeant who looked us up and down and said,'Well, you all look fit enough but, can you ride a horse?'

"Well, we had a bit of a laugh about that and soon convinced him that we could ride OK. Then we got signed up complete with our horses, we did our basic training and we embarked on a ship bound for Alexandria in Egypt.

"To cut a long story short, Bess and I had been in quite a few battles in the desert together and I thought the next one would be the last one but, I was to be proven wrong. We were given orders to attack and take a hill at a place called Tel el Saba. Thus, as mounted infantry we rode up as close as we could to the hill and dismounted to attack on foot.

"The horses were left with a handler while we approached on foot. The position was fairly strongly defended and the action took us until about 3.00pm before we finally were successful. Then we made our way back to where the horses had been held and saw a sight we could hardly believe.

"While we were gone, a German 'Taube' aeroplane had flown over, seen the group of horses and strafed the ground, killing and wounding most of the animals. Of course I rushed round looking for my Bess hoping desperately that she would be OK. Eventually I found her but she was badly wounded. I sat with her head in my arms and looked into her lovely eyes. She tried to nuzzle me showing that the love was still there and attempted to get to her feet but could not.

"She died in my arms. I cried for her as I had lost my best friend. I felt very lonely at that moment. However, the war was still going on and I had to leave her there with all the other dead animals to be buried.

"The Army immediately issued me with another horse called 'Jenny' which had belonged to a good friend of mine who was killed at Tel el Saba hill. We also realised that we had a very big problem now in the desert — we were running short of water and the horses had been out in 50 degree heat for many hours so we needed to get to water soon.

"There was no time to mourn my poor Bess."

I remember, at this point Ken had sniffed a bit and wiped his hand across his weathered face. I wondered if he was crying but he went on.

"By now it was 4.30pm and the 4th. and 12th. Regiments were assembled with the 11th. behind some rising ground 4 miles south-east of a place called Beersheba where we knew the Turks had water in their ground tanks. We had to take the place or die in the attempt.

"So, we started off at a trot and then at a gallop as we came over the top of the ridge. Looking down the long, gentle slope into Beersheba I was determined to ensure we took the town and save the horses from dying of thirst. I was travelling at a fast gallop and had almost reached the first line of Turkish trenches when my new horse, Jenny suddenly stumbled and fell dead, having been shot from under me.

"I crashed to the ground with her and quickly grabbed my rifle and checked myself but found I was only bruised. I fixed my bayonet and rushed at the Turkish trench and jumped in. I let fly two shots and got two Turks cold. Then I looked round and noticed the rest were out of the trench and running away. By this time the fighting seemed to be slowing down so, to cut a long story short — we won the battle, we took the town and the horses got the water they so badly needed." He'd then turned to me with a funny, serious look on his face.

"The reason I'm telling you all this, Gerald; I've always believed that things happen in threes. I lost two horses in the desert in that battle and I have been waiting many years for the third horse to die. Here I am working with horses again and I have a feeling that something bad will happen soon. When it does — if it does — you will understand why I've told you this very long story about the two horses that died in the war in the desert. I just don't know about the third one that has yet to die."

The funeral of Kenneth Carr, my 'father', was over and I now felt terribly cold and lonely as I had lost a friend and role model. Now I only had my mother. I was never comfortable in her company. And we had a problem to deal with.

The buck-jump show owner had asked Verna to vacate the caravan by the end of the week as he had another family coming to replace Ken in the ring buck-jumping. Our caravan was to be their home.

My mother quickly decided that everything we could not carry would have to be sold off. When this was done we finished up with three suitcases of possessions; everything we owned in the world in three pieces of luggage. Wonderful!

Fortunately, we made the deadline alright and, early one morning, after saying 'Goodbye' to one and all in the camp, we were driven to the railway station and boarded a train. It felt like we were going to another country far away.

This was the first train I had been on and it intrigued me. I had no idea where we were going. All Verna would say was that we were going 'home'. I had no idea what she meant by that. The only thing I was sure of was that this was the end of my life in this part of Australia with no prospect of returning.

I felt hollow, empty. My heart was here in this land with Yurana at Pokataroo. I felt this was still my home; nowhere else would ever feel like home to me.

We travelled for three days and nights by trains passing through small towns and big cities as we went. Over rivers, bridges, culverts and across vast expanses of open country. As we went the air grew colder and, eventually, we arrived at another big city which my mother explained was Melbourne.

"Gerald,"she expanded,"We're going to a place called Aspendale which is a suburb where you were born seven years ago."

I didn't like the place. It was dirty, noisy and there were too many people in it — like grains of wheat, everywhere.

From Melbourne we caught another smaller train then we got off that and onto what Verna called a tram which took us to the seaside town of Black Rock. Then we walked some distance, carrying the three suitcases until we stopped outside a large house painted dark colours.

My mother then walked up to the front door and knocked. The door was opened by a woman much older than Verna who just stood there staring at us.

"Oh, hello Verna," she said and hugged my mother. Then the older woman turned and pointed at me and said,"I suppose that's him?"

"Yes, mother."

"Well, I suppose you'd best come inside now." So we did.

When Verna had removed her coat and hat the older woman, turned to me and commenced issuing orders like a Tommy-gun.

"Right, young man, sit down and sit up straight. Do not speak until you are spoken to — and not before... do you understand?"

I didn't know it at the time but I had just met my loving grandmother. She looked just as I would have imagined a Jung-Moggi Kataitcha man to appear. I thought to myself 'So, this is the way you treat people you don't like in the white man's world?'

I was hurt that Verna had said nothing when Gran had pointed at me and said 'So that's him?' She could at least have said 'No, that's Gerald.' but she remained silent.

I thought that maybe my mother had been accepted back into this family and, by my coming here, I would be blamed for any break-up of the family. Since I had been raised by the Aboriginal people, I was going to be treatd as vermin, same as the poor blacks. Verna seemed to be afraid of her own mother and, as I had never met the old woman before, I wondered how she could take such a dislike to me instantly. She had never seen me or spoken to me and was obviously making a poor assessment.

I sat quietly in the room by myself while the two women shared a cup of tea in the kitchen. I realised I would never be welcomed into this white family since I had been on the lowest rung of society as an Aboriginal for the first five and a half years of my life and had received the same ill treatment before — being disliked, shunned and abused seemed to be normal behaviour by whites. I decided to be who I am inside in the 'White Society'; that is a white Aborigine.

I felt I could live with that.

However, I was to receive the same treatment all over again. This was the white man's way of getting round the fact that they don't want to understand another culture. Being rejected was nothing new to me but, having been brought up rough in the 'school of hard knocks' even at my tender age gave me a psychological shell of protection against such adversity and tended to make me stronger mentally. Even though I didn't fully understand the motivations and implications of the attitudes I encountered, I knew that, before too long, I would have the opportunity to escape the world which treated me so badly and, by golly, I would take it!

I also couldn't help thinking I'd had the same experience somewhere before. Then it came to me; back at 'Trelawney' station when I had returned to the big house from living with my beloved Yurana and wandered into the parlour by mistake. The attitude of the squatter's missus that day was exactly the same as this old witch.

"Never let me see you in here again," she had screamed at me. "Do I make myself clear? And don't let me catch you associating with my children. I don't want them to be contaminated by your Aboriginal ways..."

The memory was still crystal-clear and acidic; it was burned into my brain for all time.

Although it was a very long way from Pokataroo to Black Rock, Victoria, it seemed the same nasty attitude had transferred itself and followed me here but, even at my early age, I handled the situation quite well and I felt this time would be no different.

My thoughts were interrupted abruptly as I heard the women coming back into the front room. Gran walked straight up to me and said," I have spoken with your mother at length and I've decided that you and Verna can stay here in one of the 'flats' out the back of the house as you have nowhere else to go. But, while you are here, you will follow my rules. Now come with me and I'll show you both where you'll be staying."

We followed the old woman out the back door. On either side of the yard were two small buildings exactly the same. Verna told me later that these were holiday flats where people used to pay to stay a while on holidays. However, there were a lot of folk out of work due to the 'depression times'. This meant that nobody could afford to go on holidays so we were lucky the flats were empty.

We went inside and looked around. Everything was there, fully furnished. "Ohh, it's just lovely," Verna gushed to her mother. "We'll be calling this home for a long time, Gerald."

The next morning I asked my mother if I could go for a walk. I went out the front of the house which faced the sea and looked out over the greatest expanse of water I'd ever seen. I went across the road to the cliff-top and looked down on the golden sands below. This was a placid place called 'Quiet Corner'. I could see some fishing boats pulled up on the beach near some rocks. I sat down on a seat near the edge of the cliff deep in thought.

"This will be my escape place; a place to go when I want to be alone and, I have a feeling that this will be quite often."

After a while I returned to the house and stood out the front, observing. It was a big house, two storeys and very impressive. I could not escape the feeling that the old 'welcome mat' would not be out for me very long here. I knew that I would have very little contact with the other two children living there even though they were only a few years older, my 'uncle' David and aunty Thelma.

That didn't worry me at all as I had been instructed by Yurana that I should always be happy with my own company. That way I would never need the company of anyone else which then would make me independent and happy.

So far it had worked.

In the days that followed we had only one visitor at our flat. It was an older man who introduced himself to me as 'Uncle Jim'.

"Where do you live, Uncle Jim?" I asked innocently.

"In the big house."

"But that's where my Gran lives," I responded.

"That's right." he said "I am her husband."

I thought that through very quickly and said,"Then you're my grandfather!"

He smiled back at me and said,"Well, yes, I suppose I am in a way. Would you like me to be your grandfather, Gerald?"

"Oh, yes!" I said enthusiastically. "I have just lost my father. He was my greatest friend and he died. I need someone that I can talk to. Would you mind if I called you 'Pa'? Uncle Jim just doesn't seem right."

"Sure, why not. I don't mind at all. That would be wonderful." He smiled and ruffled my hair, got up from the couch where he'd been sitting and left us.

When he had gone, Verna told me about him. She said that after her father had been killed in a railway accident her mother had remarried to Jim Wilson and they had had a daughter who was Thelma.

"She is your aunty and my half sister."

Verna was very clinical in telling me these facts of family connection. I didn't think any more about it at the time.

Then one morning my mother told me to get dressed in my best clothes as we were going to visit her brother William and his wife and daughter, Dorothy who lived in North Melbourne. We had to travel by several trams and a train to get there but eventually we arrived at their front door to be greeted by all three who were very excited to meet us after such a long absence.

Verna did the introductions and we all went into the house. While the adults went about making a cup of tea, Dorothy and I were told to play outside in the yard. Out we went and she tried to teach me a few games she knew but were lost on me as I had no knowledge of such things.

"Would you like to eat some apples?" she said with a twinkle in her eyes.

"Oh, yeah, would I?"

Together we walked to the back fence of the property and pushed aside three palings which were loose. We stepped into the next yard and saw dozens of green apples lying on the grass under the trees. We both picked up a couple of apples and took a big bite. To my taste it was quite sour so I only swallowed one or two bits but Dorothy ate all hers.

Then we climbed back into her yard and closed the gap in the fence at the very moment that her mother called us in for dinner.

It was some time after dinner that both Dorothy and I began to feel sick with pains in the stomach and headaches. My uncle called for the doctor. By the time the doctor arrived we had both passed out so he took us in his car to the hospital with my uncle.

Since Dorothy had eaten all her apple she did not survive. She passed away that night. However, I hung on to life for four days drifting between life and death but finally pulled through. As a result of this poisoning, I have had stomach trouble ever since.

Apparently, the trouble came from a chemical that had been sprayed on trees to ward off the birds the same day and which Dorothy had taken in too much to survive. I remained in hospital for four weeks.

Nobody came to see me but, in that time I discovered what kindness was. The doctors and nurses at Royal Melbourne Hospital saw that I was getting no visitors and decided that I should have at least one visitor every day and organised themselves into a roster so that someone came to spend time with me during their duty shifts each day.

I kept wondering where Verna was as I felt she had deserted me again. Then, one morning my doctor came to see me and said that I could now go home. He said my mother would be picking me up later in the morning. When she did show up I asked her why nobody came

43

to see me in hospital when I was so sick and nearly died.

"Gerald, I now have a full-time job and I couldn't spare the time to come all this way. Besides which, my family blames you for the death of my brother's only baby girl, Dorothy.

I said to Mum, 'That's not true.' but she said, 'Well, you know how they feel about these things.' I'm sorry, son."

When we got back to Gran's place the reception was even colder than I expected. Gran would not even look at me. If ever I longed to be back at Pokataroo with Yurana it was right now.

That night, when I went to bed and was alone at last I spoke to the supreme spirit being, Baiame and asked for His help to get past this traumatic time that was not of my making.

CHAPTER TEN.

I now knew that I would never fit in with this family because of who I was and where I came from. Although Verna was a kind person, when it came to dealing with her own mother, she was terribly weak. Gran was a domineering woman however, even with all my problems, I found a good friend within the family who was being treated much the same but in a different way.

My grandfather, Jim, was an old Army man from the Great War and he liked to have a drink and smoke. These things were not permitted inside the big house so he hid away in a small shed in the yard. This was his escape area. I discovered him one day when I noticed smoke coming from the shed and opened the door to find Jim inside.

From that day on we spent many hours together in the shed talking. He told me many things about the War and I, in turn, told him about my time spent with the Aborigines at Pokataroo. He also told me of conversations in the house about me — like the time Gran said to Verna after Dorothy died, "You shouldn't have brought that boy here. He should have been left with the blacks. If you'd done so, Dorothy would still be alive!"

Apart from such irritations, life went along pretty smoothly until the day it was announced that Uncle Bill and his family from North Melbourne would be moving into the flat opposite us. This was because he had lost his job and couldn't pay the rent on the place where they were. With the 'Depression' being prevalent and no work available, there were no folk taking holidays so there was room for them at Gran's house until things looked better.

I was more than a little concerned as I wondered how he would treat me.

I had to forget Uncle Bill and all other things for the moment when, one day Gran came to visit my mother for a serious discussion. With me present, the old woman pointed at me and said,"When are you going to send him to school? He's 7 years old and has not had much formal education."

Verna was indignant for once.

"Mum, he does have a name, you know. But, in answer to your question, this morning I have received his birth certificate from the Department of Births and Deaths. Tomorrow I shall take him to school and register him."

"Which school?" the old woman demanded.

"Why, Saint Joseph's of course."

The matriarch snorted. "I will not allow you to do that. He will not go to the same school that Thelma and David attend. That would be an insult to me and to them. And, as long as you stay under my roof, you will do as I say. Is that clear?"

"Yes, Mum," Verna answered. "I understand, but can you suggest another school?"

"Of course. What about the Christian Brothers at Sandringham! Nobody will know him there."

Verna bristled again. "What do you mean 'Nobody will know him.'

"Gran explained,"Oh well, you know — the circumstances of his birth... his upbringing with the blacks. You don't want people knowing about these things, do you?"

My mother quickly replied. "Those things had nothing to do with him. The fault is mine and if you want someone to pick on, blame me, Mum, not an innocent boy. And in any case, neither school will have any idea about Gerald's background unless somebody has informed them beforehand. Would you know anything about that, Mum?"

Flustered, Gran retorted quickly." Verna, I can assure you I have said nothing about this to anyone. After all, it's your business."

The old woman rose from her chair and, without so much as a side-long glance at me, left the flat. Verna smiled at me and waved me to the chair recently vacated by Gran. It was still warm.

"Now, Gerald, I have something very important to tell you. I have here your birth certificate which we have to show when I take you to school to enroll. As you can see, it has a different name on it from how you were known previously but, nevertheless, it's yours. I must explain. You see, when you were born I gave your name as Gerald Kenneth Walshe as I was still married under the name 'Walshe'.

"When we went away to Pokataroo I told the squatter's wife a lie. I said that Ken and I were married as they wanted a married couple to fill two positions. This meant that you were known as Gerald Carr but that was not true. This meant that, because of my lie, you were living a lie. This, now, has to change. From now on when I enroll you at this school and show this birth certificate to the Brother principal your name will be Gerald Kenneth Walshe. Do you understand? I know it will be hard for you to adjust but you will have to try."

So off I went to school to be known by a different name from the one I thought I had and not liking it one bit. In the years that followed I got used to school and the school bullies and the three mile hike I had to walk because we couldn't afford the two-penny tram ride each way. But, I got used to that.

I did, however have a problem with Uncle Bill at about this time. He had obtained a rowing boat because he and my Uncle Dave liked fishing. So the family got together and made a decision that placed extra pressure on me and my mother.

Not being invited to the meeting, I only learned about the arrangement when I came home from school one day. I was simply informed that from now on Uncle Dave and I would be getting out of bed early and going out at 3.00am fishing on the Bay every Tuesday and Friday to return at 7.00am.

"That'll give you plenty of time to have a wash, get dressed for school and have some breakfast before you go." he said.

I never liked Uncle Bill. He was a cruel man and someone to avoid if possible. This was the first time I saw my mother get angry as we were not consulted in this matter and it affected us both. She normally left before me to go to work as a cook and housekeeper at a private residence but, with me getting up so very early Tuesdays and Fridays she knew this would disturb her sleep.

Although the whole arrangement upset me, I decided not to let them see how upset I was. It just made me more determined to excel at my school work and in everything I turned my hand to afterwards in life. This would give me the greatest satisfaction knowing that from humble beginnings, anything is possible if you try hard enough.

CHAPTER ELEVEN.

It was difficult and cold getting started early in the mornings but, after a while we fell into a set routine. We would go to 'Quiet Corner' where my uncle's boat was stored and pull it from the high sand to the water then load up the fishing gear and row out onto the Bay. Once there we would toss the anchor out and sit there fishing.

We would return to shore in time for me to be home by 7.00 o'clock with our catch, eat some breakfast and get dressed for school. This continued for some months in good weather and bad. Many times we were caught out on the Bay when a storm blew up from Bass Strait but nobody seemed to worry, least of all Uncle Bill.

He always said the only way to learn anything was the hard way — you have to experience it!

Well, we certainly did that! However, this experience left me with a fear of the sea and a loathing of the noble sport of fishing. This has stayed with me through my life.

The purpose of the excercise was to feed the whole family with the fish caught on Tuesday while the Friday catch was sold at the roadside on Saturday morning. The fish were displayed on top of a fruit box and kept moist with a sprig of ti-tree dipped in a bucket of salt water and then laid over the fish.

Having done this for some time we had many regular customers so the fish were sold quickly. We also kept another bucket under the fruit box with salt water and more fish to fill orders we had received the previous Saturday.

I saw many fascinating things on these fishing trips; sharks taking our catch off the lines especially when we caught snapper which were in abundance. That was always viewed as a downside to the trip. It was the grey nurse sharks which followed the snapper into the Bay. They loved snapper as much as we did.

At times we saw penguins swimming past as well as stingrays and, on one occasion we saw something that frightened both of us. There was another timber dinghy containing two fishermen close by and one of the men was pulling in a fish when a shark rose from the depths and its nose hit the boat with some force and a sickening crash.

The impact split some side planks and water started to pour into the small boat. The poor fellows called out for help so we pulled up the anchor and rowed over to rescue them. We then took their boat in tow and commenced to row ashore. By the time we hit the sand the other craft was almost under water.

The most frightening event happened in mid-winter. While we were out on the Bay the fog closed in and an eerie quiet surrounded us. Suddenly, a noise that I thought was a cow moo-ing broke the silence close by.

"What was that Uncle Dave? It sounded like a big cow..."

"I don't know, Gerald." he replied, a bit shaken. "Maybe 'tis a cow on dry land and the sound carried across the water to us."

I accepted this explanation until the water close to the boat was broken by a huge whale surfacing. The wash from its gigantic tail nearly swamped the small boat. We hung on grimly to stabilise the craft and stared at each other in horror.

Then we saw the full extent of the huge beast and another smaller shape following close by — a baby whale and its mother!

"Well, that's it for today, Gerald. We're going home." Uncle Dave rose and went to pull in the anchor but it was stuck fast below. He pulled out his knife and cut the rope and tied it to a loose plank hoping it would float and indicate where we could find it again in daylight.

Then we took to the oars and rowed for the shore as fast as we could go. When we later told some fishermen the tale they just said it was the season for whales to come into the Bay and deliver their calves.

"Oh, yes, Gerald," said one man,"They do make a moo-ing sound just like a cow."

CHAPTER TWELVE.

Although I had to cope with the fishing trips, I also had a more serious problem to deal with, not at home and not Uncle Bill but at school. For about four months, I and a few others had been bullied by a couple of fellows named Billy and Jimmy Ford when they had joined the school.

They set about worrying the boys, demanding money, searching their lunch-boxes and taking anything they wanted to eat. They insulted them and stole items from lockers and then would bash the victim if he did not co-operate.

I had watched with a sense of horror and shame and had even been a victim myself but had no idea how to stop them. I had thought of taking on Billy head-on in a fist fight but that would have achieved nothing as I didn't know the first thing about fighting. For the present, we all would have to put up with this bad behaviour until I could find a way to stop them.

The answer came quite unexpectedly in the form of Brother Luke, our maths teacher. He was also our P.T. instructor in charge of sports and sporting teams at Christian Brothers College. After class one day he asked the boys if anyone was interested in playing any sport and, if so, to meet him at the gymnasium after school today.

As I had decided to take it upon myself to resolve the situation with Billy Ford, I felt this was my opportunity to learn a skill that would stop the bully in his tracks — boxing — and Bro. Luke would be my instructor.

Thus I met the priest at the gym after school and asked him for his help to train me as a boxer. He agreed on one condition — that he would not ask me why I wanted to become proficient at the 'noble sport' of boxing if, in turn, I agreed to join the Aussie Rules Football team as they were short of players.

I thought this was a fair trade and so I agreed . I also told him that after I'd finished my training as a boxer I would let him know the reason why playing Aussie Rules was a bonus as it kept me fit. Although I did get hurt from time to time, my injuries were never serious, only small cuts and bruises. The hardest part of the agreement was not the football but the boxing.

So I began my training with Bro. Luke every afternoon after school for one hour. For the first two weeks after each session I found I could hardly lift my arms up as they felt like lead weights. The muscles in my upper arms were very sore.

Bro. Luke was philosophical about this. He said,"You have to persist. Without pain, there is no gain."

He was right of course and soon I noticed the pain grew less noticeable as I seemed to get the hang of learning to box. I knew that I'd never be a top-drawer fighter but, at least I'd be able to protect myself. I had believed that the art of boxing was learning how to deliver blows. That was not so; it also involved learning the strategy of the ring. This was equally as important as a right-cross or a left jab.

Now, some months after my training began, I felt confident enough to take on the bully, Billy Ford. One day Bro. Luke said to me "You know Walshe, I think I have taught you as much as I can. It's now up to you. However, I would like to know why you wanted to do this in the first place." I smiled and nodded.

For a few days I worried about the situation but decided that something had to be done about the bullies and tomorrow would be the day.

I was quite apprehensive when I arrived at school the next day but, I knew what had to be done so I waited 'til lunchtime when I knew the group would be active on their rounds.

Sure enough, Jimmy and Billy Ford soon approached me where I was sitting on a bench with my dinner.

"Hand over the dinner tin, Walshe!" they demanded.

I stood up and looked straight back at them and said, "No such luck."

Billy rushed forward to grab my shirt-front but I side-stepped and tripped him. He fell onto the dirt. He got up again fuming angrily.

Before he could do or say anything I said,"You know, Billy, there are rules about not fighting in the school grounds."

"Yeah, Walshe."

"Well, I am issuing you a challenge to fight me in the ring this afternoon."

He smirked and looked round his followers.

"Walshey, you must be joking. I'll kill you!"

He gazed at his cohorts and grinned hugely. They all burst out laughing. I ignored them.

"Can I take that as an acceptance then, Billy?"

"You bet it is, sucker!"

We both went to see Bro. Luke for permission to stage the fight. He was surprised when he saw whom I'd challenged but gave his approval.

He winked in my direction.

I now felt very confident about the outcome. Not so, my friends; they were quite worried. I didn't blame them but nobody at school knew about my after-hours training, not even Billy Ford. I now hoped he would be in for a shock and the element of surprise would work for me.

The boxing ring was set up in the gym for the bout. Almost every boy and teacher was there. Bro. Luke sent a message for me to see him beforehand. When I walked into his room I wondered what he wanted.

"Sit down, Walshe. I have to talk to you before you go into the ring. I need to ask you some questions. Look, I applaud your reasons for doing this. Do you intend to box him as I've taught you?"

"Yes, Brother." I answered."Just as instructed. I know no other way."

"Well, I'd like to give you one or two tips. It seems the other boy is a street fighter which means there are no holds barred — he is likely to try anything so, don't take your eyes off his for a moment. He will signal his moves with his eyes.

"And another thing, most importantly, as a street fighter he will be a 'round-house' puncher. That means he will not punch straight from the shoulder, he will swing his arms round. This is to your advantage because when he swings, he will leave himself wide open for an instant. That is when you deliver your punch — as hard as you can — to the jaw.

"Now, all this advice is well and good if, in fact, he is a street fighter. Then again, he might be a trained boxer like you so you will have to feel his style out early. Now, best of luck Walshe, and I hope it's your right arm I hold up at the end of the bout as the victor."

After the visit to Bro. Luke I went to the locker room and dressed in shorts, singlet and sandshoes. Then I walked out to the gym as it was nearly time to begin. The place was packed.

I'd never seen so many people in the gym at one time. I wondered who they had come to see. I climbed into the ring and sat on the tiny stool in my corner. My seconds were already there and Ford was on

52

his feet prancing around waving his arms in the air. Some of the crowd cheered him on.

I sat and considered my tactics for the first round. I decided that, as he was so aggressive and a bit overweight, I would let him come to me by using my feet.

The opening bell rang and we both walked to the centre of the ring where Bro. Luke stood.

"Alright lads, let's have a nice clean fight, no clinches, no hitting below the belt, no rabbit punches and break when I say to. Now shake hands, go back to your corners and come out fighting."

As the bell for round one sounded, Ford came rushing at me swinging his right arm, not straight from the elbow but round from the shoulder. This was exactly what I wanted to see. I was relieved because I now knew he was a street fighter, not a boxer.

I kept back-peddling away from him which made him angry. He kept calling out to me to stand still so he could land a blow. A couple of times I did stop only to land a punch to his face then back-peddled once more out of range. My tactics seemed to be working as I could see he was puffing heavily which meant that he was well out of condition.

The bell sounded to end round one.

I rinsed my mouth with water and spat into a tin bucket held by my seconds. They wiped the sweat from my brow and the bell rang for round two.

Again we met in the middle and I kept my eyes on his watching the signals. They were pretty obvious and I landed some more good, heavy blows to his face and body. He got me once on the left shoulder which glanced off without hurting much. Nearing the end of round two I managed to clip him full on the jaw which made him stagger a bit with eyes closed. He shook his head but stayed on his feet. I knew I'd hurt him and he appeared a bit less aggressive now and somewhat relieved the round was over.

The bell went again to end round two.

I now knew that I could hurt him but concentrating on his head would not end the fight for me quickly. I had to work a strategy of combination body blows and head punches. I thought back to what Bro. Luke had said about a street fighter throwing round-house punches and to watch the eyes for a signal.

Round three started and I could tell he was very tired as he moved slower into the ring. My chance came mid-round when he came at me rather desperately and swung a round-house 'haymaker'. I saw it coming and aimed a left as hard as I could right at his solar plexus. It connected beautifully and he doubled over, dropping his guard.

I then followed up with a perfectly timed right upper-cut to the point of his jaw. His eyes rolled back, his knees buckled and he dropped to the canvas. He lay there, quite still, while Bother Luke counted him out. He did manage to move between 'six' and 'ten' but could not raise himself from the floor.

His seconds came and dragged him back to his corner. Brother Luke walked up to me, took my right glove in his hand and raised it high.

"I declare Gerald Walshe to be the winner of this bout by TKO."

Immediately cheering and whistling broke out across the gym. It was very loud and I could hear people calling my name.

"Good on you, Walshey! You little beauty!"

I felt very proud and lucky in that I was able to help stop these people from their bullying at the College. Now, perhaps the school can get back to being the happy place it was when I first arrived.

When I arrived at school next day I couldn't believe the difference I felt with all the happy faces around me. The school had been transformed from a gloomy place to once again being a happy place of learning.

Billy and Jimmy Ford kept well out of my way. Most of their past friends had deserted them The following week the two Ford boys left the college. We were told that the family had moved away as their father had secured a job out of the area.

I was glad to see them go as the back-slapping had got to be a bit much. I did wonder if, when they got to the next school, whether they would try the same lurks. I hoped they would not.

CHAPTER THIRTEEN.

I soon realised that life never runs smoothly; it seemed to be one problem after another that required solving. I was still getting 'curry' from good old Uncle Bill. There was nothing that I did that pleased him and, if I ever was within easy reach I got a clip round the ear or a kick in the pants for absolutely no reason that I could see. He obviously still held me responsible for poor Dorothy's death.

I stayed away from him as much as I could. I spoke to Verna about this and she just said,"OK, I'm working on a plan to get us away from here."

I began to believe her as she was staying out overnight on the weekends and, when she came back home, she seemed very happy. However, she wouldn't tell me what she'd been up to.

Then, one morning when she'd stayed out all night, she appeared very happy and went to speak to Gran. When she returned to our flat she was very angry. She told me that she now had a boyfriend named Syd and she had gone to ask Gran if she would allow Syd to live with us in the flat.

"Red rag to a bull!" was Verna's summary of the meeting, brief though it was.

"No!" shouted Gran."You already have a child who's not wanted here. I do not want another one on my doorstep..."

Verna went to see the boyfriend and they decided to rent a house as he had a good job as a green-keeper at a golf club. The following week we moved out of the flat and into a house a long way from all the family.

I met Syd and, at first sight, thought he was alright. At the time I didn't realise it but, by leaving Gran's house, I had left all my past troubles behind. Well, maybe not ALL my troubles but a good many of them.

The most important ones to lose were the fishing trips every Tuesday and Friday plus being used as a slave. The nasty feeling of not being wanted or loved while living there would now disappear. Living at the new place with just Verna and Syd had to be a better life for me.

The new house was very big and spacious and, across the road was a cliff where, if you stood near the edge, you could look down on the sea a long way below. For the first time since leaving Yurana so long ago and far away, I felt free. For some inexplicable reason my body and my mind seemed to be as one and belonged entirely to me.

A strange new feeling came over me indicating that this was a turning point in my life. At last I was beginning to understand the white man's world. It was a dangerous world full of many surprises and pitfalls along the way. I would have to use every trick and instrument that Yurana had taught me about life to survive.

But, survive I would, so that I could be the person she would be proud of. I knew deep in my heart that I may never see her again but the bond we had between us insured that at least we would be one forever.

I had my natural mother who gave me life and I had a mother who sustained me through my early years. She was the mother to whom I owed everything as, without her love and nurturing, I would never have survived.

We had not been in the new house very long when, one morning when I awoke, I felt really ill. I told Verna who took a look at me and said to go back to bed.

"Gerald, honey, you look terrible. I'll go and fetch the doctor."

She left the house and walked to the doctor's place which was just up the road. When he arrived he looked at me and declared that I had scarlet fever.

"I want him to stay in bed in a darkened room for the next two weeks. I'll then come back to see him." said the Doc.

The days were long at home in a dark room. I tried to read but there wasn't enough light. Then one day, my mother said before she left, "I have to go shopping so I'll make up a bed for you in the lounge room. You'll be comfy there and warm by the fire."

After she had left I settled down to sleep but something told me to open my eyes. When I did I could see someone sitting on the arm of the lounge. The room seemed to me to be a little brighter and I could see quite clearly a beautiful young girl in a blue dress. She had long blonde hair down to her waist and she smiled at me. I asked her name and, although her lips moved, no sound came out.

She pointed down at the floor but I heard no sound. I spoke to her for a few minutes and asked her questions which she answered but I could hear nothing she said.

Then, just as mysteriously, as I watched her she began to fade away.

All the time she was present, the room was very peaceful. I was not frightened as the whole episode was so realistic. When she had gone, the room returned to semi-darkness.

When Verna returned home I related my experience to her.

"Don't worry Gerald," she said. "You were only dreaming. It's part of your illness — seeing apparitions and things."

I knew different from that and, thereafter when people spoke of ghosts, I listened and believed because I had seen a most beautiful ghost. Some time later I heard that about three months before we moved into the house, a young girl who'd lived in this house had been knocked down and killed by a car right outside. Nobody could tell me what she looked like but that didn't worry me. I had already met her.

The scarlet fever kept me away from school for few weeks but, when I returned, I was very happy to be there as I had a bit to catch up with the other boys. This would keep my mind active as I had to prove to myself that I could excel at school work as with everything else in life. I didn't want to fail to achieve my goals.

I felt that I had to prove to my mother's family at least that I was better than them at something.

One morning Verna asked me a rather strange question; "Gerald, how would you feel about having some other children living here too?"

"Why, Mum?" I asked innocently.

"Ohh, I was just wondering," was her reply and she left it at that.

When I went to school I kept wondering what she was up to but, luckily my school-work kept my mind occupied and I almost forgot the question.

That afternoon Verna approached me as I walked into the house. "Come and sit down here, Gerald," she purred. "There's something I have to discuss with you in private."

We sat in the kitchen together and I listened intently as she went about her explanation to me which, at first, I didn't understand. As she went on, I could hardly believe what she was telling me especially as, up until now, I thought of myself as her only child. I was normally prepared for many of the shocks which come with life but this one almost threw me.

"Gerald, honey, before you were born I was married to David

Walshe and, in the five years that we were together, I gave birth to three other children; a son called David and two girls — Bonny and Joyce. Then my legal husband, David Walshe desserted me and the children in a rented house with no money. I was destitute.

"When I found you were coming along, I went to my mother for advice and help but she simply advised me to hand over my son, David to her and to place the two girls in a Convent Orphanage at a far away place called Geelong."

At this point I stopped her and asked,"What does this have to do with me now?"

"Well, Gerald dear, I've been thinking about this for a long time and I think it's about time that I removed the girls from the Convent at Geelong. They've been there for over ten years and I spoke to Syd about it and he agreed with me to get them out and bring them here to live with us. I rang the Convent and arranged to pick them up next weekend to bring them home. I thought it was only fair to let you know what was going to happen to lessen the shock to you."

She sat there with her hands folded together waiting for my approbation or condemnation. Neither came. Instead I asked "Mum, if they live here, where will they sleep? We only have two bedrooms. You and Syd sleep in one and I sleep in the other in a single bed. We just wouldn't fit!"

She smiled bemusedly and replied, "I was coming to that. We have arranged to buy a double bed so that you three can share together, Isn't that wonderful?"

Verna then revealed that she'd been in touch with Uncle Bill because he had a truck. She had asked him to drive us down to Geelong to pick up the girls. He'd agreed and, early on Saturday morning he arrived. I jumped up in the back and sat down on a mattress which was there, not speaking to him in the process.

The truck was a bright red Dodge with high sides like a cattle truck. I hated the colour but, at least it was transport. We drove through Melbourne and on toward Geelong. We had about 40 miles to go when it all began to go wrong. First there was a flat tyre on the back wheels. Uncle Bill stopped and repaired the inner tube with a patch, put the wheel back and off we went again only to find another puncture in a rear tyre.

Again we stopped and Uncle Bill repaired the hole, put the wheel back and drove off. Another puncture in a front wheel about two miles down the road meant that we had run out of repair patches.

"Bad luck," he cursed and told everyone to get into the nearby paddocks and gather dead grass which he could stuff into the flat tube and give it enough bulk to carry the truck. This done, the wheel was returned to the truck and off we went again to Geelong Convent.

Eventually we reached the gates of the Convent and we sat in the truck while Verna went into the Convent to fetch the girls. They duly emerged from the establishment and I gazed for the first time on my long-lost siblings. Bonny was a bit taller than Joyce and had blonde hair while Joyce had darker hair. Neither girl spoke but stepped up into the back of the truck with me. I thought they appeared to be frightened of Mother Superior who looked to be quite calm and pleasant.

Both girls had brought with them a small bag. They waved 'goodbye' to their friends as we drove away from the institution. Bonny remained quiet but Joyce sat down and said "Good riddance! I hope to God I never see that place again!"

As we drove along heading for home, not much was said. I got the impression that the girls were not used to conversing with other people. At the time I wasn't interested in 'yakking' to them. I was more concerned about the tyres holding out til we got home. The one at the front was stuffed with grass and could have caught fire in the heat of the day. Luckily it didn't and we arrived home late in the afternoon safe and sound.

It seemed that their 'God' had been looking after the truck after all.

CHAPTER FOURTEEN.

When we arrived back home I was sore and quite tired so I decided to go to my bedroom and lie down for a while. Imagine my surprise when I went to my room and saw a huge double bed where my little bed used to be. Verna followed me into the room and explained that, as we only had two rooms, the girls were now going to share the double bed with me.

"I'm afraid that's the way it has to be, Gerald, until we can afford a bigger house with more rooms. When that will be, I have no idea, I'm sorry."

I felt cheated once again — relegated to 'third child' status. I had only been told half the story and then forced to share my room with girls whom I had never heard of before. I had no choice in the matter so I had to like it. What could I have done?

I did, however, insist that I would sleep on the right-hand side of the bed. Verna agreed for once so, for six months I put up with sharing room with the girls; one girl tidy and the other anything but...

In all that time I didn't get to know either one because they had a strange attitude. I guessed that this came about from being locked away in the institution for so many years and having to fend for themselves without a mother or other family to rely on. They had been apart from their natural mother like I was but, with the difference that, with my big 'family' at Pokataroo, I had shared the love of the greatest mother anyone could have — Yurana, my Aboriginal mother.

Now the situation had taken a strange twist; I had to look after myself as Verna was pre-occupied with giving the girls all her attention. It seemed she felt guilty after giving them to the Convent at Geelong so long ago and their having to endure the rigours of Convent life under that harsh regime. I reflected upon my mother's aspect of life; she had given away all her children twice so that she could continue her own selfish life and, now, after all these years she had regrets but not for all, only the two girls.

From my perspective, giving me to Yurana was the best thing that happened to me. My deepest regret is that Verna took me back from Yurana and for this, I will never forgive her.

As time went by it seemed that I was being pushed further into the background again. Bonny was a bit shy but she and I got on better than Joyce and I. Joyce was a forceful personality and it didn't take too long before she became mother's favorite little darling. I called her 'The Princess' as that was the way she acted — anything she wanted, she got. Being a very pretty child as well helped.

Then I discovered to my horror that I was getting accused of things I had done or said which were blatantly not true. I found out from Bonny that Joyce was telling Verna lies about me to get me into trouble as she realised I didn't like her. I therefore stayed clear of Joyce as much as I could but, sleeping in the same room in the same bed and trying to ignore her presence was a big ask.

Inevitably, the girls became family favorites and they were invited to Gran's place anytime they wanted and they were allowed to go to the school that I was not. Although I felt quite put-out by these events and privileges I decided not to worry too much about them as there were other pressing issues to deal with in my life. After all, having been on the lowest rung of the social scale when I lived with Yurana and the tribe at Pokataroo, I had also associated with people far above the social standing of these members of my family.

To help me overcome any feelings of inadequacy I decided to try to find other occupations away from the house which would keep me safe from the taunts from Joyce. As it happened, Syd had had a scheme going every second Saturday morning and invited me to help out with his secret venture.

We went to a place outside of town for the greyhound races which were held in the middle of a paddock with a strip about twenty feet wide and a quarter of a mile long where the grass had been cut very short. There were boxes at one end across the track where the dogs were held behind a spring-loaded gate. When the starter flagged them away, the gate sprang up and they leapt out and away down the track.

At the far end of the track was a hedge about five feet high (1.5m) and behind which was a strange contraption made from a push bike which Syd would sit on and peddle to wind in the rope which dragged the rabbit-skin lure from in front of the starting gate toward the hedge.

The dogs were trained to chase the lure but Syd had to peddle the 'bike' sufficiently fast to keep the lure tantalisingly ahead of the pack.

When the dogs were all ready to race, a man at the starter's end would raise a red flag to indicate that Syd should commence peddling the rope drum, reeling in the lure past the dogs. Five seconds later up went a green flag and the race was on with the gate springing up, releasing the hounds which meant that Syd had to peddle faster and keep the lure ahead of the first dogs.

My part in this was to stand beside Syd and change gears on the handlebars to increase the speed of the drum reel. It took no time at all for the race to be over and have the dogs crashing into the hedge behind which we hid.

I was to learn that quite a bit of cash changed hands on those race days and I was warned by Syd not to reveal to anyone what went on here as, if the police got to hear of it, there could be trouble for everyone involved. Thus I kept our secret and enjoyed the excitement of the day.

I had to wonder why Syd was called on to 'ride the bike' as it were so, I asked him.

"When I met your mother, Gerald, I was a road-racing champion but I had to give it away because I enjoyed eating too much and put on too much weight. But, by peddling this machine every second Saturday I lose a bit of weight and keep fit. Besides which, I sometimes have a small bet and win a few quid on the side. When I've won enough we can move to a better house with more rooms and you can have a room to yourself."

I was glad Syd told me this. It made me feel like I was someone again who mattered.

CHAPTER FIFTEEN.

My life at school had taken a turn for the better. I let nothing that happened at home deter me from achieving goals I set myself. I wanted to be better than everyone. Not from vanity but from a sense of achievement.

I felt I was very lucky too. For the first time in my life I was receiving respect from one and all at this College — students as well as teachers. I was respected for what I had done to get the better of the bullies. I relished the position that this put me in, going from the lowest rung of the social scale to the top. It gave me a real sense of pride being a student here and doing well academically also helped the prestige of the school.

I think I passed even my own expectations.

Brother Luke had been very helpful and encouraging so I decided to repay that kindness by helping him train any lads who wished to learn the noble art of boxing.

The sport had become very popular since our 'exhibition fight' and I had defeated the bully, Billy Ford but, in joining Bro. Luke in the gym, I found another side to the fight game that I hadn't seen before.

When I stepped into the ring to fight Ford I really wanted to hurt the fellow to teach him a lesson. That was the killer instinct in me then but, as I was later to learn, that was contra to the teachings of the Christian ethics of the college. They taught us that 'if somebody smite you, turn the other cheek'. In other words, don't hit back. When confronted by the likes of Billy Ford, this was a very difficult ethic to follow.

I knew that in this world there are many people like Ford — stand-over merchants — and there are people like me, happy to let others do whatever they want until, one day the stand-over men push too far and then you have to take a stand against them.

Now I found myself on the other side of the fence teaching these lads to box. No killer instinct here, just compassion to train young men in the skill of self-defence to prepare them for any eventuality which may arise in future if they encounter the likes of Billy Ford. My motivation became -'Better to be prepared than not.' I enjoyed the work as repayment for how Brother Luke helped me earlier.

Home life was getting to be a bit wearisome. I dreaded having to go to bed at night and sleep next to Joyce. I was sick and tired of picking up her things off the floor. She was a very untidy person so I asked Mum if I could sleep on the floor to which she replied "No!"

Then, one night she said to me,"Gerald, don't worry about the sleeping arrangements. Syd has some good news to tell us in the morning."

Next morning at breakfast Syd announced that next week we were moving to a bigger place which had three bedrooms. This was music to my ears. No more sleeping with the girls. At last I would have a room to myself.

My joy turned a bit sour when I discovered that my 'bedroom' was an outdoors shed with a flyscreen door which let the breeze blow through. It got very cold in winter however, it was private and it was mine.

This privacy came at a good time for me as I was studying for my exams in three weeks time and I needed to concentrate hard. These exams were my finals for the lower school and a pass with a Merit Certificate would allow me to progress to first grade in the High School where I hoped that I could work hard and finally exit with my Leaving Certificate.

This would allow me to apply for a motor mechanic's apprenticeship which was something I had always yearned to do.

For the next six months everything went along just fine. I could come home after school and disappear into my own room and study without interruption. This helped me to pass the final exam and receive my Merit Certificate. I was very pleased with this result because I was the second in the family to do so. Joyce was the first which I didn't mind as she was still part of the family.

Gran, however, was furious at the news as 'uncle' Dave and Thelma had failed to pass this exam and, because she would not let them repeat the last year of Primary School so they could try again, she had prevented them from going to High School. Although I had overcome the first obstacle in my quest to better myself, I didn't delude myself into thinking that this was the end to obstacles in life. There would be many more to come, I was sure.

My good fortune seemed to be continuing as I had joined the Navy League Sea Cadets at Half Moon Bay while we lived at Gran's place. This got me away from the family and gave me an outside interest. We paraded every Wednesday night and Saturday afternoon and we were taught everything a sailor should know such as knot-tying, signalling with flags and reading morse code both on morse key and Aldis lamp. We did a lot of marching and boat handling — launching safely as well as rowing and sailing.

It was during my time there that I almost became part of naval history, an event which came about quite by accident. It happened one Saturday afternoon in February 1939 when we had been working on our skills in the drill hall plus boat drills outside. During a break we had observed three destroyers out on the Bay going through speed trials, a normal event for this region.

To carry out these trials the Navy had placed a series of 50 ft. high white wooden triangles on the rocks at even distances of one nautical mile apart. The course covered five nautical miles. The ship on trial then would get up to speed as it passed the first triangle as viewed from a command vessel on the Bay. Its speed was then calculated on the time it took to pass the last marker. That speed was then the registered top speed for the ship.

It was late afternoon and we were ready to hoist the cutter ashore when our Commanding officer stopped us and asked if we would like to sail out to the three ships to visit.

"Is that allowed?" we asked unanimously.

"Yes, of course lads." he replied. "We'll signal with our semaphore flags, tell them who we are and ask permission to come aboard. I'm sure we will be welcome."

Thus we started off toward the nearest ship and signalled our intention and received permission to come aboard. It was a hot night and most of the sailors were on deck. As the freeboard was not very high we spoke to them quite easily from our cutter. We tossed them a line which they secured and we climbed aboard to sit on the deck and chat with the crew.

We learned the ships were HMAS Waterhen where we sat plus HMAS Stuart and HMAS Vendetta. We spent about an hour with the sailors then, as it was getting dark, we decided to leave and row ashore. We left feeling that the meeting was quite satisfying, being on the deck of a real warship.

Twelve months later we were to learn that all three ships, know as the 'scrap-iron flotilla' were engaged in running the gauntlet during the Battle of Tobruk as part of the destroyer fleet. They carried in supplies to the garrison at night and took out the wounded, a most dangerous task in the heat of battle.

Unfortunately, all three ships were lost during the action. This had a most saddening effect on the boys as we felt part of the crew whom we had met previously out on the Bay. They were gone forever.

Now, every Anzac Day I look for the marching banner of HMAS Waterhen and remember them and the ship which became, ever so briefly, a small part of my life.

CHAPTER SIXTEEN.

I was now handling my situation at home quite well. I didn't see much of Gran or her family which suited me just fine since I was never made welcome. So now, after all these years I had no desire to be accepted into a group like that. Whenever I had been in their company I got the impression that I was of a lower standing in society than they are.

What they don't realise is, I have been on the lowest rung of the ladder and, when you are there, the only way to go is upward. That's the way I'm going and will continue to go until I am so far above them they will never reach me. I have something to prove — that, from humble beginnings, anything is possible if you try.

Times were changing; the second World War had begun in September 1939 and everywhere I looked were young men and women in uniform. All the young people in town seemed to be signing up and a lot of my friends who were a bit older than me were off. I had a long way to go as I had just turned 14.

One afternoon when I had come home from school Gran was sitting in the kitchen with Verna. This was unusual as she never visited us before; it was always we who called on her. I just said "Hello" and went to my room. I had nothing to say to her.

After a while I ventured out and went to the kitchen but Gran was gone. I asked my mother what she wanted.

"I'll tell you later, Gerald" she said, "When the rest of the family are home."

That evening at the table, Verna announced that we all had been invited over to Gran's place for tea as she had an important announcement to make.

"Good luck!" I said. "I won't be going there. I have no interest in what she has to say."

Verna grew angry. "Gerald, you will do as I say. We are all going and thats the end of the matter. Do I make myself clear?"

"Yes, Mum." I answered.

The next day we all dressed up to go to Gran's house for tea. When we arrived there we went into the house but I was told to stay in the lounge room and sit down Everyone else went through to the kitchen where Gran sat in splendour.

I took a moment to look round the room. It was filled with little bits and pieces and many photos of family members, even a picture of Verna when she won a beauty contest as a young woman. There were photos of my sisters but there were no pictures of me. Well, that was to be expected.

I suppose the 'black sheep' in any family is never recognised however, the word 'black' in my case had special emphasis in this family's eyes.

I was left alone in that room for a long time before being called into the dining room to eat. Everyone was seated round the table and there was a vacant chair at the far end of the table, furthest from Gran. That suited me.

I sat and waited for the big announcement. It didn't come until we had finished the meal Gran then began to speak. It seemed that David — her 'son' — had joined the Royal Australian Navy as a stoker and would be leaving to commence his training at HMAS Cerberus, Flinders Naval Depot in a couple of days.

"So, before he goes," she went on,"I have something to tell you children and, what I have to say, goes back many years. It concerns your mother and David and myself. Nobody else knows what I am about to tell you all."

The old woman paused for effect and gazed around the table at the expectant looks from all except myself.

"I have told your mother never to say anything about what happened to David so many years ago when I took him as my own son from her and brought him up. You children have always thought of him as 'uncle David' and as a brother to Thelma and William well, that is not exactly true. Now, this is a long story and I won't go into detail right now but, suffice to say that, to Joyce and Bonny, he is actually your big brother."

Gran then cast me a cold, haughty look and shifted uneasily on her chair.

"Gerald, on the other hand, is a different thing altogether. I will let your mother explain that to you later."

When Gran had finished there was a pall of silence around the room. I quickly ran my eyes round the table but could see no signs of anyone being surprised or shocked by this revelation. Conversely, I had many questions to ask and challenge Gran's mention of 'Gerald... is a different thing altogether.'

Then we all retired to the lounge room and, while the others all went one way together, my Grandfather and I sat together listening to the others laughing and talking among themselves. I then realised that this family was born to tell lies. They lived up to the name I had given them some time before — the 'Family of Secrets'.

I resolved never to believe anything that these people told me. That news about David shattered any trust I had in them. I recalled Verna introducing him to me with Gran close by and saying, "This is your Uncle David and you will always address him by this name."

I could see now that this was a way of letting me know they thought of me as 'The White Aborigine'. I knew my place because I didn't belong here.

I had to thank my grandfather for making me feel somewhat better that night when he said to me,"Gerald, remember it's not where you came from that matters in life; it's who you are and what you do with your life that is most important."

I still couldn't stop thinking what was said around the dinner table. I always knew that, somehow, I was different in this family and now I felt entitled to know the whole truth — whatever that was. When we got home again I asked my mother about Gran's words.

"What did Gran mean? And don't just fob me off this time Mum. I am entitled to know the truth."

Verna just looked away and said," I'm going to bed now, Gerald. I'm very tired. We can talk about it in the morning."

I quickly replied, "Mum, don't think this will go away. I want to know everything in the morning."

I then went to bed also but couldn't sleep as I kept thinking what I might learn tomorrow that could explain the treatment I'd been receiving since I first came to this place years ago.

In the morning Verna and I went outside to the garden and sat on a wooden bench to talk. She began to tell me about being left with three children when her husband at the time left her; about falling for another man's charm and falling pregnant with me. When she informed the fellow, he disappeared.

She went on to enlighten me about meeting Ken Carr and to

convince him that he was my father. I gasped in horror.

"Mum!" I exclaimed,"Do you mean to tell me that I'm not really Ken's child? Does that mean that I am illegitimate?"

She reached out to stroke my cheek but I backed away a bit.

"Yes, my darling. That is correct. Kenneth Carr was not your real father. I'm so sorry." I noticed a tear emerge from her eye and roll down her beautiful cheek.

"But, why didn't you marry the man who was my father? Or even marry Ken when we were all up-country? You had already told a lie when you applied for the job — you wrote on the application that you and Ken were married. Had you married while we were there, you could have legitimised my birth and nobody would have to know differently."

Verna shrugged and replied, "I couldn't do that, Gerald. In the eyes of the Church I was already married and the Church does not allow divorce. I could never have remarried unless my first husband died."

My head was spinning at this revelation.

"So, you are saying that a woman can live with a man and have as many illegitimate children as they like and the Church accepts this behaviour so long as you go to confession? Does this help you enter Heaven when, in the eyes of the Church, you are declared pure after confession?

"But what about the children who have been brought into the world by this lustful behaviour? They have to suffer all their lives from the stigma of being known as illegitimate under the laws of the land yet, according to the laws of God, they are not unclean or stigmatised at all.

"I know what it says in the Bible,... Jesus said 'Suffer the little children to come unto me for they are without sin'! There is no mention of being born out of wedlock or in wedlock to qualify."

My dander was really up now after chewing over the situation for many years and it was time to vent my wrath. My boiler had a full head of steam and I was not going to stop until I had let it all out.

"Mum, I have listened to what you've said and I must say, some of it I do believe but the rest I do not. The parts I am trying to believe are not right at the beginning. Tell me why your husband left you in the first place."

Verna scowled at me. "You don't have to know that. It's none of your business."

"But, that's where you're wrong, Mum. If you tell me, then it might explain why you committed adultery and, as that act produced me, I feel I'm entitled to know. You said that you could not divorce and remarry as the Church forbids this as a mortal sin. However, the Church also views adultery as a mortal sin and, the punishment for both these sins, is excommunication. So, in essence, Mother, you say one thing and then believe another just to convince yourself you are doing nothing wrong.

"In fact, Mum, you have been living a life of lies and deceit all these years and I have had to suffer for it."

By now Verna was in full flood, not being able to contradict my argument with lucid rebuff. I pressed on.

"The main part of your story that I do not believe is that Kenneth Carr is not my real father. I accepted him as my father and he will always be my father to me. Nothing will convince me otherwise. Telling lies comes to you so easily, why should this not be another lie? I was convinced he was my father after you had taken me from my only 'mother', Yurana at Pokataroo long ago.

"He was a very loving, caring man and it took him no time to get to understand my situation and try to help me as much as possible. You, on the other hand, had no idea what I was going through and, I don't think you really cared that much. He was always there for me to talk to and offer advice. I couldn't imagine anyone other than my father doing this for me."

Verna was completely taken aback by my response to her story. We parted company in silence. She didn't say much after that and life seemed to go on as usual in the 'house of secrets'.

The next problem we had to overcome was moving again as the owner of the house we lived in had died and his son decided to sell it.

We moved to a house in a street closer to my school, an older place which had quite a big backyard. It, too three bedrooms but, again, I was relegated to the outdoors bedroom situated in the huge yard.

I didn't mind this so much as it reminded me a bit of Pokataroo but without the over-crowding. Constructed of timber and weatherboard, it was cosy enough and, being on my own outside, I was now free to come and go as I pleased.

CHAPTER SEVENTEEN.

It seemed that we'd just get over one problem and find ourselves with another. Syd had decided to operate as an S.P. bookie at the Red Bluff Hotel where he spent a lot of time. Naturally, in the course of his 'business activities' he found it easy or necessary to consume a lot of beer. He was now coming home drunk and very abusive.

I was the recipient of a back-hander a few times and so was Verna. He was not normally this way but he had changed. On days when he had won he was fine but that was not often.

There was a cupboard in the house where Syd had stored four shotguns. He was very proud of them and had shown me how to load them and fire when we went out shooting rabbits. Little did I realise at the time that these skills would be used at home.

One night when he came home after a heavy losing day, he was very angry and drunk. We were all sitting in the lounge room by the fire after tea when it started. Syd came into the room and, for no reason hit me with a huge backhander that sent me flying across the room against the far wall.

Verna stood up and walked over to pick me up. He then hit my mother and said, "Leave him alone!"

He then went over to Verna and dragged her to her feet and punched her again. For the first time in my life, I saw red. I got to my feet and scrambled out to the hall cupboard where the guns were kept, opened the door and reached in.

I grasped the first firearm I found and brought it out into the light, broke it open and loaded two shotgun shells into the barrels, closed it and cocked the two hammers, ready to fire.

Then I returned to the room and saw my mother on the floor, bleeding from the nose and arms. Syd was standing over her.

"Syd!" I yelled as loud as I could.

He turned and saw the gun in my hands with the hammers cocked, ready to fire. His face went white. He saw I was shaking with anger and fear.

"Leave my mother alone Syd, or I'll fire!"

His mouth began to tremble.

"I'm sorry, Gerald. Please, put the gun down."

He bent over and picked up Verna and helped her to a chair, wiped her face with his handkerchief and turned back to me.

I stood there for a while deciding what to do, watching him calm down. Satisfied that he meant no further harm to anyone, I released the hammers back to rest and took the gun back to the hall cupboard where I unloaded the shells and placed the gun back in the rack.

The night passed without further incident and, in the morning, he apologised to Verna saying that it would never happen again. To me he said nothing. In fact, from that day onward, he didn't have much to say to me at all. I often wondered whether I would have pulled the triggers.

I didn't dwell on that propect much as I had much more on my mind. It was getting very close to exam time at school and I wanted to sit for the matriculation certificate. If I passed, I was promised a job as an apprentice motor mechanic. I would be working on cars and trucks at one of two local garages; one which repaired cars and the other, trucks. Just what I wanted.

I sat for the exam and passed. I knew then my future was secure to a point even though the world was far from being secure with the war still raging overseas. Leaving school was, for me, a very sad occasion. I was leaving the place that had taught me more about living in the white man's world than anything else. I had regrets about leaving the staff especially Brother Luke.

I couldn't forget his kindness and encouragement over the years I had been there. He was, in a sense, a real big brother to me and always pointed me in the right direction when I strayed off course. I knew I would miss the other lads who had raised me high on the social ladder giving me a great sense of self worth and the will to try to understand the complex world of the white fellow.

I felt that I ought to let them know from whence I came and how proud they made me feel. That didn't happen.

The following week I went to see Mr Abadee at the Hume Garage and presented my new matriculation certificate. After the interview he gave me some more papers to take back for Mum to sign which he would send off to the Apprenticeship Board.

"Next week, young fellow, you'll be an apprentice motor mechanic. If you like to, you can start work tomorrow. Be here at 8.00 o'clock sharp!"

I was over the moon as I now had secured the job I'd always wanted and, all of my own volition. The next morning I reported for work. In those days everyone worked 48 hours a week and this included 4 hours on Saturday morning.

I was put with a mechanic and my task consisted mainly of passing him spanners from his toolbox. In this way, it was said, I would quickly learn the right spanner to use and become familiar with all the tools he used.

I was also given another task which was quite unpleasant. This involved cleaning out the gas-producing cylinders which became a war-time necessity for anyone who wanted to use the motor car during the days of petrol rationing. In those days anyone who owned a motor vehicle was allocated only two gallons of fuel per month. This was generally used just to start the engine which, when it reached operating temperature, would be switched over to gas from the device at the back of the car.

The gas producer was a cumbersome device which had to sit on the rear bumper or an extra platform fixed to the vehicle. It generated gas from burning charcoal and consisted of an oven in which the charcoal from either grey box or red gum timber was stacked and lit before the journey. The gas thus produced went first to a large canvas storage bag on the roof and thence to the engine via a copper tube where it was fed into the carburettor when the diversion tap was switched over.

However, in the process of making the gas in the oven or 'box' as it was called, there was always a great build-up of glass as a result of the very high temperatures applied to the charcoal and the presence of silica in the material.

The problem with that was that the glass residue could sometimes block the passage of gas from the oven and the result could be an unexpected explosion. Thus, it was imperative to have a mechanic chip away the build-up of glass from the oven of the cars and trucks which came in for servicing.

This entailed young Gerald, the new apprentice, taking to it with hammer and chisel, wearing protective goggles for safety. Then after cleaning out all the glass from the oven, I was to refill the box with the new load of charcoal which meant I was covered in black dust by the end of the day's work.

At least I was happy to be doing what I had always wanted to work at in an environment which gave me the knowledge to advance my career, even though I was, in effect, back on the lowest rung of the ladder in this workshop.

CHAPTER EIGHTEEN.

It was now August 1942. I had been working for some months at the Hume Garage and I was looking forward to my 16th birthday on 20th August. Then, on 9th August we heard the news that HMAS Canberra had been sunk in a battle with the Japanese off the island of Savo, north of Australia.

This was the ship on which my 'uncle' David was serving. It happened to be my sister Joyce's birthday.

We only heard that the ship was lost — nothing else — so we didn't know whether he was alright or not and we could only wait and hope for the best possible news.

Eventually, good news came through that he was saved and had been taken off the ship with many others by an American destroyer. Three weeks later he arrived home, quite a different person from the one who went to war. No longer the out-going extrovert, he was terribly introverted, withdrawn and had very little to say.

I could only hope that, in time, he would come out of this state. I resolved to think that, in war-time it is to be expected that war would take its toll.

I kept working industriously trying to forget the war but this was very difficult as more of my friends joined up and went away to fight. Every day the newspapers reported casualties. Many of my friends names appeared, some were killed or reported 'missing in action'.

1944 came round and I was in my third year of the apprenticeship. Most young blokes had now left for the action overseas and there were not many of us left at home. I started to get the feeling that I should join up too but, when I enquired, I was rejected as I was working in a 'protected industry'; the automotive trade which the Government wanted to maintain at home.

The only way in which I could leave the industry was to get a release from the boss which would entail him signing away my apprenticeship papers and issuing a paper of release. Then I could present these papers to the Office of Manpower, a Government department that controlled industry. Then I would be free to join the ranks but, where should I start the process?

I had to think long and hard of a way. After tossing and turning all night, I could see the only solution was to make myself so unpopular at work that Mr. Abadee would simply have to fire me. Rather a drastic step and right out of character for me but, I figured it would be the best bet. I had to get in and help my mates in the war effort.

Thus I commenced my campaign by turning up late for work or not going to work all day. I chose days when I knew the garage would be flat out and I would get the boss angry with me. He threatened all sorts of things to me, shouting at the top of his voice and trying to intimidate me. I wanted to respond but I kept my mouth shut which was very difficult under the circumstances.

Over the next few months I was involved in a number of arguments with Mr Abadee as well as my family who couldn't understand why I was acting this way. The strain was taking a heavy toll on me but, I could not reveal the reason for the act.

As time went by I began to have doubts as to the effectiveness of my campaign. Then, one day when I showed up for work, Mr Abadee called me into his office.

"Don't sit down." he said, "This won't take long."

He handed over some papers. I looked them over and my heart leapt. They were my indenture papers which had a word scrawled across the front -"CANCELLED!" The date underneath was Monday, 31st July 1944, just three weeks before my 18th birthday.

"Thanks Mr Abadee," I offered. I was elated and depressed all at once but I was hurt by what he said next.

Not realising the reason behind my campaign to be sacked, his tone was fearsome and full of fire.

"Walshe, I am bitterly disappointed in you. You have let me down and all I can hope for you in future is that you go from bad to worse with your life. When you look back and see that you have hurt everyone at this garage I hope you feel satisfied.

"Now, take this sealed letter and hand it to the Manpower Office in Melbourne. Now, get out of my office. Here's your final pay packet — you are sacked and I never want to see you ever again!"

Of course, he had every right to be furious but I was very sad at having won my battle and lost a good friend. He had been very kind to me but, that was the price I had to pay to achieve my goal.

The next morning I was out of bed early and off to Melbourne to the Manpower Office in Lonsdale Street where I handed in my papers with the letter from Mr Abadee. I received my release form which I would hand to the recruiting officer when I joined up.

I had already decided which service I would join. It was another act of defiance I had levelled at my grandmother.

Gran had told Verna many times that, if and when I joined up I should follow David into the Navy. It was tradition as David's father was in the Navy during the first World War. They didn't take into account that I was only a Walshe by name and my father, Kenneth Carr was in the Army.

That, however, had no bearing on my decision as I went to Suttons Motors in Russell Street and joined the RAAF as a navigator. I passed all the fitness, medical and education tests and was given a paper to take home for Verna to sign on which she gave her permission for me join up.

I had previously spoken about this with Mum and we had agreed that, for her to sign the paper, I had to agree to send her half my pay via an allotment which she would put into a bank account for me in her name. This would ensure that, when I left the service, there would be some cash saved.

At the time I thought, superficially, that it was a good idea but, at the back of my mind, I had doubts. Eventually, when my service was over, I was proven correct but, at the time, all I could think of was joining up.

With the paper signed, I reported back to the RAAF recruitment office next morning which was 22nd August 1944. I was ready to begin my training as a member of the Royal Australian Air Force.

The paper which Verna had to sign for me was parental consent for recruits who were under the age of 21 which was the accepted threshold of adulthood at this time. By signing the consent form, Verna was also awarded a Mother's Star which indicated to all who saw it that she had a son away at the war. She signed the paper.

I returned to the Manpower Office after visiting the RAAF. I expected the meeting would only be a formality however, I was disappointed to find that, when the man at Manpower read the letter from Mr Abadee, he was not impressed. I also expected that it would only be a matter of about two weeks before I was inducted into the RAAF, but this was not to happen either.

"Well, Mr Walshe, I have read the letter from Mr Abadee,"said the fellow at Manpower, "and it seems that you have been a very naughty boy in the past three months. So naughty, in fact that, I feel you should be given a job until you can report to the RAAF.

"So, instead of a two weeks holiday, my boy, you are requested to report to Hoadley's Chocolate factory in South Melbourne at 8.00am on Thursday morning, 3rd August and work there as a labourer until 5.30pm on Friday 18th August.

"On the afternoon of that day, you will report back here to this office to receive your clearance papers to present to the RAAF. Here are the papers to present to the manager at Hoadley's. I hope you enjoy the work and that you behave yourself while there. Good bye, Mr Walshe."

I left the Manpower office wondering why he had given me another job in Melbourne as I lived far away down the coast. Then it occurred to me that I was again being punished for my behaviour. I consoled myself by saying 'It's only two weeks so learn to live with it. Getting up early and coming home late will not last forever. And remember, this is your big chance to get away from the family. This is an adventure. You have finally joined up.'

On my first day at Hoadley's, I was up at 5.00am on a very cold morning. This would allow me enough time to be there by starting time as I had about two hours travelling by tram and train.

I arrived and reported to the manager and gave him my papers. He shook my hand and said, "Come with me."

"Where will I be working?" I asked.

"Production line... mostly girls and women there. Why, does that worry you?"

Confidently I replied,"No, not really." I was lying of course.

When I arrived at the factory I was nervous. Now, I was terrified as I had never worked with women before. I had only been close to four women in my life; three in the family and one other, the sister of a lad I taught boxing at college. We used to sit and talk when he was training. Unfortunately, she died of typhoid during an epidemic, after which I lost interest in girls as I thought it might happen again.

My first job at the chocolate factory was to load up a large trolley with eight shelves to carry fancy chocolates from the production line to cold storage about 500 yards away. There I would unload the trays onto shelves that extended the full length of this huge room, then return to the production line and repeat the process.

Not the most inspirational tasks but, I kept noticing the girls on the production line eyeing me every time I came into view and talking between themselves. The first four days went well as I got into a rhythm and didn't require much brain power to complete the task. On the fifth day, the whole scene was to change.

The day began the same but at about 11:45am when I had just entered the cool room to unload my last trolley before lunch break, I heard the door close behind me; something I would not do although I knew I could unlock it.

I started to unload the trolley onto the big shelves and my instinct told me to look around. I was shocked to see four girls from the factory standing there smiling at me.

"What are you lot doing here?" I asked loudly.

One lass stepped forward and said,"We just wanted to ask you a question, Gerry dear." She looked back over her shoulder at the other three who giggled. "We want to know have you ever been out with a girl before? A good looking bloke like you must have been out with lots of young girls before."

The question puzzled me a bit but, I answered "No, well, not very often."

"So, have you ever had sex with a girl?"

I was flustered wondering what came next. "No!" I answered.

"Well, we think it's about time you did some learning, Gerry dear. You've gotta learn what life's all about, don't you?"

Now I felt a bit anxious. "I don't know what you mean."

The girls then moved as one and quickly grabbed me, forcing me by weight of numbers to the concrete floor where I was held down by three while one girl undid my belt and stripped me of my trousers. Now I was terrified and began to struggle violently. I had no idea what they had planned for me but I had no desire to be quiet and find out. The 'crunch' came when they tried to remove my undies. I knew I was in deep trouble.

Although I realised it was not the accepted thing to strike a woman, I thought that the odds of four to one would justify my actions so I began to lash out. I managed to free one leg and kick one girl in the stomach. She fell groaning and clutching her abdomen, falling against another as she went down. Both fell to the floor.

This gave me time to get to my feet. The remaining two rushed me so I decided to fight them. I hit one girl I considered their leader with a straight right to the jaw. She collapsed in a heap. The second one copped a right cross and I turned to take on the other two who had, by now, got to their feet.

When they saw what had happened to their pals, they took off out

80

the door. I found my trousers and put them back on, then my shoes. I went to the girls who were still on the floor. They were just stirring so I helped them back to their feet. They gave me a strange look then slowly walked away rubbing their jaws.

I pushed the trolley back out the door and walked immediately to the foreman's office to report the incident. When it came to telling all, I faltered. He looked at me standing in the doorway, dishevelled.

"Good God, Gerry! What the hell happened to you? It looks like you've been hit by a tram."

I told him a slightly different story saying that I couldn't identify any of the girls who attacked me as the lights had been turned off in the cold storage and the girls had come at me from behind.

I asked the foreman to transfer me to another section after lunch.

"Yes, sure, no problem, Gerry. I think you've had enough excitement for one day. I admire you for not telling me which girls were involved." He smiled and made a note on his pad.

That afternoon I was working in the Polly Waffle section doing much the same routine, pushing a trolley to the cold room. I stayed there for the rest of my two weeks 'vacation' at Hoadley's Chocolate Factory.

I did, however, run into the four girls again before I left. One was sporting a black eye, two had sore jaws. Their leader named Jean thanked me for not telling the foreman who they were. She said they were all sorry for what they had done to this baby-faced lad who looked as innocent as an angel but had the courage to fight back like a wildcat when cornered.

"We all have bruises," she said," And we learned not to judge a book by its cover. Nobody could have picked you for a boxer."

She hugged me and put out her hand which I shook."I hope you are lucky in the Air Force, Gerry. Come back in one piece after the war is over. Goodbye, and thanks for your silence."

I never saw them again. On the afternoon of Friday 18th August 1944 I reported back to the Manpower office. Then I received my clearance to join the Air Force and left feeling very pleased with myself. I was looking forward to Sunday when I turned 18, the last day I would be a 'civvy' for over four years. The following day, Monday I was to report to the recruiting centre for my induction into the Service and become an airman. After that, and still in civilian clothes but wearing an armband with RAAF on it, we new recruits swaggered down Swanston Street to Spencer Street Rail Station which was to take us to Shepparton where we would spend the next month on our 'rookies' course.

CHAPTER NINETEEN.

The group of new recruits arrived at Shepparton Rail Station late in the afternoon and were taken by RAAF truck to No.1 Recruit Depot. This was another totally different world for me but, this one was to be quite traumatic for me.

Here, I would learn discipline; to do things without question and mostly, to act as a member of a team. The most important thing I would be taught was to kill. How to kill in many different ways, with all types of weapons and bare-handed as well. It was a most intensive month of training.

I remember a strange phenomenon which seemed to overcome most chaps who were in the same intake. After a long day's training I was fairly worn out and could not get to my bed fast enough however, after about an hour's sleep I would be awake and weeping into my pillow for some unknown reason.

I broached the subject with a couple of others who revealed that they, too, had experienced the same thing — late at night crying for no known cause into their bedding. That made me feel somewhat more relaxed except that I needed a positive answer. I went to ask our Flight Sergeant.

"Of course it happens to every Flight that comes through here. A percentage of young blokes cannot handle leaving home. It's called 'home-sickness'. Nothing to worry about. We will work it out of you all, in time." He smiled the smile of a crocodile who'd just eaten a juicy chook.

This explanation satisfied us however, I had to query my reasons for being home-sick as I could hardly wait to be away from my blood relatives. The only time I could recall being sad at leaving home was when I had to leave my lovely Yurana. This was entirely different.

By mid-September 1944, all 32 of us in Flight 1274 had graduated. We'd absorbed all that was taught us and were now fully qualified in the gentle art of 'kill — or be killed!'

A couple of us had actually learned a bit more than just that — how to play the kettle drum. This meant that we were in the band which played at the Passing Out Parade. Little did I realise at the time that, being able to play the drum, may mean doors would be open to me in the future.

On the train back to Melbourne wearing our very smart new uniforms, we began to speculate about how we would be accommodated at Melbourne Cricket Ground, now re-titled Rainsford Air Fore Base — No.1 Personnel Depot.

"Oh, the've probably got huts or at least tents set up on the middle of the ground ." came one hopeful suggestion.

"Nah,... I think the grass is too sacred to build even a temporary hut on it," came another voice.

"You don't think we'll have to sleep up in the stands, do you?"

"Not on your Nellie!" preferred somebody else. "It's still damn cold in Melbourne and that would be too much to bear."

Wrong!

When we arrived at what used to be the MCG, now Rainsford RAAF No.1 P.Depot, we were escorted to the stands where all the wooden seats had been removed and beds had replaced them along the tiers of concrete. In order to exclude the cold wind, plywood partitions had been erected along the front of the stands. Of course, this was to no avail at all.

The cold we experienced at night was so bad that, to a man, we slept in pyjamas under overalls on camp beds with two blankets, over which everyone threw his great-coat in an effort to keep warm. This was not enough and we asked for more blankets from the store.

"Two blankets are normal issue, lads. Sorry!" came the official reply. "Just grin and bear it!"

On our second day I was approached by a Flight Sergeant and asked if I had been a drummer at Shepparton. I replied that I had.

"Good!" he said," We're a bit short of drummers here. Would you consider volunteering to join the band?"

"Yes," I replied.

"Well, that's great. I like fellows who like to do things without being told. That saves me ordering them and makes my job easier. You can now report to the orderly room and they will tell you what to do."

I reported to the orderly room and was issued with a kettle drum and sticks. Then I received another pleasant surprise. The Officer of the Day said to me, "A/C I Walshe, all troops here are given one and a half days off per month. However, for any who volunteer for extra duty we award an extra one and a half days leave. Thus, in your case, for playing the drum in our band, you are awarded the extra one and a half days."

Music to my ears! I had been told by some knowledgable fellow, well before I joined up that, you should never volunteer for anything in service. How wrong he was!

Each day we assembled outside the main gates to march to Jolimont Rail Yards where we boarded an electric train to be taken to Brunswick Station where we got off and marched to Brunswick Tech College to begin our technical training.

After three months of this routine and, after passing our exams, we waited for orders posting us to flying units. I was expecting to muster as a flight navigator but this was not to be. We were told that all musterings had been rescheduled and we were given a choice of remustering. I chose to remuster as a flight rigger as this was akin to my prior training in motor mechanics.

The reason for the re-muster was that there was a surplus of experienced air crew who were returning from Britain. Thus, I was posted to No.1 Engineering School at the Show Grounds at Ascot Vale. This began my love affair with aircraft in general which has lasted all my life.

We were driven to our new unit and, after reporting to the orderly room, were taken to our new billets at the showgrounds. We had a big choice ahead of us — The building was labelled 'Cattle Pavilion" in letters large over the huge entrance.

Inside, it came down to a choice of either pig pens, sheep pens or cattle pens. Eight of us opted for the pig pens. Bad choice! From that day forward we were referred to as the 'flying pigs'.

The sanitary arrangements were also a bit 'slack' to say the least. The toilet bowls were situated side-by-side in two rows opposite each other with no privacy between. It was like sitting on a very long bench together and rubbing shoulders with the blokes on either side. Quite impersonal for anybody of a delicate nature. We consoled ourselves by the thought that 'it's war-time and we have to make do.'

Our technical course was to take three months covering all aspects of aircraft engineering. Exams came thick and fast throughout the course. I found I could handle the pace quite well and remained in the top four of the flight. I always had my head in a book as I wanted to excel. Time seemed to fly and, in no time at all we came to the hardest of subjects — riveting and sheetmetal work

We started this subject in our course and, by the end of the week, were well into it. Then I received a letter from 'uncle' David asking me to act as best man at his wedding the following Saturday afternoon.

I was rather taken aback. I kept asking myself — Why?

This was the first letter I'd ever received from him. Then I generously thought that the war might have mellowed him or, perhaps his future wife had had a beneficial influence on him.

I sent him a telegram saying I would be delighted to do so.

I was cleared for leave that day and prepared a clean RAAF uniform to wear; freshly washed and ironed shirt and highly spit-polished shoes so that I could present a fine picture for my role as best man at David's wedding.

After eating breakfast I caught the tram to North Melbourne where I was to meet Uncle Bill and Aunty Dot, parents of Dorothy, my late cousin.

The feelings I had at that time were indescribable but nobody had considered how I would feel meeting them here. Only Aunty Dot could see that I was uncomfortable. She put her arm around my waist and said,"I know how you feel. I have been there many times but, for today, try to rise above it for everybody's sake. Most of all, for yourself."

"Thanks Aunty," I managed to say," But, where's Uncle Bill these days?"

"Oh, he's up north somewhere. He's a driver with the Air Force."

This made me feel a lot better. To have to see him that day would have spoiled it for me. Besides, I knew I was much taller, fitter than him and able to handle myself quite well if he started anything.

David turned up in company with another sailor in 'round rig' with a white ribbon tied round his scarf instead of the usual black — normal fare for Naval weddings. He looked pretty smart except that he had specks of white paint on his shoes. Since I was now the same size as him, I suggested that we swap shoes as mine were highly polished. After we'd done so, he led me to an ante-room where, I expected he was going to instruct me in what to do. Then came a 'bombshell' I was not looking for.

"Gerald, my fiancee works in the Navy Office in Melbourne and she has decided that we should have a full Naval wedding; with everyone in Navy uniform. Frankly, I agree with her so, you see, it would spoil the photos to have you dressed in your RAAF uniform standing in."

I was almost speechless but I managed to blurt out," What the hell are you on about, David?"

He looked a bit sheepish but continued.

"You see my point, don't you, mate? That's why I've brought along a cobber to be my best man in your place."

I was furious of course. Why wouldn't I be?

"Then, why didn't you let me know beforehand?"

"Well, we only made the decision last night."

"Good grief!" I exclaimed."Thanks for nothing, David. Had I known, I would not have bothered to turn up."

I stayed for the ceremony, dressed in my immaculate RAAF uniform and paint-speckled shoes, trying to show interest in the proceedings. Again in my life, I felt like a complete outsider; exactly the same feeling I had living with Gran as the 'White Aborigine'.

I thought,"Well, nothing's changed. I should have known better."

I did, however, venture into the church which Gran and Aunty Rita would not do as they followed the dictum of the Catholic Church which forbad them going into a church of any other denomination.

After the ceremony I retrieved my shoes, turned my back on the family once more and left. This association held no joy for the likes of me. Now, I had another 'home', that was the RAAF and that suited me just fine.

CHAPTER TWENTY.

I left the wedding and the jolly guests to themselves and caught a tram to return to the only place I could now call home — my RAAF unit at Ascot Vale and the flying pigs billet. I had again been conned. Then I realised that I had been too trusting, making myself believe that 'leopards DO change their spots'.

On reflection, I remembered something that Yurana had taught me many years before when she said 'never dwell on a problem. Solve it in your mind, dismiss it and get on with your life'.

This was not difficult. My final exam was one week away and my head was full and, although it was Sunday, I picked up my books and began to study. It was quiet in the 'pig pen' as everyone was away on leave and I was determined to pass this exam to become a qualified Airframe Flight Rigger.

On the Monday morning a very hectic week began. This was a week in which, to demonstrate to instructors that what we had learned in theory, we could put into practice; hands-on exercise with riveting and sheetmetal work at the top of the agenda.

I don't know why but, I took to this part like a duck to water. It was as if I'd done this kind of work before. I could do no wrong and my confidence was at an all-time high. For the first time in my life I did not fear Friday's final examination.

The day arrived, the exam was scheduled for 1:30pm start and would last 3 hours. After the morning paper we all went to lunch and everyone was busy discussing how they thought they went or how they felt about the next session.

After lunch, we assembled outside the hut where we were to sit the next exam. At 1:28pm the Flight Sergeant Instructors arrived and we were shown to our seats. The senior Flight Sergeant sat behind a desk facing the class.

He stood up and said a few usual words about it being our final eam etc., then said that it being such an important exam, there will be no talking during the allowed time.

"Anybody caught talking will be dealt with severely. Do I make myself clear?"

"Yes, Flight!" we all answered.

"Good, then you may now begin and, good luck to you all."

A rush of adrenaline flowed through me as I contemplated the fact that, at the end of this day, I and all my Air Force pals taking this exam would be shaking each other's hands congratulating everyone for passing.

A major 'hiccup' was about to put this outcome on hold for me.

About an hour and a half had passed and I was feeling quite relaxed about my progress through the paper when a fellow on my right hissed at me.

"Walshey!"

I looked around furtively at his anxious face, my eyebrows raised in question.

"What's the answer to Question 30?"

I looked back at the Flight Sergeant up front who seemed to be pre-occupied at the desk writing something.

I turned obliquely to the right again and whispered the answer from the side of my mouth. When I looked back to the front, the Flight Sergeant was staring right at me!

He raised his right fore-finger and beckoned me to the front. I knew I was in deep trouble. I stood and made my way to stand in front of the desk.

"Your name is Walshe, right?"

"Yes, Flight..."

"Well, A/C I Walshe. when you have finished the paper, you will hand it in and then go direct to my office and wait for me there. I will then acquaint you with what will happen to you thereafter for disobeying a direct order given to everybody before the exam began; No talking in the room!"

"Yes, Flight..." I was terribly crestfallen.

I finished the paper as I knew the answers to most questions. Just lucky I guess. I handed in my papers and went round to the Flight Sergeant's office where I sat down outside to wait for his arrival and my punishment.

I contemplated what he might hand me. I'd heard that a previous offender had been given a severe dressing-down and fined a week's pay. That would suit me fine as I would plead guilty.

It was about an hour later that the Flight Sergeant arrived, went into his office without a sideways glance at me and closed the door. Thirty minutes later he opened the door and asked me to come into his office. I stood up and followed him with all the confidence I could muster. Little did he know I was shaking in my boots with a knot in my stomach.

"Sit down, Walshe." he ordered. "I won't be long."

He walked round the desk and sat, looking through some papers while I just stared at his fingers flicking the pages over.

I thought silently,"If he thinks that he's making me nervous,... he's damn right!"

Finally, he looked up from what he was doing.

"Very good." He wiped his hand over his chin and gazed at me across the desk. "Walshe, those papers I was reading were your exam papers covering the complete Flight Riggers Course. You have talent, you've done very well. Up until this last exam, you were running second in the Flight over-all. You seem to have waited until this last exam to make sure of the top position. Your pass mark is 96%,... I can't see anyone beating this mark.

"You seem to have a flair for two subjects; both pass marks were over 90%. They are Theory of Flight and Sheetmetal-Riveting. Have you had some sort of engineering training prior to joining up? Your papers show that you worked as a garage hand. What exactly is that?"

I explained as best I could what the work at Mr Abadee's garage entailed.

"Hmmm, you probably would have made a good mechanic if you'd stayed a civilian. However, I'm glad you did not. I must congratulate you for becoming a fully qualified Airframe Fitter. Well done!"

He leaned back in his chair and stared long into my eyes. I felt the storm was about to break.

"But let's cut the polite chatter. Now I've told you the good news, here's the bad news. I don't know whether you know or not but, we have a new Commanding Officer and he's a man obsessed with discipline. This, of course, affects your case and I've been instructed to make an example of you. In the past, people who've talked during exams have got off easy. Not any more!

"Your punishment will ensure that this never happens again." He smirked at the thought of what was to come. I was close to panic-stations wondering what was in store for me.

He stood and straightened his tunic, brushing off some crumbs.

"This will be your punishment A/C I Walshe; on Monday the postings will be out. All your mates will leave on Tuesday for flying units but you will not. Instead, you will leave your comfy home in the piggery with all your gear and report to the Guard House. The Sergeant of the Guard has been instructed that for the next week you will carry out the duties of guard for this unit. Your billet will be No.2 cell in the guard house.

"After that, your case will be reviewed."

I was dismissed and marched back to the piggery. I sat and reflected that having heard that dissertation from the Flight Sergeant, I had a kind of fondness for the piggery billet now that I was to leave. I revealed to all the chaps about my punishment and they said how they were sorry, especially the fellow who had started the whole thing.

"Look, chaps," I said to them all,"You blokes just get on with your own lives. I can handle this set-back. I hope to see you again some day."

Strangely, I never saw another one again. It was, in fact, our final farewell.

I moved out of the piggery on Monday morning after saying goodbye to them all and reported to the guard room. On Tuesday I stood outside the Guard House at 'Present Arms' position as their buses passed by. I was a bit sad to see them go. It was a bit like losing a family.

I carried out my duties as guard for the next three days then, on Friday morning I was told to report to the orderly room at 11:00am for a meeting. I asked who was I to meet but was told nothing, only to wear full dress uniform.

On Friday I reported as ordered and was shown to an empty room where I sat down to wait. At 10:58am the door opened and I got a shock as three senior officers marched in.

I'd never seen such an amount of gold braid before in fact, I'd never been close to any senior officer before let alone three of them. Immediately my reflexes took over. I sprang to my feet and saluted.

The salute was returned. "At ease, sit down Airman."

Squadron Leader Harman introduced himself as he took the top position at the table. "I am your Commanding Officer, A/C I Walshe. Now, we have to decide what we are going to do with you."

I swallowed hard, sure that I was in for a real caning.

"You know that the war in the Pacific is slowing down at present..." It was more of a statement than a question. "In the past there has been a pool of new aircraft assembled from crates at depots and Ops. Training Units, ready to fly when needed to the squadrons up north."

He looked left and right to his colleagues who, in turn nodded. He went on. "Well, for the past three months this practice has stopped and we have a situation now where some squadrons are operating under strength in the islands ... regarding numbers of aircraft. What they have resorted to is repairing all aircraft, regardless of their state of repair and this, in turn, has placed extra pressure on the salvage and repair units of all squadrons."

Harman permitted a slight smile to crease his face, still looking at me.

"You must be asking yourself 'What does this have to do with me?' OK, I shall get to that in a minute, Walshe, however, aircraft are being lost at present due to three things; enemy action, running out of fuel and engine failure. Then, last week we lost one when a bomb it was carrying fell off while taking off and exploded under the aircraft, killing the pilot as well.

"Then to make matters worse, two aircraft returning from action taxied into each other on the strip. Now, this brings me to the reason for this meeting.

"A/C I Walshe, you have been posted to No.78 Fighter Wing on Morotai Island. You will be a member of 78 Fighter Squadron and attached to either No.14 or No.16 Repair and Salvage Units who are at present on this island. You will assist in the repair, rebuilding and salvage of aircraft for all squadrons. Very few people get posted directly from Engineering School to active service but, in your case, we think it's warranted."

Again he sought the agreement of his colleagues. They nodded back. He cleared his throat and continued.

"You have passed all your exams with flying colours and finished top of this course. You are a good production type airframe fitter... just the sort of fellow we need for the job in hand. Now, do you have any questions, Walshe?"

"Sir, I would like to make a statement, if I may."

"You have my permission, Walshe."

"Thank you sir. I would like to thank you for putting my mind at rest. When I made the mistake of speaking in the exam room, the Flight Sergeant said that I would be severely punished. Frankly, I didn't think the punishment he handed out was sufficient, having my posting cancelled. Not leaving with rest of the course was disappointing but I expected more.

"When I was given guard duty I thought that was the way I was to spend the rest of my days in service, lugging a rifle. Now, having been told that is not the case I am very grateful."

Harman stared at me and said," With a speech like that, Walshe, I can see you are officer material."

The other two laughed loudly at this.

I was dismissed and sent to the hospital for my innoculation shots, atibrine tablets etc and thence to the clothing store to receive my tropical kit. I returned to the orderly room and picked up my orders and travel papers, packed my bags and left the unit to catch a tram to the city.

I went straight to Air Force House where I could stay until Sunday afternoon when I would catch a train going north.

On that Sunday evening I caught the 'Spirit of Progress' train at Spencer Street Station to take me to Albury. It was a fine looking machine, all gleaming blue and gold paint. When I arrived at Albury Station I was shown to a train from New South Wales on the opposite side of the platform. This was a troop train, painted a depressing dull colour. It was to carry me and a contingent of other young men to Sydney.

On boarding the train, I was shown where we slept — three tier bunks along one side of the carriage. There was no heating and the noise of some Army guys playing cards nearby kept me awake most of the night.

When I rose from my bunk the next morning, I could see the warm glow of sunrise over country pastures covered in light mist. It made me smile as it reminded me of the country around Pokataroo.

The train was slowing down and, looking out the window, I could see we were approaching a town. It was Moss Vale in the southern highlands. As the train slowly pulled into the platform I noticed a row of trestles set up on the platform with white linen covers and stacked with plates, knives and forks.

Breakfast was about to be served!

A wonderful group of young ladies were gathered around the tables all eager to help us to some early morning victuals. It was most welcome; toast with butter and jam, eggs and bacon with bubble-and-squeak or sausages and tomatoes. Rich fare for these days of restrictions and rations. Farm provisions, no doubt!

All the girls wore a uniform of blue and white and went about their task of serving with enthusiasm and good cheer. I was totally blown away!

When I had scoffed my eggs and bacon I began a conversation with one lass and asked her if the group had a group name.

"Ohh, yes," she replied with a winsome smile." We're the Blue Belles. We're all volunteers and we do this about three times a week to help the war effort before we go to work."

I was greatly impressed. "Do you enjoy getting up so early in the morning?" I asked.

"Not really," came the reply," But, we're country girls and we are used to it. Besides which, we like to help you boys going off to war."

I was moved by this confession. I took her hand in mine and raised it tenderly to my lips. "I would like to thank you so much from all the fellows on this train."

She smiled back at me and wished us all good luck. That smile went with me to the island of Morotai and, every time I think of that train trip, I recall her beautiful face.

When we arrived at Sydney Central Station I boarded another train bound for Richmond in the western suburbs. There I was to report to No.2 Aircraft Depot at Richmond RAAF Base where I would board a C47 Douglas twin engined plane for the north. I was billeted for the night at Richmond but, in the morning, boarded a C47 to begin my very first journey by air.

Upon stepping up into this 'flying tube' of a contraption I noticed that the luxury of sitting was provided for by a long bench on the right side of the cabin consisting of a tubular frame over which was a sling of webbing.

Stacked along the length of the 'bench seat' were two blanket piles for each passenger. This puzzled me so I asked the obvious question.

"When you get to 10,000 feet you will be grateful of two blankets, son!"

The rest of the cabin space in the plane was taken up with stacks of spare parts of various types — everything from canvas tents and field kitchen equipment to medical supplies and gun parts and soldiers webbing. The aircraft was on a 'milk-run' round the country, stopping overnight in Darwin where we would spend the night before catching the next plane to Morotai Island.

After some 48 hours of flying, stopping, flying we were about three hours from Darwin. I was treating the flight as a bit of an adventure. I'd seen many other cities and towns on the way and covered much of the inland areas of Australia. I had taken to flying like a duck to water.

The pilot's voice came over the 'squawk-box' and announced that he would be diverting to a remote station where a young girl had to be picked up and taken to hospital in Darwin.

We landed at the outback station and loaded the little girl into the aircraft on a make-shift stretcher consisting of a door and blankets. Her mother came with her to comfort the child. We took off again in a huge cloud of red dust headed for Darwin where an ambulance was waiting to pick her up.

There, I stepped out of the aircraft and said farewell to the crew to go and report to the orderly room at the airport. That night I spent in a tent on the verge of the airstrip with instructions to report to another C47 in the morning which would be going to Morotai Island via Biak Island. I slept very well that night being as I was a seasoned traveller with no fear of flying.

The next morning I reported to my next C47 at 6:45am and was told to climb aboard. It, too, was stacked from floor to roof with stores of various types for many different destinations. I took a seat on the wall bench and clipped my seatbelt on.

The engines were started and we began to roll forward to the runway behind two other C47's, ready to take off to — somewhere...

I looked toward the control tower and saw a long red light show. It then went to green and the first aircraft began to roll down the runway and took off. Then there was another long red light which went green and the second aircraft rolled away down the runway and off into the 'wild blue yonder'.

Then our pilot got his 'green' from the Aldis lamp in the tower. He gunned the throttles and the plane lurched forward under the surge of power from the two big, fat Pratt & Whitney R-1830 Twin Wasp engines. Stones and dust flew up all round until we had gone about 50 yards. The tail lifted and the wheels rumbled like unchained banshees wishing to break loose. Suddenly, all that noise ceased and we were airborne. The earth fell away like we had not belonged to it in the first place.

We were winging our way over water to the north-east and to the war-zone. The thought then crossed my mind; Will I be coming back? Will I be coming back in a wooden box?

Despite the tropical climate below, at 10,000 feet the air was quite chilly and we wrapped our legs in the blankets. In view of the fact that we were flying over water now, we were obliged to wear our 'Mae West' life jackets. A very comforting thought that, should we be shot down or just crash in the sea, we'd be found because we were floating instead of sinking.

I decided to settle down and monitor the sound of the synchronised revs of the engines as we ploughed through the blue sky. After some time, we crossed the shore of Dutch New Guinea. Somehow it seemed good to be flying over solid ground again.

Looking more closely at the terrain below I wasn't so sure. Rough hills and valleys dotted with miniature villages, tall, solid trees and deserted beaches were the mainstay of this landscape. To cap it off, it was at present in enemy hands!

The C47 began to climb again. The next thing I saw out the side windows was the tops of mountains floating past on oceans of white clouds. The turbulence above these mountains was a bit rough and we had to secure our seat belts again until, at last we began our descent and the engines were throttled back, popping occasionally as the exhaust gases exploded from the pipes.

At this point I decided to go forward to the flight deck and speak with the crew. I looked through the windscreens and saw a large patch of water where Japen, Neomfoor and Biak Islands lay. We were to touch down at Tawi-Tawi on Biak Island at about 1:00pm as this was as far as we were going today. The weather ahead was building into a tropical storm.

After landing, the C47 taxied into a holding bay but we didn't unload as the sky was then a deep shade of purple. This was my first experience of a tropical storm and, in my naivety, I wondered why the tents that were pitched around the airstrip had very deep trenches dug around them. After the rain had commenced it became quite clear the reason for the drainage trenches as the heavens simply opened and rain just bucketted down.

I was very glad to be inside a tent at the time.

The following morning I was up early enought to witness my first tropical sunrise. Unbelievable colours lit the eastern sky as we unloaded stores from the C47. Most were for the troops on Neomfoor Island and the rest for the hospital.

Where the aircraft stood caught my attention. It was parked on light yellow sand while, over on the strip, there appeared to be a series of green metal planks all interlocked to form a solid runway. This, I was informed , was Marsden Matting.

Every airstrip in the tropics required Marsden Matting as the sand which made up the ground here was too soft to take heavy aircraft movement.

With that to contemplate, I climbed back aboard the plane for take-off for Morotai, about 550 miles away.

Climbing away from Biak Island, I looked down on the sugar-white beaches, the light blue shallows and the darker, deep blue waters sparkling invitingly as if all was well with the world. Further to sea I could see fighting ships and transport ships riding peacefully at anchor on the green Pacific Ocean.

It was difficult to believe that, in this glorious setting, a vicious fighting campaign was being planned and waged.

All thoughts of peace were about to be dissolved when we found ourselves away over the ocean with only tiny islands dotted around. Now, I began to get a bit nervous as we had been told before leaving Biak that this region was held by the Japs and they became active from time to time.

Enemy aircraft were known to be operating from Ambon Island in long sweeps to the north and west. So, here we were, flying through what was enemy airspace, unarmed and unescorted.

I undid my seatbelt and made my way forward to the flight deck and looked ahead through the windscreens. All I could see was sky and sea.

"Are we likely to have a fighter escort, Sir?" I asked the pilot.

"What? Are you getting a bit nervous, Gerry?" he asked jocularly.

I grinned and replied, "Well, maybe a little bit."

He glanced at his wristwatch and said, "Don't worry, son, we should have some friends from your Squadron here soon. Maybe 30 minutes or so. With any luck, it will be 78 Squadron. Look for the markings on the sides — H-U. That's their registration code."

I went back to my seat feeling better. Then, engine sounds that I didn't recognise came to my well-tuned ears. Then began a sound like a garbage can being rattled with metal sticks and holes appeared in the floor and metal sides of the C47. The engine sounds intensified and I looked out the nearest window to see two aircraft I didn't immediately recognise, race past our right-hand side.

They were Japanese Zero fighters, their light-grey-bluish paint gleaming in the sunlight, the big, red roundel unmistakable. Luckily, their shots had mainly hit the stores stacked from floor to roof on the other side of the fuselage. A neat row of half-inch holes had appeared along the floor under the stores.

I watched them curve away but knew that they would be back for another pass very soon. The pilot must have realised the same and quickly stuffed the nose of the C47 down at a steep angle to lose height.

By getting closer to the sea, he stood a better chance of not being shot at from below.

I was pressed into my seat by the centrifugal force at the end of the dive. I kept thinking that the Japs would be back soon. I should pray or something.

It took only two minutes and they were back, machine guns chattering away, trying to hit the engines. I saw holes appear in the engine housing on the right-hand wing but it kept on running. The Zeros passed us by again.

By now, I had resigned my fate to a watery grave. I was not in control of my own destiny here. During the lull, I walked to the rear of the cabin and checked the 8 man liferaft in case we did put down in the sea but hoping it hadn't been shot up. That would make a farce of any use of it.

I returned to my seat and tightened my seatbelt and 'Mae West'. Just then we heard the sound of more engines coming from behind.

"Oh, God, not more of the little bleeders!" I thought.

More machine gun chatter filled the cabin air and two dark green shapes zoomed past about 50 yards away either side. They were Kittyhawks from Morotai Island. I looked closely at the side of one and saw the registration H-U which meant that they were, indeed from 78 Squadron! Beauty!

Out the front windscreens I could see the Kittyhawks chasing after the Zeros as they ducked and weaved all over the sky until they were well out of sight. They had arrived just in the nick of time.

There was a great round of hand-shaking and back-slapping in the cabin. The green light began flashing and I made my way forward to the flight deck. The pilot pointed up ahead to two dark shapes which were the Kittyhawks. They throttled back to form up on our wingtips. One of the fighter pilots pointed upward meaning we should resume our 10,000 ft. altitude. We began to climb back up.

I gazed lovingly at the sleek fuselages of our friends and marvelled at the white painted propellor spinners and white leading edges of their wings and tails. I knew I would enjoy working at 78 Squadron.

I expected our terrier-like watchdogs would escort us to Morotai but, not so. They were beside us until we got to 10,000 then they were gone, seen darting all over the sky to ensure our safe passage.

With our fighter escort nearby I felt I could relax again and consider what had just taken place. When it first happened, I had been very frightened. Then, after a while, I became quite calm as I started to think back over my short life. My head was a jumble of thoughts; Only the good die young! OK, that lets me out... Who will miss me? Will my father, Ken be waiting up there for me? Yurana might also be there... who knows?

Then I remembered something that Yurana had told me when I was very young. She said, "In the midst of life, there is death. It's a part of life, Nab. You must never be afraid of it. When one door closes, another door opens to you."

At the time, I didn't understand what she meant. Now I did.

I returned sharply to reality when the Japs decided to take another shot. I dropped these thoughts and concentrated on staying alive with self-encouragement such as 'You are not going to die young. You're not good enough!' On the other hand, I reckoned if I was to meet my fate, I hoped it would be fast.

Machine gun shots again raked the wings near the engines! The Japs were back! Persistent chappies they were. They made one pass but, curiously, left as quickly as they'd arrived. The Aussie Kittyhawks chased the Zeros from the vicinity, dodging and diving after the nimble Japanese planes.

With the departure of the Japs, the Kittyhawks formed up on our wingtips and escorted the C47 all the way to within about 5 minutes of Morotai Island. Then both waggled their wings and went down to join the air traffic circuit to land at Morotai strip.

A minute or two later Morotai Island came into view — a beautiful, dark green spot floating on a deep blue ocean bathed in sunshine. As we got closer we could see activity off-shore with warships and transport ships moving about with landing craft darting around them like chickens around hens. The white foaming water made fascinating patterns on the sheet of blue.

Later we were to learn that all this activity was due to the preparation of Australian troops for a landing on the shores of Tarakan Island near Borneo.

Our C47 joined the flight circuit and turned onto the downwind leg at 1,500 feet. I could see that there were two separate strips here; one shorter than the other. The short one nearer to the beach was reserved for single engined aircraft while twins and heavier planes used the longer one inland.

We landed and taxied to a halt near the dispersal hut where we would unload the stores. I reported to 78 Squadron orderly room and presented my paperwork.

"Good man!" exclaimed the Flight Sergeant. "Need more chaps like you. Very welcome you are, Walshe. Get your kit over to one of the tents with a spare bunk and report to the engineering hut this afternoon. After lunch will do."

"Thank you, Sergeant." I was home again, on Morotai.

CHAPTER TWENTY ONE.

I was driven in a jeep to my tent where I was to share with three other fellows. They introduced themselves as Eric — a flight rigger, Jim — a flight mechanic and Alan — an armourer. All were attached to 14 RSU from 78 Squadron.

I had been expected to replace another chap who went to replace a bloke who had, unfortunately, walked backwards into a spinning propellor on Noemfoor Island.

The following morning I was taken to the Unit where I was officially attached from 78 Sqd. to 14 RSU. I was then introduced to the crew I would be working with and shown to my first job. This was the two Kittyhawks which taxied into each other on the Wama strip near the beach in April 1945. This would be a huge rebuilding task as one had sustained 80% damage and the other 50%..

I stood a while gazing round the compound at all the aircraft in need of repairs. Then I became aware of the sound of engines approaching me from behind. Looking round, I saw the C47 which had brought me here taxiing up.

It stopped short of the compound and I could see the row of bullet holes underneath where the Japs had made their first pass. I went to the cargo door on the port side as the pilot was adjusting the steps to climb out.

"Good morning, sir." I said.

"Good grief, Gerry. What are you doing here? Are you attached to 14 RSU?"

"Yes sir," I replied. They are very busy so another pair of hands is welcome."

"Well, Gerry, I may have some bad news for you fellows. We're short of transport aircraft and we need this one repaired poste-haste. Where's the O.I.C.?"

I pointed to the compound office and he went in. Two minutes later he emerged with the Officer In Charge who called us round to hear what he had to say.

"Men, our priorities have been put back a bit. This C47 is to be first on the list. You will work as a full team on it, work day and night if you have to but, I want it back in airworthy condition and FAST!"

There were mutterings from a few men but an inspection of the aircraft showed that it was badly in need of attention. Several engineers went to work opening hatches and lifting floorboards, removing engine cowls and writing notes as they went.

It turned out that both engines had been hit, the fuselage and tail had gaping holes, the shots that came up from below had cut through some of the multi-strand steel wires in the control lines which worked the elevators and rudder. Had these been totally cut through, we would certainly have ended in the 'drink'.

This report made me shiver although the temperature at Morotai Island was then about 38C. Funny, that...

Work commenced immediately and continued through several days and nights. I was kept so busy that I lost track of day and night. When the entire job was finished I got some sleep. It was after that I realised just how important a good sleep is to a healthy body.

After that was out of the way, we got back to repairing the Kittyhawks. With tasks such as riveting and metalwork required for this, it was going to require all the skills I had excelled at in No1 Engineering School — and then some.

I didn't mind the challenge of the work. The things that worried me most were the heat of the days and the mosquitoes. I happened to mention my concerns to the Flight Sergeant.

"My boy, I can't help you with the heat. Everyone cops that however, with the mozzies, make sure you take your atabrine tablets every morning and night. Your skin will turn yellow but, they will protect you from malaria. If you go down with that, you're no good to anyone.

"Oh, yes... another thing. Don't go near the northern boundary fence at any time, especially at night. You see, we only 'own' the southern end of the island. The Japs are up north here. In fact, we're surrounded by Japanese-occupied islands here. Charming thought, ain't it?"

He cheerfully patted my head and walked away whistling to himself.

It took me a few weeks to get used to the routine here; the compound, the six-day working week, the nights we had to put in on urgent jobs. A lot of fighter aircraft were coming back from sorties with multi bullet holes and shrapnel tears in the panelwork. This was mainly on account of the different tactics they now employed; not so much air-to-air combat but bombing and strafing runs over enemy positions, convoy escorts at sea, aerial escorts, attacking stores barges which were armed, barracks, fuel dumps and other targets of opportunity.

Low level runs were highly dangerous as the pilots risked being hit by ground fire from small arms and heavy machine guns or anti-aircraft weapons. Most came back but others were lost due to running out of fuel, engine failure due to ground fire or other damage to aircraft. Generally the pilots were rescued but, sadly, some were not.

As there were no replacement aircraft to come from Australia, it became imperative that all planes were repaired fast and put back into service.

To complicate matters even more, with the impending invasion of Tarakan Island off Borneo, most of the ground staff of 78 Sqd. had gone to Tarakan to service the airstrips ready for aircraft landings. The aircraft engineers left behind at Morotai Island were then expected to carry out ground inspections daily to ensure aircraft movements could be made.

This cut well into our engineering work schedule and added to our work-load and time managemnt problems. The pressure continued for two months until July 1945 when 78 Sqd. aircraft flew to Tarakan.

CHAPTER TWENTY TWO.

Although the pace of work in repairing aircraft at Morotai Island was fast and furious, it wasn't all 'work-and-no-play'. On our rest day which was Sunday, we competed between RSU's in a volley ball competition.

Since we didn't have different uniforms to distinguish each team, some played wearing shirts, some wore hats, one wore shorts while No.14 RSU drew the short straw and were told to play naked! Luckily for us, the games were all over and done or won before 4:00pm — the time when mozzies swarmed. That would have given other teams a distinct advantage over our game form.

We also enjoyed a swim at the wharf. It sometimes became so crowded that it was difficult to find a spot to stand before diving into the cool water but, it was great fun and very refreshing on a hot Sunday. Of course, every Sunday saw the obligatory church parade form up. Roman Catholics to the right, Church of England to the left and the rest — atheists, Jews etc 'stand fast'.

When the 'believers' had marched off, the 'non-believers' went back to our tents. Although I had to wear the tag of 'atheist' it suited me to sit alone and contemplate Baiame.

Before I was introduced back into the white man's world and the Catholic Church at College, I had been taught to believe in the Supreme Being and creator of dreaming time who was Baiame. He was the creator of all things; He was not God nor the son of God. He was above them all, something which Aboriginal people have believed for thousands of years, predating any other 'supreme being' by thousands of years.

As if to reinforce this theory that Baiame looks after his people, I also learned that a pilot of Aboriginal blood had been posted to 78 Squadron. He was W/O Len Waters. I have always considered myself to be a member of the Lieillwan tribe and was excited to learn that another person of Aboriginal descent had joined me here on this remote island. Although he was a pilot and hardly ever at rest, we did have some interesting conversations after work.

I was, therefore, glad to be classed as an atheist for believing in Baiame.

A very strange thing occurred on Morotai Island. One morning as I walked to work at the compound I turned my gaze toward the wharf and noticed a ship tied up there with huge red crosses along its side — a hospital ship, no less! I wondered where it had come from and where it was headed; was it, in fact, Australian?

That afternoon I decided to investigate further. As I approached the wharf I noticed that the railings around the decks were festooned with barbed wire. I asked the guard at the wharf why this was so.

"Placed there by the Army for our protection!" came the reply.

I looked to the rear mast and was surprised to see the 'rising sun' flag flying freely. The name of this vessel was Takibana Maru. It was a fake hospital ship; a troop ship disguised as a hospital ship carrying 1561 armed Japs crowded into appallingly inadequate quarters below deck.

We later learned from a Manilla newspaper that a few men were actually sick but the ship was carrying hundreds of cases of machine guns, 2 inch and 3 inch mortars, artillery ammunition etc all marked with red crosses.

The newspaper even had a photograph of men lying across each other in a tangled heap and another with rifles stacked on the ship's bridge deck. There was no mention of the ship's destination although, it may have been involved in evacuating troops from the Kia Islands to other places where the Japs were holding out.

Nobody from our base was allowed near the wharf and then, one morning it was gone. We never saw or heard of the vessel again! It was always presumed that the reason the ship had tied up at our wharf was that the Captain had mistaken our wharf for one in enemy territory when it arrived in the dead of night. He must have been surprised when, next day he saw that he was in Aussie-held territory!

Over the next few months we worked like little beavers, day and night, repairing aircraft with all types of damage including the two Kittyhawks which had taxied into each other. Two weeks after the squadron had left Morotai Island for Labuan Island to the north of Borneo, the last four of RSU 14 personnel were classed as the rear party of 78 Squadron. We were to follow to Tarakan Island in due course.

One bright, sunny morning we were told that new postings were up and we went to the orderly room to see what was in store for us. I was shocked to see that my three companions were posted to Tarakan but I was to return to Australia to a depot at Mildura on the Murray River. It was the only unit associated with 78 Fighter Wing in Australia, No.2 Operational Training Unit.

Naturally, I was disappointed however, I consoled myself by thinking; You always classed yourself an 18 year old boy who knew nothing. You've had your overseas adventure and now, the powers-that-be have decided to bring you back to the land of your birth. Make the best of it!

Next morning I picked up my transport papers from the orderly room and walked to the C47 waiting to take off. I presented my papers. The crew recognised me from the eventful trip which brought me to Morotai. I checked the aircraft number and found it was the same one which had been shot-up and we had repaired. I was going home with people I knew and in the aircraft I knew inside and out. This made me feel a lot more comfortable.

The trip from Morotai to Biak Island was smooth as we flew over water. From Biak to Darwin we had to cross the mountain ranges of Dutch New Guinea where up-drafts and wild air currents made the plane buck and sway wildly. I left my seat in the cabin involuntarily on several occasions no matter how tight I drew the seat belt.

Eventually, we left the coastline of D.N.G. behind and flew smoothly again to Darwin where we landed in the late afternoon. I reported to the air transport office and was allocated a bunk in a tent for the night where I settled down to think back over my great adventure outside Australia.

In the morning I boarded another C47 to ride the 'milk-run' to Melbourne. The route we took called in at Daly Waters, Tennant Creek, Alice Springs, Bourke, Sydney and finally Laverton, an RAAF base outside Melbourne. I was given travel documents for train travel from Melbourne to Mildura.

"Is there any transport into Melbourne from here?" I asked the sergeant behind the desk.

"Nah, mate. Do what we all do — thumb a ride."

"What,... with two heavy kit bags and a .303 rifle to carry?"

He snorted and grinned at me. I set off out the gates and was lucky to be picked up by a passing lorry which took me to Spencer Street Station where I boarded a train for Mildura and No.2 OTU.

CHAPTER TWENTY THREE.

My train trip to Mildura was uneventful and memorable only for the lack of heating even though Victorian Railways of the day had provided a token heater in the form of a metal box which started the journey full of hot sand. It was cold before we left the outer suburbs.

On arrival at Mildura there was an RAAF truck waiting to pick up all personnel for No.2 OTU. I was among some ground crew as well as 'sprog aircrew' — new pilots who'd just graduated from training on Tiger Moths. They proudly wore their wings and a white peak to their caps instead of dark blue. This was to distinguish them from old aircrew by the ground staff, sorting the men from the boys in a way.

I reported to the orderly room at OTU and was allocated a hut with a lot of other tech staff. When my gear was put away I reported to a hangar near the control tower. As I walked along the aircraft line, I recognised many aircraft which I had worked on at Morotai.

I introduced myself to the flight sergeant who showed me through the hangar where I was to work. In a moment of historical significance, he also introduced me to the new P51 North American Mustang fighter; squatting solidly on the concrete floor and looking every inch a mean fighter if ever there was one. I gasped in admiration and walked over to run my hand tenderly along its leading edge.

"Get familiar with this one, Walshe. You'll be expected to know every nut, bolt and wire in it next week. We have 34 of them, first lot in Australia."

"Yes, Flight,..." was all I could say.

I left the hangar a very happy Leading Aircraftsman. Back at the hut I met many of the chaps I was to share with. While sitting on my bunk, a corporal entered the hut and marched straight to my bed.

"You, Walshe?"

I looked up and replied," Yes, Corporal. That's me."

"What are you doing here? Where was your last posting?"

"Actually, I was up on Morotai Island for a few months."

He squinted at me curiously. "You must be joking, son. You've just come off a bleeding course, haven't you." The statement was an insult that required clarification.

"No, Corporal, I have told you. I spent several months on Morotai Island at RSU 14 in 78 Squadron restoring aircraft back to airworthy status."

He smirked and looked about at the other men who had, by now, shown some interest in the conversation which had graduated to raised voice level.

"You're such a bleeding liar, Walshe. Firstly, you're too young to be sent overseas and secondly, you don't have the rank to be serving in the islands."

This riled me greatly and I rose to my feet and addressed him squarely to his face.

"Corporal, I really don't care what you think. That is of no interest to me. I have told you the truth."

He placed his hands on his hips and stood with legs astride. I thought to myself; A foolish stance if ever I saw one.

"Well, you'd best be interested LAC Walshe, because I am in charge of this hut and responsible for everyone in it, including liars."

I mentally measured the distance between his face and my fist.

"Not me, Corporal. I am responsible for myself and have been all my life. And why have you decided to pick on me? I don't even know you."

He looked around again to garner confidence from the expressions on the faces of others.

"I have very good reason to pick you, sonny. You see I don't like liars and I deal very harshly with liars."

By now my dander was fairly well up however, I managed to keep my temper.

"Alright, Corporal," I said as smoothly as I could," Just look at my complexion. Do you see a bit of yellowing around the gills? That's from the atabrine tablets I was taking to ward off the mozzies. They carry malaria up there in the islands, you know. Now, be a good chap and check me out with the orderly room. Take a look at my posting papers and movement papers. That might put your mind at rest.

"And, when you've done that, I'll accept your apology. If that is not forthcoming, I'll meet you behind the hut at any time you like. I've trained as a boxer and I can look after myself, thank you very much."

Later that day I received an apology. I learned also that the reason he had picked on me was that I was picked for the course on Mustangs whereas he had missed out. As it was, I had more experience than he. So I began my familiarization working on one of the most beautiful, powerful and exciting aircraft ever to grace the skies over Australia.

After the air was cleared over the confrontation with the corporal, things seemed to go along quite well. I was happy working on the Mustangs but I decided to take on another responsibility.

Motor transport division was short of drivers and had posted a notice asking for those interested in up-grading their licence to apply. I volunteered and quickly was approved to drive emergency vehicles including 4 x 4 drives.

The first incident I attended was the crash of a Kittyhawk at the end of the runway. It caught fire and was well ablaze by the time the fire tender I was driving pulled up to attack the flames. Unfortunately, the plane and pilot were both lost.

The very next day we had a call-out for the ambulance. One of our Mustangs had gone down in thick bushland three days prior. Hopes were held for the pilot's safety but we were unsure exactly where the crash had occurred.

Then we received a phone call from a timber-getter at Gol Gol saying that he thought he'd heard a crash but had seen no smoke. We had to investigate the call.

I went to the hospital garage and took charge of the Dodge weapons carrier which had been converted to carry stretchers as it was 4 x 4 drive and could travel over rough terrain easily. As it turned out, I had chosen well.

When we arrived at Gol Gol we turned off the main road onto a narrow track and headed north-east for about fifteen miles into the scrub. The track petered out after about 4 miles and from then on, we had to make our own way, crashing through heavy underbrush and dodging large saplings. With the vehicle driving through low-range 4 x 4 we made steady progress with all eyes on the lookout for steep slopes and hidden ravines or bogs. It wouldn't do to become trapped here trying to effect a rescue.

We had the assistance of another aircraft above which was to try to spot the crash site from above and lead us to it. With the scrub being so dense, this was not always possible however, from time to time we did get to hear it buzzing above and followed its direction.

I then recalled something I'd learned during the rescue course. We were told that, in thick bush, when seeking to recover a body, listen for the sound of blowflies. They are very good at locating a fresh kill. The thought came back and we stopped every two or three minutes to listen for the buzz.

Then I heard it. Unmistakable and disgusting at the same time.

The spotter aircraft was circling some twenty yards away and we made our way to a small clearing where the remains of our beautiful Mustang lay with one wing broken and lying across the cockpit canopy which was in the rearward position. This indicated that the pilot had bailed out, perhaps at low altitude. The buzzing grew louder and then the stench reached our nostrils.

We found the poor fellow still in the parachute harness and covered by the white silk of the 'chute. We stood for a moment to reflect on his demise then we tenderly wrapped the body in the silk and carried it back to the Dodge ambulance.

We followed our tracks out from the site, knowing that this would have marked the trail for the salvage crew to locate and retrieve the wreck.

Back at the base, we delivered the corpse to the hospital morgue and the others went to lunch. I didn't eat as I felt unwell having been close to the dead pilot who was only a couple of years older than us, we being around 18 to 20 years old.

I went to have a shower to cleanse my body and clear my mind. It didn't work very well as, that night I could not sleep thinking about the last moments that poor fellow must have had. The thing that worried me the most was the fact of the buzzing of the blowflies that lead us to the corpse.

CHAPTER TWENTY FOUR.

The next morning when I reported for work at the hangar I was told to report back at the Flight Lieutenant's office. He invited me into the room and I sat opposite him across the desk.

"Corporal Walshe, when you came upon the crash site of the P51 yesterday, what was your impression of the surrounding bushland? Were there any trees felled as a result of the impact and in which direction were they from the aircraft position?"

"Well, sir, my first impression was that there were hardly any trees or scrub for that matter that had been flattened by the Mustang landing. The port wing had snapped off and lay across the fuselage but, apart from that the site was fairly free of debris as far as we could see."

The officer made a note on his pad and continued.

"So, going on that summary, would you say the aircraft had not approached from a glide? More of a spin, perhaps?"

I didn't have to think much about that.

"Well sir, I'm no expert but, from what I've been told about air crashes, I would say it appears to have spun in rather than glided as there were no damaged trees nor bushes behind the aircraft. But then, as I say, I'm no expert."

"Fair enough description Walshe." He made more notes and thanked me for the report. I left his office to return to work.

A few days later we received another call from a farmer near Renmark, a short distance from Mildura. He said another Mustang had crashed close to his property and the pilot had actually bailed out, again.

This particular case really shook me as I had been responsible for aiding the pilot into the Mustang that morning. He was to test the aircraft to 25,000 feet for high altitude performance. I had strapped F/O Milledge into his seat and cleaned the windscreen as he went through his ground checks.

He took off and I went to the tower to check his reports as he went higher. That P51 was the only movement for the day so we had no other jobs to attend of any importance.

I sat in the tower and listened for his calls which came back loud and clear two or three times saying that his climb was going as planned and all was OK. He was due to return at about noon and at 11:35 hours we heard his call that the aircraft was climbing through 22,000 feet and he had a problem but he was working on it. He signed off saying he would call back when it was fixed without saying what the problem was.

There was no further transmission.

At about 13:35 hours the farmer rang to say there had been an aircraft crash on his property. An emergency was called and I ran to the hospital to collect a crew for the ambulance — two doctors and two sick-bay attendants. We left the base with the breakdown truck headed for Renmark about 40 miles away. We arrived at the property at about 14:55 hours.

The farmer pointed us to the far paddocks and off we went to find the remains of the aircraft scattered over a vast area of land. I felt quite strange standing there looking down at the mud-spattered windscreen which, some hours earlier, I had polished to gleaming clarity.

The engine was nowhere to be seen, having been driven deep into the soft, ploughed earth. The pilot was also missing. We spread out to find him but with little hope of finding him alive. His watch was found hanging from the limb of a tree, its glass broken but still working.

To our surprise we found the pilot's body a little further away from the tree still strapped into the parachute harness. I went back to drive the ambulance closer to lift him into the vehicle however, when we went to pick up the body, it felt just like a mass of jelly.

The doctor said that he thought every bone in his body must have been broken; the only thing holding him together was the flying suit. We, therefore, had to roll the corpse onto the stretcher and carry it carefully to the vehicle and strap it into the back, covered by the 'chute.

The whole event came as a terrible shock to me, having been so close to the pilot just hours beforehand and now, to see his broken body so badly injured as a result of the accident. At the hospital, after unloading the corpse, I complained to the doctor about feeling nauseous. He said I was suffering from shock and gave me an injection telling me to go and lie down for the afternoon.

I took his advice and woke up the next morning, still dressed in my overalls.

Following the second Mustang crash, training on P51's ceased at Mildura. The ground staff had been transferred to 84 and 86 Fighter Squadrons at Ross River and Bohle River near Townsville. Unfortunately, I was to remain at Mildura as a driver which didn't impress me one bit. I felt let down after all my training and experience. Anyone with an ounce of brains could be a driver!

It was 13th August when I was told to report to the Transport Officer. I had been selected to do a special driving job at the bombing range near the town of Wentworth. RAAF had been using the range for quite some time and, as the war seemed to be winding down, there was little use made of the range now. Thus we were to comb the sand dunes and locate any unexploded ordinance and dig it out, strap a charge of TNT to it and explode the thing, rendering it harmless. Well, that was the theory, anyway.

I was given the company of some bomb-disposal experts and went to pick them up along with all their detection and other equipment. And so, it was off to Wentworth Bombing Range to begin work.

I was to be included in the digging party so was handed a long-handled shovel. Along with the picks and shovels we had a series of long probes made from thick wire. With these we were told to shove the pointy end deep into a depression where we thought there was a bomb, locate the device and estimate its depth. Then the experts would come along, strap a block of TNT explosive to each side of the shell and attach electric wires which ran back to another trench where lay the plunger.

This was an electric generator. When the plunger handle was raised, the circuit was made active. When the plunger descended rapidly, an electric charge ran to the detonator fixed to the TNT and — WHAM-O! — up went the lot. The most dangerous part of the deal was the shrapnel which always flew in unpredictable directions; pieces of hot steel with jagged edges, some the size of a saucer whizzing through the air to slice into any flesh or other soft material in its path. Not a pretty prospect!

Therefore, all other personnel were moved well away from the bomb site until the explosion was over and the area declared clear.

Work proceeded well the first day and we came back for another go on day two. After mid-day break we were informed that some Kittyhawks were coming over to make some bombing runs at the range so we cleared off to give them a free run at it.

At about 3:00pm four aircraft appeared overhead and we communicated with them via the tower radio. All was clear on the ground.

The first three aircraft came in at shallow angles, attacking the outline of a warship, and released their bombs which went off like Guy Fawkes Night. It was real poetry to watch as these graceful warbirds swooped down to 1,000 feet, released their bombs and pulled away to the left or right of the 'target'. The pilot of the fourth kittyhawk, however, decided to perform a steep dive and came down from about 5,000 feet howling all the way.

At critical altitude, we heard the pilot's voice over the squawk-box screaming,"Can't pull out! Can't pull out!"

We all watched in horror as the Kittyhawk slammed into the soft earth. The bomb exploded throwing wreckage plus a spume of sand and small bushes in every direction. The shock wave was felt for miles around. I'll always remember the fact that this particular aircraft's underbelly was painted light blue while the others were painted light grey. Was there something in that?

Later, when we had a chance to investigate the crater that the Kittyhawk had made, there was not much of the aeroplane to be found while the only recognisable body part of the pilot was the middle finger of his left hand.

This was ceremoniously placed into a full-size casket and given a military funeral.

The following day we ran into another problem. In the afternoon we had dug up two bombs close to the surface. The experts calculated that the shrapnel would rise high upon explosion but were unsure how far away the crew should be for safety. I was told to move the truck to the perimeter fence. This was far enough away from the point of explosion to ensure safety.

Thus, I parked the vehicle close to the fence, side-on to the detonation spot and, just to be sure, I decided to crouch down behind the furthest wheel from the explosion.

The first bomb went off and the shrapnel from it peppered the truck from one end to the other, tearing the canvas cover and breaking the driver's window. I heard it smack against the mudguards and the bonnet, thankful to be hiding where I was.

When the 'All-clear' sounded, I inspected the damage. Nothing serious, I thought so the second bomb was detonated. The bits then flew high, well over the truck and smashed a few saplings across the road.

After that, I drove over to pick up the rest of the crew and, as it was getting a bit late, the Sergeant called a halt to the day's work. We were headed back to Wentworth for a good night's rest.

Then, about 7 miles from town it happened. BANG! The right-hand front tyre blew out and the steering wheel was wrenched from my grasp. The truck veered to the right and went into a ditch, hit the embankment and rolled over, landing upside down.

I kicked open my door and crawled out, helping my two companions out as well. We stood up and checked ourselves for damage. Nothing bad. We then went to the back of the vehicle and looked in. It was dark but I'd taken the torch from the glove-box and shone it into the void. The two blokes in the back had fallen over each other and needed a hand to get out.

We were all bruised and a bit bloody but intact. I was then 'volunteered' to march into town to call for help. Off I went tramping along this dark country road until I could see the lights of Wentworth up ahead. As I got closer I could hear the distinct sounds of revelry and loud music.

When I got to the pub I was greeted as a hero. Stunned, I had to ask the barman to tell me what the celebration was all about.

"The bloody war's over, mate! The Japs have had enough!"

I couldn't believe my ears. He handed me a beer and waved the money aside. "Have this one on me, matey! The yanks dropped a bomb on them yesterday that made them chuck in the bloody towel." His face glowed with delight. I was elated looking round this tiny pub in the middle of nowhere; simple folk were celebrating the end to what had been the most horrific conflict in human history.

We borrowed a truck to drive out to pick up the other chaps and take us back to town. Later we were to learn that, during the second last explosion at the range, a piece of shrapnel, no more than the size of sixpence, had penetrated the wall of the tyre which blew; something I'd failed to spot when I checked the truck.

The whole crew were given two days leave after the accident but that didn't help much. Back at the range we found that digging and shovelling was the best therapy for sore muscles. We finished the whole task by the first week of October 1945 which meant that we would not be there during the heat of summer.

CHAPTER TWENTY FIVE.

M y stint at the Bomb Disposal Unit was over and I was told to report back to the Transport Office. When I arrived at the T.O. on the first morning there was a great flurry of excitement with people running in every direction and waving their hands.

"What's going on?" I asked the Sergeant behind the desk.

He went a deep shade of purple and stammered,"Bloody Oldsmobile ute's bloody gone! Disappeared altogether,... and so's a 44 gallon drum of fuel, gone off the base. There's gunna be Hell to pay!"

The Oldsmobile utility truck was one commandeered from a local citizen for use by the RAAF during the war-time emergency. It was the pride of the fleet of light vehicles in the garage we maintained at Mildura Base.

The Sergeant had taken the trouble to check with the guard at the main gate to ascertain whether the ute had left the base and was told, "Yes, it drove away about 2 hours prior."

"Who was the driver/"

"LAC Peter Ridell," was the reply. "And I noticed a 44 gallon drum in the back as well." offered the hapless fellow.

The Service Police had been called out and they required a designated driver to take the base Police sedan in pursuit of the runaway vehicle and apprehend the culprit. Being an endorsed driver, I was given the task of driving the high-powered 1938 Ford V8 car after the villain.

As it turned out, Ridell had applied for compassionate leave some two weeks prior but was turned down. Repairing a broken romance was not a good enough reason to take leave and go to Melbourne.

So, he'd decided to take matters into his own hands and steal the best looking, fast vehicle on the base.

Thus I was ordered to take the Ford V8 and get after him. I had always admired the vehicle from a distance but, until I actually got behind the wheel, didn't realise just how powerful it was. And built like a tank! Heavy and sturdy, it would be just the ticket to carry three burly policemen and me to Melbourne in style and at speed in reasonable safety.

Out the gates we went and hit the road to Bendigo. The car swayed a bit on corners and threw up gravel as we cut some corners short making a sound like a machine gun spraying the mudguards from below. I was too intent on watching the road ahead to notice the speedo reading however, I was told later that the wheels almost left the road going over some of the hills and dales we traversed.

Down through Ouyen. Lascelles and St. Arnaud we went, horn blaring as we went through towns along the way. I'm sure it gave the locals something to chat about in the pub that night — the Service Police car shooting through town at breakneck speed.

Eventually we reached Melbourne where I suggested we call in at Suttons Motors which was the G.M. Dealer to fill up the tank and ask about the Oldsmobile ute.

As luck would have it, Ridell had called in there and sold the spare wheel from the ute for ten pounds spending cash. They also informed us that he'd mentioned going to pick up his girlfriend. We knew she lived at Mornington but didn't know a phone number there so we were obliged to drive down there to see if he was still there.

Upon arrival at the girl's place we were told that he had left to return to Swan Hill. The policemen decided that we should find a place to eat before we drove off again so we found a small cafe and ordered toasted ham sandwiches with mustard. With these placed handy on the seat beside me, we set off again toward Ballarat.

There, the Police Sergeant rang the Mildura Base to see if they had any news of the fugitive. He was told that there had been a sighting at RAAF Flying Boat Base at Lake Boga near Swan Hill.

We drove off again, up through Castlemaine and Bendigo. As it was getting on a bit, the Sergeant asked me if I thought we could make it to Kerang. I glanced at the map I had and calculated that we could be there by about 8:00pm if we maintained the high speed we were doing.

"Right-o, son. Do what you have to. Just get us there in one piece." was his firm reply.

Away we went and arrived at Kerang just before 8:00pm. We found a pub open which had accommodation available and checked in for the night. The Service Police gave the publican a chit for the meals and beds. We slept pretty soundly as we all had been tense for most of the day during the drive to Melbourne and back.

We left Kerang early next morning and headed for Lake Boga RAAF Base to speak with the person who had reported the sighting. He was a RAAF Sergeant and he told the police Sergeant that, when he'd seen the Oldsmobile, it was heading back toward Kerang to the south-east.

The police Sergeant decided that if Ridell was to drive to Mildura now, he would best go through Swan Hill. Therefore, they decided to set up a road block on the Swan Hill road just north of Lake Boga.

At the chosen site, I was ordered to park the Ford across the road to block the traffic as much as possible. Although the road of the day was not very wide I positioned the vehicle as best I could and stepped away into the scrub to watch.

We didn't have long to wait as the utility came into sight round a bend 100 yards away going like fury. The policemen all waved at the driver to slow down but he took no notice. Instead, he drove right at the big Ford and, at the last moment, swerved magically round the front end and along the shoulder, missing me by a matter of a few feet. He was away again!

"Get in and give chase!" came the voice of the police Sergeant. We all piled back into the Ford, I gunned the motor and we sped away up the road after the fugitive.

Eventually, and after much hair-raising driving, we got to within about 60 yards of the Oldsmobile and were approaching a bridge over the Murray River. It was solidly blocked at the far end by civilian police cars. Ridell could obviously see the problem and decided to leave the road and headed for the river bank where he pulled up and leapt out.

He sprinted for the river and dived in, probably hoping to race to the other side or float away downstream. Seeing this, one of our Service Police stripped off his tunic and boots and raced to the water's edge and dived in after the runaway Ridell. He caught him and persuaded him to return to the bank where he was dragged from the water looking very contrite, tired out and ashamed. As well as soggy wet!

As we drove back to Mildura RAAF Base, I silently contemplated the last 24 hours adventure I had just experienced. It seemed to be cut straight from a B Grade Hollywood movie; the pursuit, the trail of evidence, the decisions made and the rescue from the river all seemed too fanciful yet, I was there alright!

Peter Ridell did time in the cooler. The ute was returned eventually to the lucky owner and the book was closed on that episode; something I will never forget.

CHAPTER TWENTY SIX.

The war was over and it now seemed somewhat pathetic to see the way that morale around the base was running down. Compared with the way we all marched, exercised and went about our work, repairing, cleaning, arming and training on aircraft prior to the Japanese surrender, it now took on the air of a British holiday camp. There just wasn't the same sense of urgency as before.

Yes, we still saluted officers and swept out the hut each morning and played the occasional game of table tennis but, with the majority of personnel being either de-mobilized or transferred to other stations to fill gaps where de-mob had taken a toll, we had lots more 'elbow room' every day.

Most of the P51 Mustangs had gone and so had the trained ground staff. Since there was no flying, there was no monthly intake of pilots but, the loss of 50% of personnel also meant that an extra workload was placed on those left behind to maintain the Base.

I was enjoying the new freedom of being classed 'driver' and hoping that nobody would discover that I was actually classed Technical Personnel. That would have meant being sent to an operational depot to work on aircraft again, something I was, by now, glad to give up for a while at least.

So, life on the Base continued as before but, perhaps with less formality. I cannot be sure why the accident took place. I just know that it became another very painful experience in my short life thus far. It happened this way;

It was the weekend of 13th and 14th October 1945 and I was rostered on for guard duty as the driver. My duty was to drive the truck for the guards on Saturday night and Sunday morning.

I had reported for duty at 5:30pm Saturday at the same time that the guards were being issued with their ammunition quota. I then drove the guards to their respective posts at 6:00pm for their first 3 hour shift. They would do 3 on and have 3 hours off.

At 11:00pm the Orderly Officer and the Orderly Sergeant got into the truck with me to go round the Base and check out the various guards at their posts. We toured the area with success until we were approaching the bomb dump compound which was some 200 yards from the main gate.

I was ordered to turn off the lights and the motor and let the vehicle coast to a stop close to but not within earshot of the post. This I did and brought the truck to a silent stop, no handbrake used but left in 1st. gear to prevent it from rolling on.

The three of us descended from the cab and walked stealthily toward the tiny guard house. There we could see the fellow supposed to be awake and alert for intruders, sitting on the step against the doorway. His rifle was in front of him, bayonet fixed and plunged into the soft earth like a monument. He was sound asleep.

"Right, we'll fix this fellow," whispered the officer. "You two, gather two handsful of gravel and creep forward. When I signal, chuck the stones onto the tin roof and see what happens."

This we did and crept up to within ten yards of the hut. The officer waved his hand and, up went the small stones. They hit the tin with the sound of a light machine gun being fired at close quarters.

The guard was instantly awake, leapt to his feet and ran all round trying to find his rifle. The officer had him caught in the stark, white beam of his flashlight.

"That man there!" yelled the officer at the top of his voice,"What are you looking for? Forget your rifle,...I have it. Move over to the fence and stand to attention!"

For the next two minutes the air was thick with expletives and commands. The poor airman was on the verge of wetting himself with shame and fatigue. At last, having shouted himself hoarse, the officer gave up and let the man go back to his post.

We three got back into the truck and drove back to the gatehouse guard room. I felt sorry for the poor chap but said nothing to anyone at the guard room. The officer chuckled all the way back.

In the morning at 6:00am I did the rounds and picked up the men from various posts and took them to their huts. All except one chap, Kevin Bowd, who was a close friend and had served at Morotai Island at the same time I did. He was a permanent guard and I was to take him to the emergency landing strip at 7:00am. This was to be his posting for the following 3 hours.

We headed off to breakfast in the guard room. As we drove along he told me about his girlfriend. They had planned to marry in 3 weeks time and he asked me to post three letters for him. He said they were on top of his locker in the hut: one to his own mother as she was arranging the wedding, one to his best man and the last to his girl. In it, he told me how he had said that the 3 weeks couldn't go fast enough for him and that his love for her would be forever undying.

I said,"Kevin, you don't have to tell me that! I can tell how much you are in love..." I looked him straight in the eye and followed with,"Of course I'll post them for you."

"Thanks, mate. I knew I could rely on you," he said and we went into the guard room to have a cup of tea. Most of the fellows from last night had left to go back to their huts. The corporal of the guard was standing at his desk counting back the unused .303 bullets from the rifles used last night. The rifles stood leaning against the wall close-by.

Kevin and I sat on a bench near the pot-belly stove to warm up. There was a big teapot on the stove brewing the tea. I poured two mugs of tea and handed him one.

"How long have you known your girl, Kev?" I asked.

"Just about all my life, Gerry. Her family lives only two doors from mine. It's like one big family at times."

He'd just finished this sentence when the guard from the main gate walked into the room, picked up one of the rifles from near the doorway and jokingly pointed it at us.

"Go for your guns!" he yelled, grinning wildly. There was a loud BANG! I heard the thud and Kevin stood straight up, clutching his chest. His face was a ghastly white colour and he staggered a few steps toward the man with the firearm.

"Christ... what have you done?" he managed to murmur. He then dropped to the floor and a large pool of crimson began to form around his torso. I just stood transfixed, not daring to move.

The next thing I remember was the Guard Commander and the Sergeant telling me to move the truck from the bay in front of the building to allow the ambulance to park there.

The doctor arrived with the ambulance and bent over the body.

"Who the Hell stabbed this man?" He was looking at the exit wound in Kevin's back, a great gaping hole.

"He was shot, sir" came the answer.

"Oh, I see." muttered the doctor and ordered the body to be placed

120

on the stretcher and into the ambulance.

Poor Kevin was taken to the hospital where he was officially pronounced dead. Although I was in a state of shock, I must have moved by rote. I went to his hut and retrieved the three letters he'd mentioned and took them to the post office, put stamps on them and into the mailbox.

I then walked in a bit of a daze, away into the scrub and sat under a large gum tree to consider the past few minutes.

Why him? Why not me? He had everything to live for, lovely girl to marry and rest of his life to live in peace.

It just didn't stack up right. Had that rifle been aimed a few inches to the left, the bullet would have hit me, not Kevin Bowd. It seemed terribly unfair to have happened that way at all.

My head was, by now, just about spinning with questions and — "What if's?" However, I eventually came to the conclusion that there really wasn't anything I could have done to prevent this from happening. The fact was that the damned rifle should not have had a live round in the breech, let alone be left with the action cocked and ready to fire. Not even having the safety catch applied would have justified that scenario.

Rule One: Treat all firearms with respect and assume that it is loaded and ready to fire.

Rule Two: Never point a firearm at anyone unless you intend to shoot.

Both rules were obviously broken by the unfortunate fellow who chose to sky-lark instead of respecting the rules of firearms handling.

After I'd spent some time in the scrub grieving for Kevin I decided to return to the hut and return to a normal life. I remembered something that Yurana had taught me about being confused. She always said, "Go and talk to Baiame. He may not talk back to you but He will listen to you."

This I did and, feeling a surge of new life, went back to camp ready to talk to people.

In later years the people of Mildura erected a plaque on a boulder outside the War Cemetery in town to commemorate all who died on active service from No.2 OTU RAAF Base. Kevin Bowd was listed along with pilots and the other men.

The following Monday I was given a new honour and a new designation. I was handed a peaked hat in place of the blue forage cap that I normally wore as I was now a driver; proficient, Class 1.

I was then told about my new task — to pick up all the unexploded ordinance and accessories for transporting to the rail head at Mildura where it would taken by rail to Melbourne for storage and/or destruction.

It was nice to know that the RAAF had sufficient faith in my driving capability to safely carry their lovely explosives. And, to have the peaked cap as a badge of office too. That was my big day indeed.

CHAPTER TWENTY SEVEN.

My promotion up the transport ladder had been a slow but interesting climb. Now, instead of wearing the petite forage cap of lowly airmen, I was permitted to wear the jaunty peaked headwear of somebody important.

I was designated an experienced driver!

I was shown to a monstrous 6 x 6 GMC truck which stood well above my head at the front tyre with a fully enclosed cabin, hooded headlamps and an enormous front bumper bar which also carried a gigantic winch, capable of pulling the 'Titanic' from the Atlantic Ocean, no doubt.

This was the vehicle, together with a 4 ton dog trailer, which I was to take to Mildura rail yards loaded with surplus explosives and live bombs. It should, however, be pointed out that not all the aerial bombs were the explosive type. Some were smoke-making bombs which contained chemicals which, when exposed to the air, immediately commenced to generate dense clouds of white smoke, very useful stuff to cover the advance of troops over open ground. In practice, they also showed a pilot how his aim was to a target.

The dog trailer was a huge square item with steel gate sides and four wheels, the front set of which swivelled to follow the tow vehicle easily. Its brakes were air-operated with a 6 second delay. This meant that, when the actuating handle was applied in the driver's cabin, it took 6 seconds before the effect took place at the trailer wheel brakes.

The 500 lb. bombs (explosive) were loaded into the truck first for safety. Not that it made me feel any safer knowing that right behind my kidneys were several thousand pounds of high explosive material which, if not treated with respect, would not leave much of me. On top of that went the packs of TNT and detonator wire and other minor materials.

The trailer was then loaded with the smoke bombs and various other bits and pieces in wooden crates which I didn't take much notice of. When all was tied down and vouched as secure on board, we set off for Mildura railway yards to offload onto a rail car bound for Melbourne.

And someone else's problem!

We had a fairly uneventful drive to Mildura town. Other vehicles we approached gave us a wide berth as the signs across the front, sides and tailgates warned the public that the load was 'EXPLOSIVES — KEEP CLEAR'.

Driving along Deacon Avenue, Mildura toward the railway yards, a passenger bus suddenly shot out from Merbein Street on my left. Not wishing to risk a collision, I quickly wrenched the steering wheel to the right, heading for the central garden which divided the traffic in the Avenue. I applied the trailer brakes immediately.

I judged the turn nicely so that, as the front wheels of the truck scraped the edging bricks of the garden, I turned the wheel back to the left and the trailer brakes pulled the combination vehicle to a stop.

Unfortunately, the rear wheels of the trailer had caught the bricks and jumped the kerb, dumping some of the smoke bombs onto the roadway. As I looked around the street from my vantage point high in the cabin, I could see people jumping from the bus which had pulled up almost beside the truck.

Other folk who had been going about their normal business and shopping, ran for cover as the street began to fill with acrid, white smoke. Unbridled panic set in and men, as well as women were screaming as they ran.

The officer with us in the huge cabin decided to take charge of the melee and stepped from the truck.

"Come on, chaps. Let's get these things back onto the trailer and down to the jolly railway. They can have it from there."

We leaped from the vehicle wearing leather gloves for protection, picked up the smoking devices and placed them back on the trailer. With the mess cleared up, I managed to straighten up the vehicle and drive away with no more fanfare than a rousing cheer from some fellows standing outside the pub.

Frankly, it was a most interesting way to break up an otherwise boring trip to Mildura. I took to the GMC truck like a duck to water, left-hand drive and all.

CHAPTER TWENTY EIGHT.

Working as a transport driver certainly appealed to my personality and I was enjoying my daily chores when, one afternoon I was told to report to the orderly room at 'Bull-dust Castle' — Squadron H.Q. building. This I did and was asked to wait for an interview with two senior ranking officers.

Presently, I was shown into a room where two senior officers sat, a Group Captain and a Wing Commander. "Please sit down, LAC Walshe," I did so, wondering what this was all about. "We would like to discuss your future plans with you, if you don't mind," said Wing Commander Bradshaw.

"Yes, sir. What would you like to know?" I asked.

"Well, it would seem that you've been previously employed in a variety of tasks from repairing aircraft up in the islands to bomb disposal and now transport driver. Is that so, airman?"

"Yes, sir."

"OK, then how would you like to volunteer for a further extension of your duty in the Air Force under our new service structure?"

I was lost for words as I had not heard about any changes to the RAAF as we knew it. "Well, sir, I am enjoying my life in the Air Force. It's the only life I know and, frankly, I don't fancy returning to civvy street."

"LAC Walshe, that's exactly what we wanted to hear," said Bradshaw. "Now, this is what we propose but, before we go on, we have to give you some background . The Australian Government has decided that, in the wake of the last war, they are going to create a permanent Air Force. This may take about two years and, meantime we need to ensure our personnel numbers and we are asking our present people to sign on again for a period of 2 years while the transition occurs.

"Now, that gives you an idea why we are here but, there is a further reason that we are talking to you. The Government has joined forces with a number of other countries to form an 'Army of Occupation' in Japan. This will ensure that certain law and order issues are maintained." He took a sip from the glass of water on the table before him.

"Our commitment to this force will be No.81 Fighter Wing with 3 Operational Squadrons of Mustang P51 aircraft; 76, 77 and 82, 481 Maintenance, 381 Base Squadron and No.5 Airfield Construction Squadron. Some of these aircraft will come from this unit. The Wing at present is stationed on Labuan Island off Borneo and we intend keeping this force in Japan for a period of two years or more. This is where the second document comes in.

"LAC Walshe, we will be asking you to sign two documents here; one to signify that you agree to stay on in the RAAF and the other that you agree to go to Japan as part of the Occupation Forces. What do you think?"

This proposition hit me with unexpected force. I sat silently for a moment gathering my thoughts.

"How long would the posting be in Japan, sir?"

"Two years minimum. Then you will be given two weeks leave in Australia. While you're in Japan, we will send you to an advanced course in airframe engineering ."

'Not bad at that,' I thought.

"Sir, which aircraft will I be working on there?"

"Mainly P51 Mustangs and C 47 Dakotas. I believe you've worked on both these aircraft?"

"Yes, I have, sir. OK, let me sign those papers. It sounds like another adventure to me. Life's been getting a bit hum-drum around here of late. Going to Japan might be a good tonic for my soul."

I signed the documents and the next day I reported to the orderly room to receive my transport papers out of Mildura RAAF Base and on my way across the globe.

My ride out of Mildura was with a Beaufighter bomber going to Laverton flown by Flight Lieutenant Peter Oliver. After we had introduced ourselves he handed me some chewing gum.

"You'll need this later," he said and climbed into the aircraft through a small hatch. I followed with my kitbag. The observer had already taken his seat in the aft cabin and the pilot slid into his single seat up front. I closed the hatch and stood on it right behind the pilot, hanging on to the frame of his seat.

"Sorry, chum," he called over his shoulder. "Only 2 seats, you'll have to stand."

"That's OK sir," I yelled back. "If I need to I can sit on my kitbag here."

He busied himself with preflight ground checks and started the engines. Pretty soon we were taxiing out along the apron, past the tower and onto the runway. We turned into wind and the green Aldis lamp signal came from the tower, indicating clearance to take-off.

Oliver gunned the engines and the Beaufighter surged forward, the tail rose from the surface and soon we were aloft with the ground dropping awayquickly. Past the end of the aerodrome the aircraft did a wide climbing turn still on full power to about 2,000 feet. Then we commenced a slow descent toward the runway where we had just left. Boy — oh — boy, was I in for a surprise!

Standing on the small entry hatch behind the pilot, hanging on for grim life, I had a fine view of the ground rushing back up at the aeroplane at about 200 miles an hour. It was enough to make a person grow old.

The Beaufighter levelled out at about 120 ft. and flew down the runway, raising dust and blowing small stones left and right. On the ground, people waved delightedly. In the Beaufighter, Gerry's knees shook.

At the end of the run, Oliver pulled back on the control column and the aircraft climbed away at a steep angle. My head suddenly became quite heavy and my fingers clung desperately to the frame of the pilot's seat as the aircraft screamed to about 5,000 feet.

There we levelled out and the throttles were pulled back a little to cruising revs. The pilot smiled back over his shoulder at me.

"How about that, Gerry? Great feeling, eh?"

I think I managed to smile weakly back at him and nod. I concentrated on chewing the gum he'd given me a moment before we took off.

When we arrived over Port Phillip Bay the pilot turned the Beaufighter back toward the line of wharves at Williamtown. There the Beaufighter turned toward Laverton where we joined the circuit area and landed.

The trip to Melbourne had taken about 2 hours and we rolled to a stop near a service hangar.

"OK, Gerry. Let's hop out." said Peter Oliver rising from the pilot's seat. "Open the hatch, my son."

I bent down to unlatch the hatch where I had stood for most of the trip. It would not budge. Oliver tried and I tried again. I drew my trusty pocket knife and tried to 'jemmy' the latch. Nothing happened.

Oliver went to the slicing window to call a ground crew. Two engineers came running with screwdrivers and pried the latch open from outside. The hatch exploded open and we leapt out.

Looking back at the aircraft, Oliver noted, "Geez, Gerry. That hatch latch might have been your undoing, had it been too easy to open,..." He strode off whistling merrily.

'Just call me Lucky!' I thought.

I picked up my kit bag and reported to the orderly room, there to receive my transport papers which would take me to Japan, land of the Rising Sun.

CHAPTER TWENTY NINE.

I left Australia for Japan in December 1945, flying in a C47 Dakota aircraft from Melbourne to Darwin via Alice Springs then on to Timor, Ambon, over the jade green sea north of Borneo to land at Labuan Airstrip. We were to join 81 Fighter Wing RAAF where there was work a-plenty as P51 Mustangs were being damaged left, right and centre on take-off and landings.

Unfortunately, one of the negative characteristics of the P51 was that the torque of the mighty Merlin engine tended to throw the aircraft off line to the left on take-off and to let it drift to the right when landing as the pilot reduced the power. Any pilot who didn't allow for this was liable to get into trouble — quickly.

The Mustang was a most unforgiving aeroplane and many pilots came to grief on account of their inattention to the torque tendencies.

The line-up of aircraft at this establishment was quite remarkable. We had a long silvery line of Mustangs, Beaufighters in drab camoflage and another fast-looking twin engined aeroplane which I didn't recognise immediately.

It turned out to be the De Havilland Mosquito, a fabulous, smooth-skinned beast which, surprisingly, was constructed mainly from timber framework and plywood covering. With two Rolls Royce Merlin super-charged engines driving it along, this aeroplane was the scourge of the Luftwaffe in the latter stages of the war in Europe. It was largely occupied in fast reconnaissance photo sorties and 'path-finder' flare drops at night, leading the night raids into enemy territory.

Thus, I reported to the orderly room and was allocated a bunk and told to report to the training school in the morning to take up a position as assistant instructor on airframes to train the airmen posted to P51 Mustang maintenance. We were kept very busy with the aforementioned incidents and accidents to Mustangs.

Early in 1946 we were told to report to the sick bay to receive our innocculations for typhoid, cholera, tetanus and encephalitis to follow in Japan. With all these jabs going in we got very excited thinking we would be off to Japan soon. In fact it took another month before we got going by sea.

The convoy taking us to the home islands appeared at anchor one morning in the bay. They were corvettes HMAS Warramunga and HMAS Murchison, 3 LST's, SS Murrumbidgee and the flagship, HMS Glengyle.

The next morning we were transported from the beach to the fleet by Indian Army barges. Fortunately, I was standing with the group from 77 Sqd. and we were taken out to the flagship 'Glengyle' instead of onto an LST. We had to climb aboard via landing nets over the side but, later during the trip north, we had a much smoother ride than the poor devils aboard the 'big barges'. Just days out from Labuan, we were hit by a typhoon which made many chaps quite ill.

Some days later we found we were steaming up the coast of Japan's home islands. Presently, we turned into the Bungo Strait between Honshu and Shikoku Islands and continued through to the southern end of the beautiful Seto-Naikai — The Inland Sea.

A mist hung low over the water. In the lee of Shikoku it looked like a lake with both shores visible and the hundreds of tiny islets dotted about with fishing boats. The sight was spell-binding; the dark green of the islands contrasting with the azure blue of the water and the distant ridges topped with snow.

I remember the cold. We had been warned that the temperature was well down but, coming from a tropical climate as we had, it seemed somehow more intense. The views, however, were a fine distraction.

As our vessel closed on the western shore, we could clearly see houses, shrines and people moving about on the beaches. The hills were covered in crops of various colours in fields or paddies that reached down to the sea. The stench from the fertilizer that the farmers used here reached our nostrils and reminded me of the warning not to eat uncooked vegetables.

Now and then we passed the visible signs of sunken Japanese ships, sent to the bottom by either USAAF bombers flying from Okinawa or carrier-borne fighter-bombers in mass attacks with torpedoes as well as bombs during the closing stages of the war.

We were passing the Harima ship yards where a long, sleek cruiser was being systematically stripped of its fittings and superstructure.

One of our crewmen pointed out that this vessel had been the 'Aoba' — 10,882 tons — and had been involved in the sneak attack on allied shipping in 'The Slot' at Guadalcanal when my brother David had been aboard the 'Canberra' which had sunk.

'How ironic,' I thought, 'Three and a half years after that action I was so close to one of the ships which almost took my brother's life.'

Later that day we docked at Kure wharf. There was plenty of depth of water here as the terrain ran from the top of a mountain behind the town straight down to the water and on at the same incline, giving the anchorage plenty of draft for large ships.

Close by we could see an aircraft carrier which was listing heavily to port but still afloat. It was being scrapped at the nearby shipyard. This was the 21,000 ton 'Amagi'. Further down the way was a large battleship with just its superstructure visible. This was the 'Haruna', sunk at its mooring with the loss of some 1,200 men.

Looking around the foreshores and over toward Eta Jima island where the Japanese Naval H.Q. had been situated, the devastation was horrific. Twisted and blackened steel frames marked the spots where, previously sat workshops, dry docks, holding pens and slipways. A row of black cigar-shaped vessels caught my eye. On closer inspection they turned out to be 70 ft. midget submarines, the same type which attacked shipping in Sydney Harbour in 1942. Strangely, I always thought they were smaller.

Early next morning we disembarked and, in full battle dress including overcoats and gloves on account of the snow, we marched through the war-torn streets of Kure to a bus station. There were no people to be seen as they had been warned that the 'gorsu' people from Australia would exact our barbaric vengance; raping the women and eating the children. How far from the truth could they be?

We caught a bus to take us to the railway station. I was interested to note that the bus had a gas generator on the back just as we'd had in Melbourne. Inside the bus there were no seats. It was deemed better to remove the seats so that they could carry more people at a time.

We stood at the rail platform at Kure station and watched the dilapidated trains pull up and pack more passengers into the carriages, some hanging out the doors and others sitting on the roofs. Very precarious mode of travel.

Looking past the trains to the shops visible outside the station, I noted how the shopkeepers displayed their wares on woven mats outside the shop. Anyone who ventured into the store was immediately harangued with a torrent of bartering. This cacophony filled the air as the civilian population moved up and down the streets with an air of dejection, being poorly clad, undernourished and badly in need of a wash.

At any time that a serviceman tossed away a cigarette butt, a stampede began with Japanese people diving for the discarded smoke. A row of bamboo rickshaws stood by like taxis waiting for a customer, drivers patiently standing or sitting between the shafts.

I was totally fascinated with the way that the trains were being run. They would approach the station with people hanging out the doors. When those who were getting off had done so and the others who were boarding got on, a fellow in uniform would take hold of the handrails either side of the door and place both feet against the last passengers and push them inside in order to close the doors.

It didn't always work but, it was an interesting technique.

Then, along came the B.C.O.F. Express, reserved for the British Commonwealth Occupation Forces as we were. It was nothing at all like the general run of carriages for the public. The outside paintwork gleamed in beautiful blue and gold livery with the names of Cities of Australia painted on each one. We stepped into the luxurious, warm enclosure of the 'Canberra' carriage and sat on the plush green velvet upholstered seats. Our boots made no noise on the deep pile carpet. It seemed a bit odd sitting there with our .303 rifles and uniforms in this quaint oriental splendour.

I even imagined that this might be similar to travelling on the Orient Express, perhaps?

The train moved off very smoothly toward our destination of Iwakuni about 50 miles along the track and without the assistance of the platform guy having to shove the last man inside the door. 'Terribly civilized', I thought.

CHAPTER THIRTY.

The landscape through which we now were travelling became somewhat monotonously beautiful or beautifully monotonous with lofty mountain peaks running straight down to the sea, rice paddies and groves of decorative trees dotted about with picturesque villages or farmer's cottages all much the same design as if bought in a box from a department store.

Where the train ran alongside the road we saw women working to repair pot holes. As the train passed they all stood up and waved to us. We waved back.

All along the track toward Hiroshima we could see the semi-submerged remains of huge battleships, cruisers and smaller vessels, their decks twisted and blackened, their rigging tangled and smashed. The emotional and psychological impact must have been horrendous seeing the pride of the navy sink before their very eyes.

Eventually the train emerged from one of the many short tunnels through which we had to pass and we took our first glimpse of Hiroshima about a mile distant. It is situated in a valley about five miles wide and five miles long, it is surrounded by hills about 1,500 feet high on three sides with the Inland Sea across the fourth side.

The train slowly approached this once beautiful city and I could not believe what I was seeing. The devastation was absolutely staggering, the desolation was almost total. With very few exceptions, every building as far as the eye could see was flattened or burned. A few solid structures such as chimneys remained vertical but, even they had a lean — away from 'ground zero'.

The train slowed to walking pace passing through Hiroshima Station and stopped along the track. We were told that the train would require some repairs and it would take about an hour. We decided to take a walk, leaving three fellows in the carriage to mind our gear.

Walking along the rail line toward the city we encountered some Japanese soldiers, still wearing uniforms but without their badges of rank or unit flashes. They looked particularly depressed and scruffy as we passed. I was glad to have my rifle over my shoulder and a couple of spare magazines of live rounds in my day pack. We were told that they were battle-hardened veterans from China and they gave us some filthy looks as we passed.

Next we encountered a gang of young boys and girls who ran to us giggling and holding out their hands in friendship. As they got closer I could see that each one had what looked like warts on their arms, legs and faces. They were keloids, possibly caused by being caught in the open when the atomic explosion went off in August. Their clothing was virtually thread-bare and most had no footwear. They certainly looked cold.

I searched my day pack and found some survival rations which I gladly gave to the kiddies. Among the gang of youngsters were some who had club feet, withered arms and legs where the tendons had been so affected by the hot blast that they simply contracted into useless matter. It broke my heart to witness this legacy of the brutality of war. They knew nothing of the politics yet were to pay an enormous price. Some would not live past the next summer.

Back in the train carriage later, I found myself mulling over the sights I had seen and tears flowed easily down my cheeks. My mind went to my relationship with Baiame and I couldn't help but wonder why this sort of carnage could be perpetrated on poor little kiddies who now, might have been without parents or other relatives to look after them. I felt quite nauseous thinking about their plight.

The train repair was completed and again we started to move, heading for Iwakuni Railway Station.

Along the way we looked out on terraced hillsides, Buddhist shrines and pagodas, toriis or collections of stone grave markers where the dead had to be interred in the upright position as the land was too scarce to take up more space lying down.

Mile after mile of highly cultivated rice paddies went by. On the roads we could not help but notice the ubiquitous 'honey carts', so called because they collected the community night-soil to spread on the cultivated field and rice paddies. The warning about not eating raw vegetables came racing back to my mind.

We finally arrived at Iwakuni Station and left the train to board trucks which would take us to our billets at what used to be a Japanese

Naval Air Base. There we found a concrete runway still intact, slipways into the Inland Sea and many two-storey huts, accommodation for over 4,000 personnel.

The majority of huts were badly in need of repair however, despite their neglected condition, they proved to be more comfortable than the tents we slept in at Labuan Island. Broken windows and the lack of steam heating were minor faults compared with the luxury of having somewhere that was dry and we might get a good night's sleep.

After stowing my kit, I went for a walk around the base and was surprised to see Australian kurrajong trees planted all round the place as well as along the road into town. It made me a little bit homesick just to see them.

We didn't have to put up with the short-comings of the huts at Iwakuni for very long as the base soon bcame overcrowded with men from other nations; RAF Poms, RNZAF Kiwis and RIAF Indians. We had been told to standby for movement to another camp when 12 silvery Mustangs landed from Labuan. This was 78 Sqdn., the first Aussie lot into Japan. Just to see them made us feel better. The Poms called them 'pregnant ducks' but, to us, they were graceful young ladies.

Within 5 days of this, we were told to get ready to move out. We packed up and got aboard buses back to Iwakuni Station and aboard a train to take us to Bofu Camp, about four hours away down the railway line to disembark at Mitajiri Station.

CHAPTER THIRTY ONE.

We arrived at Mitajiri Rail Station in our luxurious blue and gold carriage named 'Adelaide', there to disembark and board some army trucks. Big contrast in travel conditions there!

The airfield at Bofu Aerodrome consisted of one long concrete runway and several timber huts which were in a terrible state of neglect. They were going to require a great deal of work to bring them up to standard.

We noted also that the topographical layout of the place was not conducive to bad weather flying as the 'drome was almost completely ringed by some very high hills. We learned later that the 'hills' were originally islands in a sea and that the 'drome was built on reclaimed land that now sat well below mean sea level.

This also meant that, to save the area from flooding, the industrious people here had built some walls high enough and strong enough to hold back the seawater from invading the reclaimed territory. There were many places that were manufactured the same way in the Land of the Rising Sun.

On arrival at the living quarters at Bofu Base I was interested to note that the area was ringed with a shallow moat about 40 feet wide. We drove over the bridge and stopped amid a group of two-storey wooden buildings. When we had stepped down from the trucks we gazed at our new lodgings and asked the Corporal in charge, "What are the knotted ropes for that hang out of the top floor windows?"

"That, my friends, is your best friend in case of fire. These huts will go up like a packet of crackers if they start so, get to know where your rope escape is located in every hut."

He was absolutely right. Only three days into our stay here and the hut next door went up at midnight, the dry timbers crackling and spluttering like a bonfire on Empire Day. I had a grandstand view of semi-naked men leaping out of windows and working their way to the ground on the ropes. They had lost everything including their clothing and personal effects. In total, four huts went up in smoke that night.

Following this event, life in the barrack huts became a case of 'get used to it — 'cos there ain't any relief coming soon that we can see.'

For the chaps who had escaped from the burning huts, they were obliged to share with those of us who still had a bed and some clothing. This meant that almost every bed in the remaining huts was a 'doubler' and each man had to get used to sleeping with the smelly feet of another chap for conversation and a kiss goodnight. It was almost enough to put me off ever sleeping with another person in my lifetime.

It wasn't until six weeks later that work commenced replacing the damaged huts. Extra issues of clothing and other stores came sooner but, at the time we did our best to accommodate the unfortunate ones.

In March 1946 we had most of 76 and 82 Squadron aircraft at Bofu Base. The 24 P51 Mustangs of 77 Sqdn. had departed Okinawa on 21st March and were expected at Bofu on the afternoon of the same day. We were, however, somewhat apprehensive as a week prior, on a ferry flight from Okinawa, 82 Sqdn. had lost 3 P 51's and their Mosquito escort in a fierce storm off cape Tsuru, southwestern Shikoku Island, just short of their destination.

As luck would have it, all our Mustangs arrived over Bofu Base safely and put on a fine display of formation flying which sent the local farmers running from their fields. With the arrival of these fine aircraft, we now had something to work on.

I soon learned that the Japanese people have a love of nature and they express this admiration through their cultivation of flowering trees. The most honoured of these is the beautiful cherry blossom tree. These trees do not produce any fruit but are planted simply for the brilliant display of flowers during springtime when they hold the four day Cherry Blossom Festival — Hana-Matsuri.

This is the time when women dress in their finest and most expensive kimonos and family groups spend the day strolling through parks and sitting by lakes and rivers underneath the cherry trees admiring their glorious colours and profusion of blossoms.

During this season I took the opportunity to climb nearby Mount. Tenjin from where I was able to view the entire valley below. The pale pink haze of the cherry blossoms stood out against the green of fields and, in the distance, the seawall holding back the Inland Sea scribed a dark yellow line across the end of the valley. It was easy to imagine how the 'valley' must have appeared ages ago before the land was reclaimed to form this part of the country with small islands dotting the waters.

For the next 3 months the Base settled down into a routine of daily flights of Mustangs on surveillance duty, aircraft servicing and supervision of building work on the aerodrome. The aircraft were keeping watch over the prefectures of Hiroshima, Yamaguchi, Shimane, Totori and Shikoku west, looking for smugglers and illegal entry to Japan by Koreans across the Tsushima Strait.

Unfortunately, with all these movements of aircraft, the concrete runway at Bofu began to deteriorate and, by late June the 'drome was closed to all operational flying. We had to call in RAAF No.5 Airfield Construction crew at Iwakuni to rebuild the runways, a job that would take at least 30 or 40 days — more if the weather turned nasty.

While the repair crews worked at putting the runways to right, five of us airmen were given 5 days leave and we decided to get on a train to visit the volcanic districts of the island of Kyushu. The steam train took us a s far as the southern tip of Honshu where we boarded an electric train to travel the under-sea tunnel to Kyushu. We emerged from the tunnel into broad sunshine in the city of Kitakyushu. There, we boarded another steam train and continued to the City of Beppu where we had booked into a hotel type of building which was located next door to the palace of a prince, high on a hillside overlooking this amazing place.

There was plenty to see and experience on Kyushu — the volcanic Mount Aso, 40 miles west of the city had begun to erupt and the night-time view of this was quite spectacular. The mud pools at the hot-springs venue were something to experience as well as behold. Called 'jigoku' or hells by the locals, they were driven by underground thermal activity and came in different colours which depended on the composition of the minerals in the clay. One was dark green and two were shades of crimson while three were a pretty blue hue. The temperatures varied from about 170F to 195F and they bubbled continuously, rising four inches above the surface to burst and subside back into concentric circles.

In a park near the centre of town we also found a couple of pools where, on one side the water was hot enough to boil an egg and right next to it was a cool pool about 6 feet away.

We walked into a statue of Buddha and climbed the stairs to the head where, one could view the city below. Our luxurious accommodation was typical Japanese. Each room had its own bath with a house-girl supplied to scrub the back and shoulders. This was a requirement of all who wished to bathe in the thermal pools.

Of course the rooms were designed and built in the traditional style with sliding screen doors or 'shoji', woven reed mats — 'tatami' and cushions to sit upon and 'futons' where we put our heads down at the end of an exhausting day of sight-seeing.

One concession to western culture the management afforded us was the addition of a mattress for the 'futon' which made sleep all the more restful.

After five days of being pampered, buried in hot, brown sand to tone up the skin and having the back scrubbed several times, it was time to return to Bofu Base. We walked through the sulphurous air of Beppu to the train station and boarded the train back to the tunnel, the eleven mile under-sea tunnel and the steam train back to Mitajiri.

We would never forget those five wonderful days spent in pampered luxury. Although we had the opportunity to inspect the city of Nagasaki where the second of two atomic bombs had been delivered by the allied forces in August 1945, we declined to do so. That would have been pointless and voyeuristic to say the least. Enough sadness and pain was experienced seeing the survivors of Hiroshima to last my lifetime.

CHAPTER THIRTY TWO.

A fter our return to Bofu Base, the next few months were a virtual 'dog's breakfast' — nothing was going right. We detected fuel contamination in drums, we had a shortage of BTM magnetos for the Packard Merlin engines and some foul weather set in.

We did, however, have some good luck. The whole wing was engaged in routine surveillance patrols which covered the entire BCOF region and, wonder-of-wonders, there were no sightings of smugglers nor any unsual sea traffic to worry about. Maybe the villains had decided to have a rest or perhaps they were victims of the inclement weather too. Whatever was the case, it gave us a break as well.

At this time, we did take the opportunity for a bit of engineering to suit a pressing problem. As the district was rural and crop-producing it was heavily water-logged and a great place for breeding insects of various types. Of course the insects had a most annoying effect of the troops so, in order to keep their breeding in check, we undertook to fit some P51's with liquid spraying equipment.

The aircraft also carried supplies of DDT in their drop-tanks which seemed to work marvels in killing the wee beasties but, it also had a disastrous effect on personnel who came into contact with this most dangerous chemical. I was affected but, the negative result did not show up until I had returned to Australia and been married a while.

I was diagnosed as being sterile.

The aircraft continued with their spraying activities during August 1946 over the areas of Okayama, Bofu, Iwakuni and Kaitaicha. I guess many other men at Bofu were equally affected, to say nothing of the locals.

During this period the wing set up a group of volunteers who were named Disaster Guards. Any who volunteered for this group were told they would receive extra benefits. Thus I volunteered.

Our duties were simply to be able to cope with any disaster or emergency which occurred. The booklet we had received upon arrival in Japan nominated some of the potential emergencies we might encounter; earthquake, typhoon, tidal wave, floods and fires.

We had already survived one disaster in the fire which consumed four barrack huts but we were hardly very experienced to handle the other emergencies when we were alerted in mid-1946 that a typhoon was developing in the Marianas Islands with torrential rains and high winds exceeding 100 m.p.h. in strength. It was moving rapidly northward toward the Island of Kyushu and Bofu base lay directly in its path.

All local leave was cancelled and all aircraft were covered and lashed down by three anchor-points. All buildings were made secure with windows battened shut and any loose materials found outside were secured. Fortunately for us, after a couple of hours of heavy rain and high winds buffeting the base, the typhoon changed direction and moved out over the Sea of Japan to expend its fury.

This event turned out to be a valuable rehearsal for us as, on December 21 at around 4:30am, Honshu and Shikoku Islands were shaken violently by earthquake to be followed by a tidal wave. Everyone was woken by the sounds of windows rattling and doors banging loudly. The whole barracks hut shook and the wooden floors rippled like a sheet in the wind making it too difficult to walk anywhere so, we tried to stay in our beds until the rocking and grinding ceased. This was only partly successful as the floor heaved and rolled like waves at sea tossing the beds around like corks. Most of us landed unceremoniously on the floor in our pyjamas.

Expletives exploded in the darkness all around me as men realised their predicament and fumbled about looking for torches and clothing, stubbing toes on chairlegs and preventing lockers from toppling onto other chaps. The grinding roar of the 'quake continued like a huge wild animal all around us for some minutes. That, in itself, was enough to give rise to fear in the superstitious among us.

I found myself sprawled on the cold timber floor and groped madly for my flashlight which had been on the small table beside the bed. I found it under the bed and turned it on. The sight which then greeted me was frightful; bodies and furniture at odd angles all around the room.

"Is anybody hurt in here?" I yelled above the grinding noise.

"No, mate, not here but what a bloody shock, eh?"

"Let's get outside in case the roof comes down," I suggested and there was an immediate rumble of agreement from the men.

We donned our greatcoats over pyjamas and slipped into gumboots to make our way more by feel than sight down the timber stairwell to the concrete apron. There, we all stood in the pouring rain, watching the building sway and window glass snap out of its frames to fall to the ground, adding to the cacophony all round.

Eventually the quake ceased and the roaring noise subsided. We checked each other for injuries but none were reported so, since there was still a few hours til dawn, we trouped back into the hut.

There we straightened the beds up and pushed furniture back to more or less the positions it had occupied beforehand. Everyone lay on his bed still half dressed, rather than get into bed, hoping that there would not be a sudden repeat performance. The chatter around the room in the dark was quite interesting and largely was of the impressions of the fellows as they woke to experience the earthquake and witness the strange lights in the sky.

In the early morning light we began the task of cleaning up the mess created during the night. When that was out of the way we went to breakfast in the mess hut. There, we discovered that, not only did we have an earthquake but also a typhoon and a huge tidal wave which had done an impressive amount of damage for miles around.

It was the worst wave to hit the islands of Honshu and Shikoku for ages and the shipping docks at Kure had been severely damaged. The rail line south from Bofu was buckled and closed to traffic while fire had destroyed numerous buildings in Kure City including the Chogoku Electrical Works.

Three landslides had blocked the trainline between Tokyo and Kure and would take several days to clear and repair. In Iwakuni many homes were destroyed by fire when the hibachi stoves had overturned. Part of the seawalls had collapsed and the land had become flooded as a result. There were reports of many deaths and loss of property. Approximately 1,700 fishing boats were missing, presumed swept out to sea by the receding wave action. A few sizeable ships had even been carried considerable distances inland and stranded there in farmers' fields.

Naturally, as a volunteer Disaster Guard I realised that I would be in line for duty as all Disaster Guard Units had been called into action early that day. We were instructed to report to the Service Police unit. There we were given orders to report to the hospital to load equipment and medical supplies packed in specially designed cane panniers onto a truck. Each pannier contained basic medicines, instruments, drugs and dressings.

These supplies were destined for Kochi City on Shikoku Island where the 2nd Dorset Regiment, a British Army unit were stationed. One of our C47 Dakotas would fly over to deliver the supplies, the pilots risking heavy rain, low fog and possibly damaged landing strips to get there.

We had been told that the Military Government had commandeered schools, hospitals, warehouses and other public buildings to shelter the homeless civilians. Morgues had been set up near hospitals to receive and register the dead while the small hospitals would cater for the injured population. The death toll at this early stage was estimated to be around 2,000 with a further 3,000 injured. About 200,000 Japanese were left homeless and the BCOF troops were put to work searching for survivors and clearing debris from roads and streets.

The truck was loaded at the hospital and, with 6 Disaster Guards aboard, we headed off to load the C47. The rain pelted down unmercifully, making the miserable task even more miserable. When the aircraft was loaded we climbed back into the truck.

"Hoy, you men!" It was the Flight Lieutenant in charge." You fellows are going with it to Kochi. Get aboard the aircraft, now!" he barked. We did so.

The loadmaster locked the double doors and went up front. The pilot started the engines and we taxied out to the runway and, off into the heavy, grey, wet sky. We flew north a way then turned east to head for Shikoku Island. The clouds were very low and the pilot kept the aeroplane below 1,500 ft. looking desperately for the airfield.

Presently we found it through the gloom and the aeroplane descended to make a low pass over the strip to ascertain its suitability. We could see puddles and streams of water rushing across the tarmac but it generally seemed to be intact. The pilot pulled away and climbed to 1,000 ft. to fly a circuit and land.

In due course, and due to the skill of our pilots, we landed at Kochi City airstrip and rolled to a halt near a couple of huts where men came running through the heavy rain to help unload.

Instead of a truck to receive the supplies, we were surprised to find they had driven up with an Army DUKW, an amphibious landing craft capable of carrying 2.5 tons of goods over land or water.

Just the ticket! I thought.

The aircraft was duly unloaded and we were, by then, quite exhausted as we had not eaten since a very early breakfast. We sat on the floor of the aeroplane and speculated about getting back to Bofu for a hot shower and hot lunch.

"You men, there!" A loud British accent drove such thoughts from our minds. A Captain of the Dorset Regiment stood at the doorway and bellowed at us. "Get your backsides out here. We have work for you. No sitting down now, there are people to rescue and debris to clear away."

We hopped out of the C47 and were shown to the DUKW aptly named 'Sunshine Girl'. On such a fine day? No way! Not much sunshine today, I fear.

Away we went aboard the DUKW sitting atop the boxes and panniers, along boulder-strewn roads, across flooded fields and rivulets with water rushing underneath us. At last we arrived at the outskirts of Kochi City at what looked like a school built on high ground.

After unloading all the stores at this place we then headed off to scout for dead and injured civilians. The DUKW headed for the shores of a lake where we went to work picking up bodies of men, women and small children. One child in particular was to alter entirely my perception of the Japanese race.

Arriving at the designated site which looked like it might have been a school or basketball stadium, we unloaded our precious cargo and then headed away toward a small lake where we could see many bodies lying about exposed to the elements.

We drove the DUKW into the water to reach many of the injured and dead. Although I had seen many dead bodies before during the war, I had never had to pick up any and the experience was quite unnerving to me at first.

We had been at this unpleasant task for about an hour when I sighted what looked like a small child dressed in pompei bloomers, a white shirt and a jumper lying across a wooden box. I jumped into the water which was waist-deep and waded to her, picked her up in my arms and made my way back to the vehicle, pushing flotsam aside as I went.

As I reached the DUKW I looked again at the child's face and saw that it was a different colour from those of dead people we had already on board the vehicle. I checked for a pulse and, to my surprise and delight, found there was a slight beat. This made me quite excited so I put my ear to her tiny mouth to check for breath as I didn't have a mirror to check for mist.

She was still breathing!

I then did something completely emotional and yelled to the crew to take the child while I scrambled back into the DUKW. Then, when I had settled, I removed my top clothing and stood bare-chested in sub-zero conditions. Then I asked the others to strip the girl's wet clothing from her frigid little body and place her against my own then dress me again with singlet, shirt, jumper and greatcoat while I clutched the tiny, cold body to my torso.

The memory of my lectures in first aid came flooding back — Hypothermia: Body to body contact is best to reinstate a victim's bodily heat.

Thus, I sat at the back of the vehicle, unable to move any more during the search and held the child to my body, hoping against hope that the warmth of my own flesh would transfer to her small body and cause her to survive and live.

The DUKW eventually returned to the hospital and morgue where we unloaded the supplies and I was aided from the vehicle to the ground, still clutching my frozen human cargo. Some mates helped me to waddle as best I could manage into the reception room and find a doctor.

As luck would have it, I found an Australian Captain from Kure who regarded me curiously and asked, "Airman, are you hiding something there that you want to tell me about?"

"Yes sir," I answered, "I have here a child suffering hypothermia. I have carried her here from the disaster area held against my body to try to warm her up a bit."

He gulped and peeked inside my greatcoat. "Good grief! You'd best bring her into this examination room." He pointed the way and I followed, waddling like a pregnant duck.

He then took the little child from my coat and placed her on a bed while I got dressed. With her body taken away I felt a bit warmer but still pretty cold and wet. We waited outside the room while the hospital staff went to work on her. They wrapped the child in blankets and began to wash the putrid muck from her face and hands.

My mates and I sat outside the room for some time before the doctor put his head out and declared," She's a real fighter! She's hanging on to life by a thread but, now we have her, I think we can save her. Thank you boys, you've done an excellent job here. Very commendable too." He winked knowingly.

"I should like to keep in touch with you if you don't mind, sir," I said. "I feel terribly responsible for this child. She may not even have any parents left and I would be grateful of any news you can let me have from time to time."

"That will be OK by me, Airman. You look like you could do with a hot meal yourself. Try the 2nd Dorset Regiment barracks." He nodded at us and went back into the room.

We boarded the DUKW again and drove away from the hospital with its gloomy corridors and overcrowded halls. The vehicle drove along a visible road for a couple of miles then, down a dip and into water where the driver paused to change from road travel to water propulsion. Then, we were away, pushing a bow wave like a boat.

We arrived back at the 2nd Dorset barracks where we were treated to a hot cup of cocoa and told to report to the clothing store. There we were given dry army uniforms, woollen underpants and singlets, socks, pyjamas, shaving kit etc and shown to the shower block where we had the most glorious hot showers.

A hot meal followed and, by about seven o'clock we were all in bed and exhausted. I tried to go straight to sleep but, the picture of the little girl clinging to dear life kept returning to my mind.

Eventually, I must have drifted off. I awoke next morning with a feeling of urgency coursing through my bones. I dressed quickly, ate breakfast on the run and went to the assembly point, ready for another day's scouting for survivors.

"Gee whiz, Gerry, you're dead keen to get going today," someone remarked.

"Well, after yesterday's find, I guess you could say that. Maybe there are other kiddies out there who need our help. Let's get going!"

We leapt aboard the DUKW and drove off. On the way I asked the driver to make a stop at the hospital so that I could see how the child I'd found was coming along. I felt she would definitely pull through, now being in the capable hands of Aussie medical staff .

We duly pulled up at the hospital and I leapt from the vehicle and went quickly to the examination room where, the day before I had left her in the care of staff. The bed was empty!

My heart sank. I felt sick. A nurse walked toward me

"Can I help you there, soldier?" she asked.

"Yes,... that little girl I brought in here yesterday,... is she alright?"

The nurse smiled at me. "Oh, yes, she's fine. We moved her to the general ward. She's been taking a little warm soup and sleeping a lot but, she will be OK it due course."

"Oh, thank you nurse. May I see her while I'm here?" I asked.

"Of course, come this way."

She led me to another ward and past a dozen beds where people with various injuries lay or sat. We stopped beside a petite figure on a bed and I looked down at a tiny mite. Her face now had better colour than the previous day, her lips were pink and her hair was freshly brushed. She looked like a sleeping angel.

I reached down and took her little hand in mine. The fingers were cold but not icy. I stooped over and kissed them. She didn't stir but my eyes began to blur with tears. I sniffed them back and turned to the nurse.

"Thank you Sister. She certainly looks a lot better today. I'd best shove off. Ohh, incidentally, I'm Airman G K Walshe, dressed like this on account of my wet clobber from yesterday." She smiled.

"Sorry. A natural mistake to make. Do call again." She waved as I turned and left the hospital, satisfied that the child would recover and live on. I would be back another time to make her acquaintance.

CHAPTER THIRTY THREE.

When I returned to the DUKW everyone wanted to know how the little girl was today. I related my meeting with her, brief though it was. They all cheered and, on that note, we set off once again to locate more victims of the tsunami and typhoon.

We headed for Kochi city which had been heavily flooded. We could see a huge open space where the harbour was and wrecked buildings which were up to their 1st floor windows with putrid water. The stench was overwhelming, the rain had ceased and the insects had begun to swarm.

There were quite a number of bodies to be retrieved here and we worked away without a break for some hours, pushing through chest-high muck in our duck-hunting waders, sometimes tripping on hidden obstacles which always brought a roar of protest from the unlucky individual who usually scored a good dollop of muck inside the water-proof suit. It was a most unusual and perilous activity.

The vehicle's deck was almost filled with bodies and parts of bodies which now needed to be encased in rubberised body-bags. Several trips were made into the city to unload our ghastly cargo at a reception point — through the 1st floor windows!

On a subsequent trip later in the afternoon, I saw what I took to be a hat floating on the turbid waters. I volunteered to wade to it and retrieve it in case there was a body attached or close-by. The DUKW drove toward the object and I slid carefully into the muck. I reached out for the hat and froze as I lifted it.

Beneath the rim was the face of a beautiful Japanese girl of about 18 tender years. Her slightly suntanned face told me instantly that she had worked in a rural pursuit. As I grasped her clothing to lift her aboard the craft, I almost threw up. There, attached by straps over her shoulders was a baby basket containing her child of no more than a few months.

I gagged and shouted for help. Two comrades came to my aid and helped me to lift the duo onto the deck of the huge vehicle. I felt like I was losing my mind. I began to shake involuntarily and sob uncontrollably. My mates tried to console me but, to no avail. I wished only to end this horror and go home to have a long, long sleep.

The image of that delicate face and the tiny baby strapped to her back stayed with me through all my days. I could not avoid contemplating the terrible vision of the pair being thrown into the surging waters and struggling for very life as the tsunami overwhelmed them both. Not even Yurana's comforting words could allay the pain I felt when I recalled what she had said to me; "In life there is death. It is a part of life!"

I was distraught. The only thing I could see that would keep my mind focussed on saving lives and doing my job was the fact of my little girl back at the hospital. She was my 'beacon on the hill' and I had to stay sane to see her get well and thoroughly recouperated.

Being late in the day, it was then decided that we should deliver the latest 'load' to the morgue and head back to base. I argued for a deviation via the hospital so that I could check the progress of my little patient. I had to see her once more.

With the delivery completed, we drove to the hospital. The waters had receded quite an amount by now and this made the journey by road a bit faster. The DUKW pulled up at the hospital and I leapt to the ground, removed my waders and walked into the ward where the girl had been the day before.

To my surprise, next to her bed I could see three women standing and chatting together. One was the Australian ward sister and two Japanese ladies in western clothing. The nurse saw me approach and turned to greet me.

"Hello there, Airman Walshe! I'd like to introduce these ladies to you."

It turned out that one was an interpreter and the other was the little girl's mother. When my name was mentioned to the mother, she let out a yell and came running toward me with arms held out. I was taken aback since this was most unusual behaviour for the reserved Japanese people.

Mama-san threw her arms about my waist and hugged me, yelling in Japanese all the while. The interpreter tried to maintain pace with the verbal torrent but gave up and just stood there admiring the scene and clapping her delicate hands in approbation. The Aussie Sister joined in. I looked all around, amazed at this display of unfettered emotion, something that Japanese women would never do under normal circumstaces.

"Domo arigato gozaimasu!" Mama-san kept repeating.

Eventually the turmoil of our initial meeting subsided and I moved closer to the bed and sat. Then the little girl was introduced to me as Miyoko. She was standing beside the interpreter, holding her hand. I asked the mother, "May I touch Miyoko, please?"

She nodded agreement and took Miyoko by the hand, leading her to me. I stooped down and picked her up, kissed her on both cheeks and hugged her closely. I felt like a newly introduced father must feel to be connected to a long lost child. I felt that, although I had not been present at the original birth of the child, I had been present at the re-birth of this precious little girl.

I placed her gently back on the floor and stroked her jet-black hair. She turned her delicate face to mine and smiled widely. I could feel the rise of emotion beginning to well within and knew that, before too long the tears would commence.

I turned to the Sister and said, "Well, it's certainly good to see that everything turned out as well as it did. I couldn't be happier. I'd best be off now. Got to get home and have a shower and a meal. Goodbye, ladies. Sayonara, Miyoko." I choked, turned on my heel and walked quickly from the ward, out into the gathering night and leapt onto the DUKW to ride back to b ase.

Our trip back to base was quite maudlin since nobody wanted to carry on a conversation. This was quite understandable after what we had experienced over the past few days.

This was especially poignant for me, having found the poor drowned mother and baby and then to be re-united with my 4 year old baby, Miyoko. Terrible thoughts raced through my mind; aspects of the war conflicting with the way we had found the general population of Japan afterwards. The workmen who willingly helped repair the huts in which we slept, the girls who tirelessly washed our backs and tended the mud-baths at Beppu, giggling at our stupid mistakes but never doing anything to offend, and the people who ducked for cover each time they saw an aircraft zoom overhead. This all contrasted greatly with the stories we'd heard about the way in which the military government of Japan had psychologically bludgeoned their political opponents into agreeing to wage war in the first place.

To prove a point of national pride perhaps? It never works in my book. It only creates heartbreak, tragedy and poverty.

However, out of all this I would remember the blessing of having saved Miyoko from the jaws of death. She would remain part of me forever.

Some days later when I was still considering the rescue and survival of Miyoko, I came to the conclusion that I had been selected and guided by Baiame to perform that act of rescue. There were a couple of other Christian lads aboard the DUKW doing the same Red Cross first aid course but, it was me who saw her tiny body, plucked her from the freezing waters and held her to my torso to maintain enough body heat to resuscitate her and give her a chance to survive.

The seven days that we spent at Kochi rescuing and retrieving bodies etc left a terrible impression on me, being as I was, a 20 year old lad. I desperately needed to be able to speak to someone in confidence to air my grief but, this was not to be. I sank into a morass of mental anguish, unable to concentrate on small tasks without having the visions of Miyoko or the other girl with the baby strapped to her back haunt my mind.

It certainly altered my perspective of the Japanese people but, these visions still haunt me today.

CHAPTER THIRTY FOUR.

When we arrived back at Bofu Base we were asked by many who'd remained there where had we been for 7 days. They didn't believe us when we told them the truth. I could not see any point in trying to convince them so I decided to remain silent on the matter.

December 1946 was a bitterly cold season in Japan and, as there were snowstorms virtually daily, there was not much flying done as it was too treacherous. On 31st December we were told that all Disaster Guards would be granted 5 days leave in Tokyo at a posh resort called Kawana Hotel. It sounded fine by me; the reality was even better.

After an all-night train trip to Tokyo we arrived at Ito Rail Station, there to be taken by bus to the hotel. Upon stepping from the bus, I thought I must have died and gone to paradise.

Built on a grand scale for the political hierachy and well-to-do Japanese business community, it featured an 18-hole golf course (of course!), 25 metre heated indoor swimming pool, billiard room, plush wet bar, sheets on the beds, and house maids at our beck-and-call who kept our rooms tidy, washed and ironed our clothes daily, and bowed to us deeply every time we passed.

After what we had been through at Kochi, we reasoned that this was about as close as we could expect to get to Heaven. The food was pleasant, mostly seafood but plenty of it and the atmosphere was conducive to sound sleep after we retired at night.

However, like the ring-master always says at the end of a circus performance, all good things must end and, for us the 5 days ended all too quickly. Once again we boarded the train for Bofu and watched the countryside slide past in the snow.

In February 1947 the replacement period came that would see many of the previous serving members of the Wing returning to Australia for discharge while others were sent south to enjoy a period of leave before returning to Japan for a further tour of duty for 12 months.

At Bofu Base many troops were packing up to leave for Kure where they would board a ship to return to Australia. I felt a bit down-hearted as there were many mates among the soldiers. I was not going with them.

I was told to report to the orderly room. There I received a surprise; I was to pack my bags and be ready to get aboard a C47 in 2 days for flight back to Australia. This was the 14 days leave promised by Wing Commander Bradshaw at Mildura.

Early on Friday morning, 14th February I boarded the Dakota parked at Bofu airstrip. It was covered in snow and, all about the countryside looked like a postcard of Fairyland. To clear the strip of snow the aircraft taxied from one end to the other twice to blow away the stuff before we could take off. This done, the pilot gunned the throttles and the sturdy aeroplane leaped forward, tail in the air and swept along the concrete to finally take to the freezing sky and set a course for Okinawa, some 450 miles to the south-south-west.

On landing at Okinawa we were taken to the USAAF mess for lunch. This was a hurried affair unfortunately as we had a flight plan to maintain but, having eaten well and had the aircraft refuelled, we took off again for Clark Field, Manila where we landed just on dusk.

Being obliged to stay overnight sounded to me like a bit of a 'junket' until it was pointed out to me that, although the mess was only a 15 minute walk from the barracks, we were not to walk there but would be picked up and driven there by Military Police truck.

I had to ask why.

"Well, son," drawled the tough Marine Sergeant, manoeuvering his fat cigar from one side of his mouth to the other, "You see, round here we got bandits, call theirselves 'Huk' freedom fighters. Commies, you know? Well, you see, they'll take a shot at anything they see move on the base at night."

I considered his remarks timely and pertinent. "Gee, thanks, Sergeant." I walked to my billet and laid out my kit on a bed.

Outside I could see aircraft I recognised — B17 Flying Fortress, B29 Superfortress, P51 Mustang and P47 Thunderbolt. The one I hadn't seen before I was told was a C54 Skymaster transport, a fine-looking, 4 engined heavy aeroplane from Douglas Aircraft, a big brother to the ubiquitous C47.

In the morning we had a typical huge but welcome American breakfast and packed up early to board the C47 for the next leg to

Darwin. Aboard the aircraft waiting to take off the pilot handed me a route map and said it might be of interest to follow our passage as we went. I agreed and thanked him as I had been a bit bored on the way from Japan.

We took off and flew over countless islands of the Philippines Group, making note of landmarks such as Bataan Peninsula, Corregidor Island, Luzon Island, Bantigui Point and the distant islands of Los Negros and Cebu. I made note of an active volcano spewing dense clouds of black and yellow smoke into the clear sky from below the surface of the sea and then, we left Philippines behind, heading for Morotai. My curiosity was peaked as I wondered what would be left of our base.

I didn't have long to find out.

We joined the circuit at Morotai Island and landed on the longer strip of Pitu and taxied to a stop, just short of the control tower. The pilot came out of the flight deck and announced that we would spend the night here as there was a tropical storm heading for the island and, before we went anywhere, we were to help tie down the C47.

This done, we reported to the orderly room and were given tent accommodation for the night. The storm built up slowly in the north-east and by dusk, we were treated to a fierce electrical display in the heavens. Sleep that night was not possible as the storm hit, buckets of rain came down flooding the tents and making life miserable. The flashes of lightning illuminated the outside walls of the tent bringing to mind the ghosts of those who had worked, flown and died here in the past few years.

The morning light brought scenes of devastation all round with trees pushed over, roads washed out and tents collapsed. Luckily, the C47 was OK except for slight skin damage to the starboard wingtip. We were able to scrounge some tools and sheet 'alclad' to effect a repair and, as there were three Airframe Fitters among the group, we had the work done by lunchtime.

We then scoffed a quick lunch of sandwiches and tea and, back into the aeroplane and off to Ambon so that we could refuel and reach Darwin that night.

As the C47 approached Ambon a flight crew member came back into the cabin and reminded us that, as we had just crossed the Equator, King Neptune required that we pay homage.

"What from 10,000 feet?" I queried the fellow. He laughed and went back up front.

At Ambon I decided to take a bit of a stroll and see the sights while stretching the legs. A couple of C47's caught my eye parked near the tower. On closer inspection they showed they were painted with a red stripe and a white stripe and the word 'Garuda' painted down the sides. This was the birth of the Indonesian airline.

We fuelled the aircraft and took off again for Darwin and home. Flying over Bathurst and Melville Islands I began to get quite excited. Looking down on the lush green I could just make out tracks carved in the landscape going in all directions from the coast.

The aircraft touched down at Darwin and rolled to a stop. The side door burst open and a cannister was flung into the cabin with dense, white smoke pouring from it. Instantly we began to choke and cough madly. The door slammed shut.

I could not see, tears streamed from my burning eyes and the other fellows in the aircraft began to pound on the door and scream.

It took some thirty seconds for the door to be opened again then a voice called out,"OK, chaps, step out here and walk away."

We all stumbled to the light and managed to scramble down the steps to the pavement where we fell about wheezing and choking. Someone grabbed my sleeve and led me with burning eyes and throat past a row of men in uniforms toward a hut where more uniformed people stood staring at us as we tried to recover some semblance of normality.

When, at last, I regained some composure, I asked a uniform, "What the hell was all that about? That damned smoke bomb was some welcome back to Australia. Whose idea is that of Guy Fawkes Day?"

"Nothing of the sort, sir. Each and every aircraft what touches down here is subjected to the very same treatment on account of we don't want no creepy crawlies or foreign diseases brought back with youse lot to this here country of ours. Thus we smoke out the little bleeders before they gets a chance to breed, like. You know?"

His 'official-ese' was totally comical but the message was quite clear. This was the birth of border quarantine regulations. What they were using was a powerful disinfectant driven by a pressurised cannister of CO_2.

We were examined by Customs and our papers individually scanned. When this process was finished a small bus pulled up to take us off-base to the 300 bed Qantas Hostel at Berrimah, 4 miles away.

"Whatever happened to the 112th Army General Hospital?" I asked.

"Ahh, yes, laddie. That was the hospital,... now it's the brand-new Qantas Transit Hostel. You'll find it very comfortable there. Good luck!"

He was right. Walking into the foyer was like walking into somebody's comfy loungeroom. The sleeping quarters were fairly basic; twin beds per room with carpet on the floor and one small wardrobe with dressing table attached.

The showers were most welcome, lots of steaming hot water for a close shave and shampoo. We dressed for dinner our tropical drabs — khaki uniform of light cotton material and shoes.

Dinner was very popular with the BCOF men who had been fed mainly seafood and other Oriental fare overseas. A juicy steak with three vegs and apple pie for dessert. Beers were served at the bar which made us really feel at home. With all that safely tucked away we hit the sheets early, folded our wings and put our heads down on soft pillows for a well-earned rest.

CHAPTER THIRTY FIVE.

Early next morning after breakfast, we were driven back to Darwin airport to our C47 which was parked in a long line with others from various airlines. Ex-military C47's — now designated DC 3's — in civilian livery of Australian National Airways, Qantas Empire Airways and Trans Australian Airlines plus another rare 'bird' which I had not seen much before, a De Havilland DH86 .

These aircraft were loaded and we joined the queue as we crept along the taxiway to await the green Aldis lamp shot from the control tower, signalling clearance to take off.

Our turn came and we sped away down the strip, tail up then, wheels lifted away and we were once again airborne. The under-carriage thumped back into the wheel wells and we settled down for the ride to Alice Springs, next stop-over.

I dozed off during the trip south and was woken by the excited yells from a fellow passenger who shook my shoulder with, "Look, Walshie! Alice Springs down there!"

Gazing out the window I could see in the distance the roofs of a town shining in the morning sunlight. Yes, it was 'The Alice' alright, sitting in a shallow depression surrounded by low hills. Our pilot said we would refuel the aircraft here but, because the weather between Alice and Melbourne was stormy, we would spend the night here too.

We checked into a hotel near the centre of town and had lunch and a few beers at the bar. Afterwards I decided to take a look around the place. I happened upon a park where there were groups of Aboriginal men sitting under some trees so, innocently enough, I decided to wander over and strike up a conversation with them, not fearing rejection on account of my up-bringing at Pokataroo.

"G'day, fellers," I began quietly. They turned their woolly heads and regarded me curiously. "How's things with you today?"

I hardly expected the diatribe that came forth from one who appeared to be their spokesman. Without rising from his seat he filled the air with denunciations of the white race and peppered his delivery with expletives enough to make a sailor blush.

It was clear that I was not wanted here among the people that I normally would have considered to be my tribal brothers. I didn't need a second serving of that so I walked away as calmly as I could manage. Apparently, the tables had turned from the way things were in my youth at Pokataroo. Was this reversed racism of a kind?

In the morning we loaded back into the refuelled aircraft and took off for Melbourne, climbing into a cloudless blue sky. I was glad to be out of the oppressive heat of the Alice and rugged up as we climbed higher to where the air grew colder.

Landmarks went by as we flew; the rail line to Port Augusta, Lake Eyre shining like a sheet of silverpaper and onward to the Murray River with Mildura on the right. I knew that Melbourne was then only 360 miles away.

We arrived over Laverton Base and joined the circuit pattern on the downwind leg. The pilot throttled back the engines, lowered the under-carriage and first stage of flaps. The C47 gently descended to turn onto the crosswind leg and then short final approach, over the boundary fence and touch-down.

We rolled to a stop on the line in front of the tower and I was glad to be able to hop out and stretch my legs after such a long journey. I said farewell to the crew and reported to the orderly room to present my papers. In turn, I was issued with a leave pass for 2 weeks and some travel documents to present to RTO at Spencer Street Station, there to receive a rail ticket to Sydney and rail ticket to Clarendon Platform which would then put me across the road from Richmond RAAF Base. After my leave was over, I was to join the BCOF detachment for transport back to Japan.

With all that paperwork safely tucked away, I made my way back to Black Rock to see the family again. Alighting from the tram, I stood for a moment outside the house. It seemed to me to be smaller than I remembered it. It also looked a lot older now.

I went around to the back door and into the kitchen where I found Verna. She appeared to be as happy to see me as I was to see her. After we had embraced she said, "It's been a long time, Gerald."

"Yes, Mum, that it has. Two years in fact."

"We didn't expect you for another two weeks but, never mind, you're here now."

She phoned around and informed most of the family of my return. They turned up that evening and I handed out the presents that I'd brought with me from Japan. Some were pleased with their gift, others not so happy. I was not concerned with their reactions; I had done what I thought was the right thing to do.

There was a lot of chatter round the table that night but it all centred on Uncle Dave and Uncle Bill and how they had suffered during the war. Not one of them asked me about my experiences or what I'd done or how I felt. The only reference to me was from Verna who kept repeating,"My, my Gerald. You've certainly changed, haven't you?"

I had to agree with her. I surely had changed. Now, I could see through people whereas, before I could never see anything cynical or underhand which allowed others to take advantage of my better nature. Looking around the room I realised that nothing much had changed here.

I stayed there four days visiting other friends then, one night I just packed up and left in the morning for Pokataroo.

I had decided to travel back to Collarenebri and Pokataroo to see if I could locate my mother, Yurana and my little sister, Adori. It had been 15 years since I was dragged back into white society away from them and I missed them badly now.

At 'Colly' I booked into a hotel in the main street which looked exactly the same as when I'd left. I ate alone in the pub and went straight to bed. The next day would be the time to start looking for my family here.

In the morning I hired a taxi to drive out to the Barwon River at Trelawney Station. "What do you want out there?" queried the driver.

"Maybe I'll tell you when we get there, my friend," I answered cryptically. He shrugged his shoulders and kept on driving along the dusty road, gravel flying up at every corner.

When we arrived at the old camp site I recognised the sandy beach and the bend in the river, the giant gum trees with their roots sticking out of the water where we used to catch fish. I got out of the cab and stood gazing all around. There was no sign of any huts or even a bark lean-to. Not a sign of any habitation anywhere. It was as if they had never existed.

I thought I could feel the presence of Baiame here. The breeze rustled the leaves high in the gum trees.

The cabbie had stepped out too and stood beside me, looking around curiously.

"So, what did you expect to find here?"

"Actually, I was looking for the Lieillwan Aboriginal people who used to live right here."

He looked at me a moment."Why?"

"Mate, it's a long, long story. Can you tell me what happened to those people? Did they just up and leave? They had everything they needed here."

"Well, from what I've heard round town, the place was sold up a few years back and the new boss decided they were not wanted on the property and he told them to pack up and leave." He held his hands out in a gesture of resignation. "They protested wildly so the squatter got in the police and they took to them with batons and drove them away out of here."

My heart sank. "Any idea where they moved to?"

"No, mate. As far as I know, they split up and moved to other yambas near other big towns in this region. But, why do you want to find these people?"

I shrugged, remembering Yurana's lovely face. "I am looking for someone I knew a long time ago."

He moved a step closer, speaking confidentially.

"Let me give you some good advice, matey. Don't mix with these people or you might get into big trouble." He smiled, showing his dirty, brown front teeth with one missing.

"Thanks a lot." I replied and got back into the cab."I'll remember that."

We drove back to town and I paid him off. As I was walking back to the hotel I saw some Aboriginal folk in the park sitting under a large tree. I wondered if any could tell me about the Lieillwan tribe so I approached them cautiously, remembering my experience at Alice Springs.

"Hello there, fellers. I wonder if you can tell me where I can find people from the Lieillwan clan?"

"Why, are you a copper or somethin'?"

"No, I'm just an airman. I'm in the Airforce and I'm looking for someone I lost long ago."

The man looked me up and down, smirking.

"I bet it's a woman, eh?" All the men began to laugh.

"Well, as a matter of fact, it's my mother and my sister who are members of the tribe."

"Hah! Now I know you're lying." he said."Anyone can see you

have no Aboriginal blood in you whatsoever!. Get lost pal. We can't help you." With that, they all rose as one and wandered away.

I then hired another taxi and drove around all the yambas near 'Colly' to see if I could spot a face I recognised. I found nothing so, I returned to the hotel, very sad and disillusioned. The thought running through my head was that I would never again see Yurana or Adori. I would therefore have to live with my memories of the time long ago. This was some consolation.

The next day I caught the train back to Sydney and reported to the RAAF Base at Richmond as my 2 weeks leave from Melbourne was, by that time, expired. At the orderly room I was informed that our transport back to Japan was HMAS Kanimbla, at the time in dry dock being refitted for sea. That meant that, until she was back in the water and revictualled and fuelled up, we would have to remain at Base and work at various menial tasks.

Although we were highly trained aircraft tradesmen, we were not permitted to work on any aeroplanes at Richmond as we were not attached to the base. We were labelled 'gypsies' as we seemed to have no visible means of support and found our accommodation in Nissen huts outside the perimeter of the base, across Windsor Road where a huge sign identified us as BCOF troops with a large cut-out figure of a Japanese girl in kimino standing near the gate.

Our next weeks at Richmond were then filled with menial tasks to keep us occupied since we were still paid service personnel and classed 'general hands'. This gave the Base Commander licence to use our time in any way he saw fit.

During the first week of this 'limbo', I was made a 'pearl diver' at the Airmen's mess. This was the colloquial term for pot-scrubber which began work at 3:00am. It took me a couple of days to get used to the routine but, thereafter, I found the time to myself very fulfilling. It gave my brain a rest from worry and I only had to use my hands.

That episode passed and I reported back to the orderly room where I was given guard duty. That didn't phase me since I had done the same at Mildura. The only fly in this ointment was the fact that the base now had some guard dogs to replace men at specific places around the base. One was the hangars where a long wire was strung each night and the dogs were attached to the wire with lengths of chain from the collar.

This allowed the animals to patrol up and down the length of the wire unimpeded and they alerted the guard if they surprised an intruder with their barking. The dogs in use were not Alsations but Dalmations

— big white animals with black spots and a nasty disposition.

The guard Sergeant must have had a strange sense of humour. He insisted that new guard recruits should take the round which brought them into the realm of the dogs' patrol area. Of course, he never told the recruit beforehand.

The shift I was on began at midnight and went for 3 hours. I was dropped off and began my patrol in the pitch black. After the truck had left I was pacing in front of the hangar when I stopped to listen to a sound I couldn't quite identify. It sounded like a distant phone ringing — Ching! ching! ching! It seemed be coming at me from the dark of the next hangar. I flicked on my hand torch and swept the area.

Suddenly, out of the dark the animal leapt at me, fangs bared. It frightened ten years growth from me. I dropped the rifle but not the torch. I backed away as quickly as my legs would allow. For the rest of the 3 hours I stood in the shadows watching the damn dog stand over my rifle, drooling at me.

At 3:00am I went to my pick-up point, minus the rifle, and waited for the truck to come by. The truck was on time and the Corporal stepped down, shone his light on me and asked, "Where's your rifle, LAC Walshe?"

I related the sad story to him. "Still under the dog, Corporal."

He laughed loudly as did the other chaps with him.

"Alright, we have to retrieve the rifle, don't we? Give me your torch. I'll walk back along the dog wire and cause a noise to get him to move away from the rifle. When he does, you get in there and grab the rifle. Then we'll go back to the guard-room."

In the morning the guard Corporal reported the incident to the guard Commander and they both had a jolly good laugh at my expense. The guard Commander then gave me extra duty as punishment for dropping the rifle. My punishment was to stand guard 4 hours a day at the main gate beginning straight after breakfast. This really knocked me about by midday but I had learned my lesson the hard way. It would never happen again.

When the weekend came round I decided to go to Sydney with a mate and stay at Air Force House in Liverpool Street. I didn't much like Sydney for a couple of reasons but I'm sure I would have felt the same in any city; the traffic was very noisy as the trams rattled along all day and night and the girls I'd seen, to me, seemed to have too much make-up plastered on their faces. This gave them a look of porcelain dolls. Perhaps this was just a comparison with the women I'd been used to seeing in Japan where they wore very little or no make-up in the street and their natural complexion was slightly yellow going on beige.

That Saturday night we went for a walk around Sydney town. We were fascinated by the sight of the 'toast-rack' trams, quite unlike the trams in Melbourne. I had to feel sorry for the conductors on these trams as they had a narrow plank to walk along outside the tram and needed to hang on to the handrail while collecting fares from passengers. And even on the move!

We were disappointed to see that the CENEF Canteen that once sat at Hyde Park, dispensing tea and cakes to soldiers was not there any more. As we walked back toward Air Force House we noticed that some trams carried lady conductors instead of men. We decided to catch a tram. We looked for one going south with a romantic-sounding name.

Along came a tram labelled 'Rosebery'. We hopped aboard and settled down for a ride to what we thought might be romance.

Rosebery, it turned out, is an industrial suburb with the glamorous aromas of tanneries and iron foundries belching fumes into the atmosphere day and night.

We rode the tram to the end of the line and, while the vehicle was being turned around, the conductress perched on the seat opposite us and asked, "Getting off here, boys? Or going back?"

I had to explain to her that we were from the southern capital and had no idea where we were going but liked the look of the name.

She laughed. "Well, fellas, you can ride back to town free if you like. That's really funny. Wait 'til I tell Percy, the driver."

We offered to pay the extra tuppence fare but she refused our cash.

"Look, if you want to see the best parts of Sydney, get yourselves on a tram to Watson's Bay. That way you'll get to see the foreshores and some great houses too." Despite our best intentions, we didn't get to see Watson's Bay until we were aboard the troop ship heading out to sea.

On another day we had an amusing experience when we decided to catch a ferry to Manly. We knew that we had to first catch a tram to take us to Circular 'KEY' so, we took up a position in George Street to wait for a tram going to Circular 'KEY'. Trams came and went but none had the destination label that we wanted. An hour passed.

In desperation I asked a policeman walking past, how often do trams go to Circular Key?

"Oh, every ten minutes, mate. Look, here comes one now." He

pointed to another green and yellow monster rattling along the street.

"No," I argued, "That says 'The KWAY'.

He laughed. "That's how you spell Quay, my friend. That's your tram. Good luck!"

Stunned at our naivety, we leapt aboard the rattler and rode to Circular Quay. We enjoyed our day at Manly all the more as we couldn't stop laughing at our time wasted waiting for the wrong tram to come past.

Back at Richmond Base, the week following was taken up with being a gardener — cutting grass with a heavy push-pull mower, pulling weeds and planting new seedlings to a carefully drawn design. It was hot, back-breaking work but, again I enjoyed it being left to my own devices with time to think about private matters. This gardening was the task I liked most of all.

It was too good to last! On Thursday afternoon we were informed that on the following Tuesday we would be loaded onto trucks and taken to Captain Cook dry dock in Sydney where we would board HMAS Kanimbla which had just been released from a refit. She would then take us back to Japan for another stint with BCOF.

It was therefore decided that we should spend the coming weekend in Sydney and enjoy our last days of freedom for 12 months.

O Friday afternoon we arrived at Air Force House at lunch time and later went to a pub for a couple of quiet beers to celebrate returning to Japan next week. While we sat there chatting quietly between ourselves, three men walked into the public bar and took a seat at a corner table. One big fellow came straight up to our group and began to stare at our uniforms, swaying slightly.

"What do we have here, eh? Four bloody 'Blue Orchids' and still in uniform. Bludging are you,... 18 months after the war's over!"

We tried to explain that we had volunteered to serve with the Occupation Forces in Japan and we were leaving on Tuesday.

"Oh, nice! Bloody Jappo lovers, are youse?" Some choice phrases followed and his mates tried to calm him down. He would not be placated. Time and again he returned to try to stir us into a fight.

Several times he took a round-house swing but kept missing. I could only see one way in which to subdue the poor chap. I grabbed his shirtfront and let him have a short right jab. It caught him on the jaw and his eyes rolled back. I then helped him to a seat and apologised to his mates.

"That's OK mate," they both offered. "He had it coming. Been like that ever since he came home from the war. I see from your medal ribbons you served during the war too."

"Yes," I agreed," Morotai Island mostly."

Both the others stood and shook my hand.

"Don't worry about him, we'll make sure he gets home OK."

They picked up their friend and left. We downed our drinks and headed back to Air Force House. I left my pals and went to sit on my bed. I needed time to examine my reasons for hitting the fellow in the pub. I agonised alone for some time, trying to think whether it was the world that had changed so radically or was it me?

Visions of dead bodies kept flooding back into my mind — the young mother with the baby strapped to her back in particular. Miyoko's sweet little face, too, came floating to me in the twilight.

I was roused from my reverie by the blokes who returned from the games room to announce they were going out after dinner to a dance at the Trocadero Ball Room.

"You'd best come with us, Walshie,... get out and find a girl tonight. It might be your last chance for some time."

"Fellers, I don't know, really. I don't feel much like dancing tonight."

"Bad luck, matey. You're going, even if we have to carry you there. We won't take 'NO' for an answer." I could see how excited and determined they were so, to keep the peace, I agreed.

At the Ball Room I sat quietly with an orange drink for company, listening to the band. My courage seemed to have deserted me and, when I looked across the room at the line up of young ladies, the sight of their over-painted faces gave me the horrors. They frightened me.

My pals returned to my side after finishing another dance and told me of their success with getting girls to dance with them. There was a group of four girls and the three lads needed another chap to make up the fourth couple.

"Come on, Gerry. Come and meet Dawn." They cajoled me sufficiently and I relented. We walked back to the dance floor and joined a group of four young ladies, nurses from Canberra, in Sydney for a 'silly weekend'.

I was introduced to Dawn. I could not take my eyes off her.

The author (left) and Sgt Rocky Morrison,
Japan 1946

Kittyhawk P40 as flown against Japanese Zeros 1938-1945
(Photo courtesy of 'P40 The Kittyhawk in Service'
by Geoffrey Pentland).

Truck turned turtle following tyre blowout near Wentworth NSW.
VJ Day 1945

P51-D Mustang, typical of the aircraft of 77 Squadron at
Bofu Base, 1946

Mustangs of 77 Squadron shortly after arriving in Japan

Servicing aircraft on Morotai Island at night. Trucks provided light
for ground crews with their headlamps.
(Photo courtesy Geoffrey Pentland)

Catholic church, Hiroshima — still conducting school classes and
serving the congregation amid post-atomic rubble

CHAPTER THIRTY SIX.

I just stood there transfixed. Dawn was such a lovely girl, about my own age with long, dark shining hair, clear skin and wearing very little make-up except for lipstick. When she smiled at me her beautiful lips parted to reveal perfectly white teeth. She looked at me with grey eyes that seemed to soothe my very soul.

She stood as I approached and held out her hand. We shook. I'm sure she could tell just how nervous I was so she asked me to sit with her. That felt a bit better so I apologised for being nervous. I explained that I had not had a steady girlfriend before.

"Please, don't ask me to explain." I said. "Maybe later?"

She gave me one of those looks that only girls have that said — OK, later, but don't forget!

"Now then, young man, do you know the foxtrot?"

I looked down at the floor but answered, "Well, yes I do."

"Then ask me to dance, please." She gave me a winning smile. How could I resist?

We started to dance but, being so nervous, my legs did not wish to follow my brain. My co-ordination was shot to Hell. I was embarassed. Dawn kept encouraging me.

"Don't worry,... it will come back to you."

She was absolutely right of course. By the end of the number, we were getting along fine. Not Astaire and Rogers but we were OK together.

She carried on a conversation while we danced; more of a one-way street as I was feeling gloriously happy, self-conscious and somewhat intimidated all at once so, topics of discussion didn't flow easily from my side.

She told me that she and her friends were nurses from Canberra Hospital and had come to the big city of Sydney for a week's holiday.

They were to return to the capital next Wednesday.

That evening was wonderful. It had been such a long time since I had held a girl in my arms — and so close — I was ecstatic with a feeling of unbounded joy. I felt so lucky to have met this wonderful young lady who had accepted me as I was and put me at ease so quickly without asking for background information or explanation.

We danced together all night until the Trocadero Ballroom closed. When the band packed up and the lights dimmed and the patrons were leaving, we asked the girls if we could see them home to Bondi. They agreed willingly and we all trouped out into the cold evening air to catch a tram to Bondi. We had no idea where the Hell that was or how to get there but the girls agreed to show us the way.

The tram ride took us to Campbell Parade along the beach front. When we hopped off it was just a short walk to their flat. At the front door they invited us all in for a cup of tea.

Inside the sparsely furnished lounge room, Dawn and I sat close together. I somehow got the feeling that she wished to have a more private conversation with me which was almost impossible in a room full of people. She stood and went to the window, looking out toward the beach.

"Oh, look, it's raining," she said. "Gerry, do you like walking in the rain?"

"As a matter of fact, I do!" I replied enthusiastically.

Dawn found a large black umbrella and beckoned me to the front door. Turning to the group she called out, "We won't be long. Don't leave without Gerry, will you!"

That night we strolled back and forth along the promenade at Bondi Beach for what seemed like hours in the rain. She clung to my upper arm and we conversed on many diverse topics. I felt as though I'd known her all my life. I revealed to her my upbringing, my school days, the apprenticeship and joining the RAAF. My whole life encapsulated into one short interlude and a half of recollections. When I spoke of my experiences in Japan she gripped my arm all the tighter.

Then there came a lull in conversation and we stopped walking. She turned slowly toward me and tilted her lovely face to mine.

"Gerry, do you believe in love at first sight?"

This puzzled me so I replied, "Dawn, I don't even know what love is. I have been out with a few girls but I've never had a serious relationship. However, let me say this, as far as you are concerned, I am very attracted to you, even in the short amount of time we have known each other. I've told you things I have never mentioned to anyone else. I feel completely at ease with you because I know you are a person I can trust. I don't know why,... I just feel it.

"I would like to see more of you. Will you come out with me tomorrow? We could spend the day together — my last day here. Perhaps a trip to Manly on the ferry,..." Her answer rang golden bells in my head.

"I would love to do that. Meet me at 10 o'clock at the flat." She slipped her hand into mine and squeezed it, exciting my inner man. I remember my breathing was now somewhat restricted. I took a deep breath.

Dawn continued, "I think we should return to the flat, now. The others will be waiting. Besides, the rain seems to have stopped so we have no excuse to stay out. May I say one more thing before we go back. I have listened to what you've said regarding love and I still believe in love at first sight."

When we arrived back at the flat, my friends said they had asked the girls out the next day and they had decided on a day at the Zoo. They asked Dawn and me if we would join them, but we declined as we had already decided to take a ferry ride to Manly.

"OK then, you go your way and we'll go ours but, don't forget, we have to meet back at Central Station at 4:30pm to catch the train back to Richmond RAAF Base."

We then said 'goodnight' to the girls and made our way back to Air Force House.

In the morning we had a quick breakfast and boarded another Bondi tram and arrived back at the girls' flat where the ladies were waiting ready to go. Back on a tram and we headed for Circular Quay where the other three couples boarded a harbour ferry to Taronga Zoo and Dawn and I got on a big Manly ferry for the 7 mile ride to the other side of that glorious harbour.

The ride to Manly was smooth until the ferry 'South Steyne' was crossing the water between the Sydney Heads where the swell from the open ocean rolled through. Standing on the upper deck out in the open we got a good idea of how a ride on the 'Big Dipper' at a fun park would be with the vessel rising and falling with each powerful wave that crossed our path.

After arriving at Manly Wharf we strolled along The Corso and eventually found our way to the point of North Head where there was a bench. We sat and gazed out across to the Sydney city skyline. All this time we chatted away about life, love and the things I had done during the war as well as my time in Japan.

"But, Gerry, how old were you at that time?" she asked.

I had to confess that I was only 18 when I joined up and now, aged 20. She took my face in her warm hands and stared long into my eyes.

"Gerry, you have seen so much pain, experienced so much hurt and you have the face of a baby. It's hard to believe you have gone through so much in your short life."

I had to change the subject so I asked her to tell me about herself. I sat and listened to her relate her own experiences, her articulate, clear voice soothing my edgy nerves. I tend to think that it was while I was being lulled by the dulcet tones of Dawn's sweet voice that I fell in love with this young woman, there and then.

Time slipped away and we seemed to realise at once that we were hungry. We walked back to a small fish cafe on The Corso and enjoyed some fresh battered fish and chips and a cup of tea with lemon. This pleasant meal simply topped off an already perfect day out.

The ferry ride back to Circular Quay was uneventful except for the fact that we clung to each other warmly. Then followed a tram to Liverpool Street where I retrieved my kit bag from Air Force House. We made our way up to Central Station and met up with the other chaps waiting with the nurses from Canberra. We then had 10 minutes to say our last 'farewells' before the train left for Richmond.

My bag was already on the train so I stood on the platform with Dawn, holding both her hands. She looked intently into my eyes. I said, "You still believe in love at first sight, don't you?"

"Yes, Gerry, I'm afraid I do."

"Well, young lady, I would not have you any other way." She squeezed my hands. A railway guard in black uniform began to blow his whistle — one minute warning!

I took Dawn in my arms and kissed her delicious mouth. I whispered in her ear, "Thank you so much for a lovely day. And, also for a lovely night last night. Those moments I will treasure forever."

She reached up with both hands, taking my face in her grasp and kissed me for a long time. "Thank you, my sweet. This will not be the end of things, you know. Just the beginning!"

The train began to roll. I kissed her again with passion. "That's a 'goodbye' kiss," I said as I turned and sprinted for the door. "Until we meet again. Don't forget to be at the wharf on Tuesday!"

I leaped aboard the carriage and waved to her all the way down the platform until we were round the bend and away down the line.

CHAPTER THIRTY SEVEN.

A s I sat on the train going back to Richmond Base that evening, my mind was totally confused. The events of the last 2 days needed to be sorted and I had to set my mind on which direction to take with Dawn. I had always been afraid of commitment to emotional ties. That, to me, was the most difficult task to deal with. I was on the threshold of another tour of duty in Japan, travelling into the unknown and, the next 12 months work must take priority.

The following morning I awoke to the reality that I could not wander from the path I was currently on. I needed complete concentration on my duty to the RAAF. After that, who knows?

On the Tuesday morning we were out of bed early, had breakfast and waited for the trucks to pick us up to go in to Garden Island and board HMAS Kanimbla en route to Japan. When we arrived at Garden Island Dockyard we were taken aboard and allocated bunks in the bowels of the ship. We stowed our gear and went top-side to get away from the dank, humid atmosphere of the cabin and get some fresh air.

There were some 800 service personnel aboard, a mixture of Army, RAAF and, of course, Navy. We crowded the rail to watch the activity below on the wharf and see if we could spot any familiar faces.

This was pretty unlikely as the time was only about 10:30am and sailing time was down as 3:00pm. Visitors would probably not turn up 'til about 2:00pm. An hour went by and suddenly we noticed the boarding plank being removed and hawsers cast off the bollards. We felt the throb of the engines from way below and, to our astonishment, the ship began to move away from the dockyard wharf.

The troops down on the wharf and the visitors with them became quite agitated and showed their disapproval in typical Aussie fashion. Alas, to no avail. The ship continued away from the wharf and half a mile out into midstream where she dropped anchor. We now had no chance of seeing the girls if they turned up. They would have been most disappointed, as were we.

A news article printed in the Sydney press later was sent to me in Japan by Dawn. The headlines read; 'Bungled Farewell to Troops.' and the article went on to speak of the confusion and outrage felt by many visitors who came to wish us well only to be told by Navy officials that HMAS Kanimbla had already sailed.

A few who had the presence of mind, hired a launch and followed the ship out to its mooring and went aboard for 2 hours. Naval authorities were savagely criticised by all who had literally 'missed the boat'.

I didn't see Dawn again. From our vantage point high on the top deck we could see the wharf but could not make out any recognisable people. Perhaps as a gesture of mollification, the Navy put on a superb spread for luncheon. This was most welcome as we had not eaten since 6:00am and it was now approaching 1:00pm.

The ship remained at anchor for about another 2 hours and eventually, weighed anchor and left at about 3:00pm, the original sailing time from Garden Island wharf. As we passed ferries and private yachts people waved and hooted, wishing us good luck and 'bon voyage'. It was great to witness this display of patriotism and support to servicemen going overseas to serve their country.

Out through the Heads we sailed into the Tasman Sea and turned left to head up the coast. Japan seemed so far away. The excitement and disappointment had left us and we all felt quite worn out. We had been up for 9 hours and the sea began to rise as we went further out from the coastline. We thought it to be a bit rough — not so the Navy. They called it a 'moderate sea'.

We decided to take advantage of the bright sunshine and lie down on the deck. What a mistake to make! It wasn't long before we had soldiers, not used to the ship's movement, standing at both lee and windward rails, trying to lose their lunch. It began with a small number but grew to many as we went further north.

One poor soldier, looking decidedly green, asked a sailor how to alleviate the sea-sickness he felt.

"You see that hatch over there," said the tar. "Go and lie down there and look up at the masts. That ought to cure you, matey."

I managed to catch the fellow before he did so and advised him not to do what was proposed. "It doesn't work," I pleaded.

The soldier ignored my advice and lay down staring upwards. In 2 minutes he was at the rail, wishing to die.

I have always been lucky in that I have never been sea-sick nor air-sick. Why? That is a puzzle to me. As the line-up of sick soldiers grew we decided to leave the deck as it was becoming quite foul and went below where the air was close but not disgusting.

For the next 2 days we sailed up the east coast in beautiful weather and a calm sea. My days were spent sitting around with my pals talking, reading books from the sparse ship's library and looking over the bow of the vessel at the flying fishes. They are very interesting creatures as they rode the pressure wave in front of the bow and would suddenly leap from the water en masse and travel air-borne for long distances.

Late on the third day I was given the task of checking the lashings of the lifeboats. The reason given was that we would run into bad weather later that night and it was required that the lifeboats be checked for safety reasons.

The weather did begin to deteriorate as the afternoon wore on. The wind picked up and the seas began to rise. The Navy told us it was only a moderate sea. "Just wait 'til the cyclone hits, boys!"

Comforting words, indeed.

"What do we know about sailing into a cyclone, fellers?" I asked naively.

"God knows!" came the answer.

"Maybe we shouldn't eat too much dinner then," I suggested. "And, be sure to eat slowly."

By the time we decided to bunk down for the night, the ship was pitching and tossing like a proverbial cork. Very quickly I discovered why sailors preferred to sleep in hammocks which, unlike fixed bunks, swing with the movement of the hull allowing the sailor to get a restful night's repose.

Not so us land-lubbers! We hung on for dear life to the edges of the bunks. Even if we could forgive the movement of the vessel, the howling of the wind echoed throughout the ship and the crashing of waves against the ship's sides was deafening. With the lights out, we lay in the dark hearing sounds with which we were not familiar and thinking the worst. Then, as if ordained from below, we heard the definite sound of 'sloshing water' inside the cabin.

I grabbed a torch and shone it toward the floor. Sure enough, water was coursing through the small space of our quarters like a demented river — at once this way, then that.

"Are the portholes closed, men?" I called in the darkness.

"I can't close mine, mate!" came one voice, then another , then another until we discovered that almost all the portholes which operated on a worm-drive closure and opening system, were jammed half-open as the salt build-up on the screw had frozen solid.

What the hell had the re-fit at Captain Cook dry-dock been for if the portholes had not been checked for proper operation?

The ship was now rolling at a rather dangerous angle (I thought, anyway) and the sea water poured into the cabin with every dip. Bunks were being inundated and men were standing about in ankle-deep salt water having abandoned their sleeping quarters.

"Bunk up together, boys!" came the cry from all round.

Thus, the night progressed with men sharing bunks, feeling uncomfortable and angry.

When day broke and the cyclone died a bit, we were able to examine the situation more closely and, with the aid of borrowed tools from Navy stores, we managed to put the problem to right, forcing the worm-drive mechanisms to unclog and work smoothly to open and close the portholes.

The wet bedding was another problem we dealt with in typical RAAF style and ingenuity. The blankets, pillows and mattresses were stripped from bunks and taken down to the engine room where, with the aid of some stokers, we stacked them and hung them out to dry in the heat of the room.

The rough weather lasted another day and then we broke free into clear skies and sunshine. In the tropics as we then were, we slept on deck until 5:00am when the Navy decreed that the clean decks that we had yesterday needed another hosing down today with high-pressure water. We didn't want to argue with sailors armed thus so, we began our day early.

It was discovered that the cyclone had actually blown the ship off course to the east and we were then short of drinking water. We therefore had to head for Samarai Island near New Guinea to refill fresh water tanks. Thereafter, we sailed on up the northern coast of New Guinea past Milne Bay and the D'Entrecasteaux Islands of Normanby, Fergusson and Goodenough to Dreager Harbour on the Huon Peninsular near Lae to re-supply HMAS Tarangau, the RAN Shore Depot situated there.

The evening before we arrived at Dreager Harbour, our skipper, Capt. Snowball called for volunteers to assist with unloading of the cargo at Tarangau. 250 men were required for the task. 200 Army and 50 RAAF types put up their hands. Each man was then promised 2 bottles of beer for the job on completion.

The entrance to Dreager Harbour was quite narrow and the ship made very slow progress to the wharf where we tied up in the late afternoon.

At 5:30am next day we were up, fed and at work on the dock. The Navy brought a refrigerated barge alongside the ship to receive the frozen goods which were to be transferred to Tarangau. Our contingent transferred to the barge to handle the slings full of goods and store them aboard the barge. It was back-breaking work as the tropical sun rose and heated the day. After an hour of this we were told that the refrigeration unit on the barge was unserviceable and the frozen goods should be taken direct to the wharf for loading onto Army trucks.

This was then done and the cranes carried the frozen stores from the barge to the wharf where several large trucks stood ready to receive. During this operation we had 3 RAAF men and 6 native boys working as a team handling slings of goods when, suddenly, a shout caused us to look skyward. There we saw a sling begin to tear apart, letting heavy boxes to fall to earth.

"Under the truck!" somebody yelled. We dived for cover as boxes hit the ground, splitting open and sending bags of foodstuff everywhere.

Apart from a few skinned knees and cut shoulders, we seemed to be safe. We crawled out from under the truck and examined the scene. Broken boxes lay scattered and smashed in all directions. Among the wreckage we also discovered an unfortunate native boy who had caught a heavy box and been killed. The body was taken aboard the ship for official identification. The rest of the natives walked off the job.

The RAAF contingent of the work party conferred about the safety aspect of the job and we declared that, as it was, it was too dangerous to continue. We decided to sit down.

After 15 minutes of no work being done, a Navy Lieutenant appeared at the rail of the ship and called out for us to resume working.

His command was rebuffed with typical Aussie humour and in colourful language. Red-faced, he left and returned some time later wearing a pistol and holster backed up by four armed sailors bearing rifles with fixed bayonets.

"I again command you men down there to resume your work."

He received the same response from our group. His next move was to march down the gangway at the head of his four armed sailors with the Webley .38 revolver in his hand acting something like Captain Bligh of HMAS Bounty fame. He ordered his men to round us up and march us in single file back onto the ship.

"You men have disobeyed a lawful command given you by an

officer of His Majesty's Royal Australian Navy. You are, therefore, in contempt of this lawful command tantamount to mutiny and I am placing you all under arrest to stand trial, the penalty for which will be determined by the court martial, Naval judiciary, at a time to be fixed.

"Take them below to the brig." He smirked as we were led away.

The dungeon on an old vessel like HMAS Kanimbla is not a pretty place. It is deep in the bilges of the hull and has either nil or very little air circulating. Being close to the engine room, it is smelly, hot and, as we found, not big enough to hold 50 men at once in any kind of comfort.

The light was extinguished and we sat disconsolately in the semi-gloom with two armed guards at the bolted door. All I could think about was my memory of the film, 'Mutiny on the Bounty' with Chas Laughton. Even that was ghastly enough to compare with our predicament.

An hour or so went by before a Commander and two Lieutenants arrived to renew the pronouncement of our dire guilt.

"You people must remember that, while you are aboard a ship of His Majesty's Navy, you are governed by Naval discipline. The punishment for your crime is either imprisonment or death. You will be kept here, under guard, until the Naval Board on this ship decides your fate."

After he left there wasn't much discussion. Now we all knew just how crestfallen the early convicts must have felt; in the hold of a ship, accused of a crime and expecting execution.

About 6 hours later another Naval officer turned up to announce that we were to be released with no charges laid. We hurried from the confinement of our prison. When we hit the deck, the free, humid warm air was an elixir of life compared with the fetid, stale atmosphere of the bilges.

The following day a senior RAAF officer marched all RAAF personnel off the ship to a distant clearing in the bush and addressed us on the matter of the incident of the day before.

"Men, yesterday I did not have the evidence to bring a defence before the Ship's Board however, now I do and I did. It turned out that the cranes used on the wharf should have been handled by qualified engineering people from the ship. Instead, they were handled by ordinary seamen with little or no experience on lifting devices. This was in breach of Navy Code.

"When this was brought up at the investigation hearing, Captain Snowball had no alternative but to drop the charges of mutiny against you all. This was most embarrassing for the Navy. I am proud of the way you all acted in this case."

A loud cheer went up and we shook his hand and thanked him for his interest in our plight. Despite the fact that the Navy lost face over the incident, they came out ahead — we never got our 2 bottles of beer. But, I'm sure they had a drink on us.

CHAPTER THIRTY EIGHT.

I rose early the next day to witness another fabulous tropical sunrise and also to see the sights of Lae. Sunrise in these parts is a most wonderful, colourful sight with all shades of red, orange, whites, greens, purples, and other colours mingling in the heavens as far as the eye can see. It's a sight that remains with a person throughout life.

Phil Cadd, who was a mate of mine, and I decided, after looking around Lae, to try to find a swimming spot which had fresh water as the ship's showers were converted to salt water during a stay in port to conserve the fresh water stores.

We stopped a passing jeep driven by a sailor and asked him for information.

"Sure thing, pal." he said. " There's a water hole back in the hills behind Lae where everybody swims in the clean, fresh water. I'll be going close to it so, if you like, I can drop you off. You can catch the bus at 14.00 hours to get back to the wharf."

We thanked him and jumped into the jeep. Along the way we passed the airstrip where four black PBY Catalina flying boats were parked. This indicated to us the presence of a RAAF squadron as well as the Navy depot.

The jeep headed inland and we drove along a rough road while the sailor extolled the virtues of the water hole.

"Boys, you won't get malaria here,... nor any of the other bloody wogs that thrive in the tropics. You see, the water comes in at one end of the pool and rushes out the other end. Doesn't allow the little buggers time to breed. You'll be quite safe. Believe me, I swim here a lot."

We felt reassured by this and willingly entered the water where we had a whale of a time, skinny dipping with gay abandon. We left the gigantic tub with plenty of time to catch the bus back to Lae. We discovered that the reassurance by that sailor was misplaced as I later came down with a bout of malaria and, in Japan, suffered from 'tropical ear' all due to the water of the jungle hole.

HMAS Kanimbla pulled away from the wharf exactly on time, as was the Navy way. However, rather than turning round and moving bow-first along the channel and out to sea, since the channel was very narrow, she was obliged to reverse all the way to the entrance and then turn 180 degrees.

We were now on our way to Morotai Island to deliver a brand new Halvorsen Brothers motor launch to Air-Sea Rescue. It sat in its cradle on the deck, all shiny and clean with its dark blue and white paintwork gleaming in the morning sunshine. This was to be a 'milk-run' round the islands.

The ship continued sailing up the east coast of Dutch New Guinea. I had been seconded for guard duty until we reached Morotai Island and wondered what there was to guard aboard a troop ship. Apparently, bars of chocolate had been disappearing from emergency stores on board the lifeboats and liferafts.

The rafts were stationed between the lifeboats along both sides of the top deck and positioned so that, with one swing of an axe to cut the lashings, the rafts would slide into the water. Each raft could carry 28 persons.

It was the first time I had pulled guard duty and not been armed. Instead I was issued with a wooden clip-board where all my instructions and regulations were listed plus a very heavy 4 battery torch. I was rostered for the first shift from 6:00pm to 8:00pm, then take 4 hours off. My second shift was from midnight to 2:00am.

The first shift went by without incident. On the second shift I was not so lucky. On board the ship we had a compliment of stage performers going to Japan to entertain the troops with concerts. Of course, the concert party also contained dancing girls — eight of them — housed away from the troops but in special cabins in the Naval Officers' section. I was about to meet one that night.

At about 1:00am I heard somebody talking as they walked slowly toward my post. I waited until they got closer then I turned on my heavy torch. The white beam of light showed me it was a Navy Officer and one of the young girls from the concert party.

"Who goes there?" I challenged them.

"Drop the tone, guard. I am the Commander of this ship."

"Sir, with respect, I must ask you what you are doing in this restricted area which is under my protection."

The officer then became a bit overbearing and pushed the girl behind him, drawing himself up to full height.

"Look here, young man, I have told you who I am and, as such, I can go anywhere I choose to on this vessel."

I was unmoved by this. "Sir, this is a restricted area and NOBODY is allowed here besides me. Those are my orders." I held his face in the glare of my torch all the while, noticing him glow red.

"Well now, guard, I will give you an order as senior officer. I do have the rank. Don't you agree with that?" I agreed. "Alright, I am ordering you to stand aside and let us pass."

I held my position. "Sir, I'm sorry but I cannot do that. Your order cannot countermand the orders that I have written on this board I have in my hand. I must ask you to leave this area at once."

I thought I detected a sound like steam being released from a boiler. His face went a deeper shade of red, he looked at the girl and back at me then, without another word, left for the Officers' Quarters below where, I assumed, he carried on as planned but in more comfort.

I reported the incident to the guard Corporal at the end of my shift as did 3 other guards who'd had the same experience. The guard Commander relayed the report to a senior Naval Officer who assured us it would not happen again. We had no more trouble. It seems that the girls and the Navy officers were in party mood. The 800 troops were not amused.

In daylight hours it was not necessary to mount a guard over the liferafts and their chocolate bars. There were always people close by so nobody in their right mind would want to risk it. This meant that we had plenty of time for other diversions — like deck hockey — which we organised to play against the other services in a round-robin of 6 teams. We were competing for a trophy to be presented at the end of our trip. The teams were made up from Army ordinary ranks, Navy ratings and RAAF airmen against officers from the three services.

Our team were hardly the best at this game but that didn't concern us at all. What we were really looking forward to was the fact that the Navy officers team included the same overweight, overbearing Lieutenant who had given us a hard time at Dreager Harbour. Revenge is so sweet!

The day came when we were to play and, for some reason, our guys began to play like they were absolutely inspired. 'Tubby the Tuba' was a marked man and, even though the puck may not have been anywhere near the man's bare shins, everyone seemed to think it was and took a friendly swipe.

WHACK!...OWWW...

The agonised cries came thick and fast. The fellows watching fell about laughing like drains until the poor chap was so badly beaten he had to be carried from the game, much to the disgust of the Navy ratings who must have hated the man as much as we did.

Our team actually won the game that day but, thankfully, we never saw 'Tubby the Tuba' again during the remainder of the voyage. That suited us just fine.

We were now sailing calm waters and it amused us to stand at the bow and watch the porpoises as they caught the bow wave to ride it like a surfer at Bondi. As well as this we noted an extraordinary phenomenon called phosphorescence which gave the water ahead of the ship an unearthly glow during daylight or night. It was caused by tiny animals in the water getting excited by the passage of the vessel causing them to bunch together and glow. Such a beautiful sight to see.

Shortly thereafter, the ship approached Morotai Island. It was the first time I had arrived by sea but the anchor was dropped about a mile from shore. It was difficult at that range to make out any landmarks I recognised.

A Dutch Police patrol boat approached the ship just as we were unloading the Halvorsen launch over the side. I made note that it had three props which would have given it very high speed over water. When it had settled in the water, the crew stepped aboard the new boat and started the 3 engines which gave a deep throaty roar.

At a given signal, both vessels circled the ship a couple of times and then took off back to shore. The ship then got underway again heading for the Philippines and on to Japan. It was the last time I saw Morotai Island.

CHAPTER THIRTY NINE.

On leaving Morotai Island, our last landfall, we made way for the east coast of the Philippines and thence to Okinawa. From there, we headed for the beautiful Inland Sea of Japan and Kure. Through the Bungo Straits we went between Kyushu and Shikoku Islands; the Inland Sea opened up before us. It was wonderful to behold the looks of soldiers and airmen who were experiencing Japan for the very first time. This was a classic, cultural introduction to them.

For me, it was also difficult to act as though it was my introduction to the Land of the Rising Sun as any indication that I'd already done a tour here previously, would have led to a barrage of questions every day from the novices who needed answers to questions. That, I could easily do without however, I somehow managed the performance of another new chum.

As we closed on Kure Docks it occurred to me that something was vastly different from the last time I was here, 12 months prior. Gazing around the waterways it came to me. Most of the sunken ships and the 30 midget subs had been taken away and broken up for scrap metal.

On shore all the bombed-out buildings had been rebuilt. Very little physical damage showed in any part of this town. The wharves had been repaired after the earthquake before Christmas and the place looked like a postcard scene.

I would have been one of few aboard HMAS Kanimbla who remembered the place as it had been 12 months ago. When this contingent of troops set foot on Japanese soil they would be excited to be at last able to see for themselves the other side of the coin.

We walked to a line of buses waiting to take us to the railway station. No marching this time. As we drove past the Kure No. 4 Dry Dock we could see the 300 ton cranes lifting sections of the very ships that went to war against the world, being cut up by the same shipbuilding crews who first assembled these gigantic sea-going war machines. Ironically, they were working in a dock three times the size of our Captain Cook Dry Dock at Garden Island.

It had been here at Kure that most of the pride of Japan's fleet had set sail to do battle with the Allied ships in the Pacific Ocean. Sadly, not many of the young sailors who sallied forth aboard ships like the massive 65,000 ton 'Yamoto' were to return alive. I considered myself priveleged to have seen this part of Japan. Oh, how the mighty have fallen!

On the way to the railway station, jammed into buses like so many sardines, we drove through areas of Kure which had previously been simply masses of twisted, blackened metal and rubble. Now, as I observed the neat rows of buildings, I couldn't believe it was the same place. Shops, bustling with customers, were thriving and prosperous. Shoppers were conversing along the paved footpaths and dressed in neat clothing instead of tattered rags and shoeless.

At the railway station luncheon had been prepared for us. Tables were set along the platform and guarded by Red Caps — British Military Police. While we dined on succulent finger food and miso soup, trains came and went; still the same dilapidated carriages with passengers clinging to doorway handrails and being shoved into doors by railway guards. I refrained from telling anyone about the BCOF trains we would be riding.

When the delightfully painted blue and gold carriages pulled into the platform, the looks on the faces of the other men was a real picture. They stepped into the unabashed luxury of the carpeted floors with plush green velvet upholstery on seats and threw their kitbags onto the highly lacquered luggage racks overhead. They then settled down to enjoy the ride like Sultans of India and gazed out the perfectly clean windows at the picture-book Japanese countryside rolling past.

When we reached the last of the tunnels before Hiroshima, the contrast the men experienced when emerging from the dark was extraordinary. From fairyland cute, we gazed upon a scene of total devastation despite the fact that work had already begun on clearing the rubble and repairing some of the infrastructure of the atomic target city.

Hiroshima was, in fact being rebuilt but, everywhere we looked there was evidence of folk scrounging for building materials or other usable objects to help put together some sort of shelter. I sat back on my plush green velvet seat and listened to the comments of the other men. I closed my eyes and could see the little kids who'd approached us before, covered in keloids and blisters. I began to weep silently. I took out a handkerchief and pretended to blow my nose.

The men were busy gazing out the windows at Hiroshima.

The train continued across the flat plain toward Iwakuni, through the rubble of Hiroshima and out again into the relatively clear, country air where farmers tended their crops and fisher families caught the daily catch for the village market.

Although the staples of Japanese diet seemed to be rice and fish there were parts of the countryside which spoke to me of other industrial activity. Dark smudges on the landscape belonged to coal mines and steel factories where life was not nearly as pleasant as it was around Kure or Iwakuni.

However, for all its contrasts, Japan was proving to be a fascinating place to be in 1947, the trains being a particular example of the contrast.

The lights in villages that we passed were being switched on as night was falling and the rural picture now took on the aspect of twinkle town. I settled back into my seat and relaxed, sure that we had some way to go before having to leave the train at Mitajiri Station.

Eventually, the train slowed down and the men around me began to pick up their kit bags, ready to disembark. I was home again at RAAF Bofu.

CHAPTER FORTY.

So far, I had been away from Australia for quite some time, had travelled thousands of miles, seen many interesting places and met many fascinating people. Now that I was back at Bofu, it all seemed like a dream and I had just woken up.

I stepped down onto the railway platform feeling a little stiff after being so long in the train. We headed over to the buses and trucks to take us to 81 Fighter Wing Base. Only another 6 miles to go!

At the Base everybody stood in line to be allocated accommodation. Not Gerry! I picked up my kit bag and walked toward Accommodation Block No.2.

"Hey, Gerry! Where do you think you're going?" somebody yelled after me.

I stopped and turned back toward the line of novice airmen.

"Gentlemen, I am going back my barracks — where I was on a previous tour last year. Sorry,... I couldn't tell you beforehand. Your questions about Japan would have driven me nuts! I'll see you all at the mess in 30 minutes."

I waved cheerily and walked away to the howls of disgust, disappointment and faux outrage which rose from thirty men lined up at the orderly room door.

At the table for dinner, all was forgiven as we joked among ourselves at my subterfuge and acting skills. The meal was fair dunkum Aussie fare — tomato soup, real roast lamb with vegetables followed by tinned fruit salad and cream. Nothing ever tasted so good, especially as we had not eaten since 2:00pm at Iwakuni station. It was a meal to remember.

After tea I returned to my accommodation, Block 2, room 6 upstairs and entered in the dark. I undressed in the dark, determined to surprise my previous room-mates in the morning with my unheralded reappearance. This was not to be. In the morning, the joke was on me.

Of the original five who'd shared the room with me before my departure back to Australia, only one was left. However, we soon got over the shock and disappointment and formed a firm friendship all round. This was important to our future together.

Later that morning I reported to 77 Squadron orderly room and, for the first time I was welcomed back as a hero, something that hadn't happened to me before. This made me somewhat suspicious as I was still only what is termed an 'erk' — a lower rank. I was ushered into the Officer-of-the Day's office where I was greeted by Flight Lieutenant Wilson.

"LAC Walshe, sit down please." he began. I sat.

"Looking at your service record here, you had experience at Labuan Island working on repairs to P51 Mustangs and also at OTU No. 2, Mildura where you were given temporary rank of corporal. Is that so, Walshe?"

"Yes, sir. That is correct," I replied.

"You were appointed Airframe Instructor?"

"Yes sir."

"Well, LAC Walshe, you will once again be required to carry out the same duties here as you did at Labuan." He picked up a set of stripes and handed them across the desk to me. "Congratulations, Corporal Walshe!"

I froze for a moment. Then the reality hit me and I scooped up the insignias with glee.

"The reason is quite simple. As you know, the beginning of 1947 was the change-over period during which many longer serving members of Fighter Squadrons of 81 Fighter Wing were posted out while others were sent south to enjoy some leave before coming back to Japan for another tour of duty.

"You were one of the latter, I believe."

"Correct, sir."

"OK then, we have suffered a massive loss of trained personnel. The Wing's experience level has dropped considerably which necessitates training programmes to be commenced immediately. When you leave here, report to Flight Sergeant Potter, our senior instructor at HQ building to begin your duties under him.

"You will find everything you require plus the personnel there waiting for you. Apply your stripes and, jolly good luck, Corporal Walshe."

I stood and we shook hands across the table.

The next few weeks were very interesting as ground training continued inside heated classrooms. The new pilots were put into the air flying familiarization sorties around the Yamaguchi Prefecture whenever the weather permitted. A lot of days it was too foul to get aloft.

For the next months snow storms set in and low cloud kept the aircraft grounded many days. This weather lasted until the middle of May when the warmer air cleared the skies enough for patrols to resume with emphasis on rocket dives and formation flying. By this time all the ground crew were fully trained up on P51D aircraft. However, during this resumption of flying, it was discovered that the concrete strip had again deteriorated to unserviceable status due to the rain and freezing temperatures which tended to expand the frozen water under the slabs of the runway. Movements were again curtailed until the repair work was finished in June.

Since returning to Japan I had been kept very busy but, now the workload was diminishing. I had completed my time as an instructor and now returned to the Squadron as a Fitter 2A, only to find very little work available due to the bad weather and few aircraft flying.

I was, therefore, given a transfer to 481 Maintenance Squadron which suited me as all the maintenance was carried out in a heated hangar instead of outside in the cold and windy conditions we had before.

At this time in my life I was feeling quite contented and relaxed. I couldn't remember feeling this way before and put it down to being back with the people who understood me for what I am, not where I came from. I was getting mail from Dawn twice a week to which, of course, I replied in kind. In the letters we confided our innermost thoughts to each other and revealed intimate details of our lives.

I explained my early up-bringing and childhood which she accepted with the kindest of words when she wrote; 'I don't care what went on in your life before I met you. I only care what happens to us from now on. I know you don't believe in love at first sight but that's the way I feel about you and I can only hope that eventually you will feel the same way about me.'

As time passed I found myself warming to the concept of 'love at first sight' since receiving Dawn's letters became an absolute necessity to my life. I looked forward to her lovely letters so much. She had the gift of writing words that made me think, words that went direct to my heart. I found myself thinking just how much I missed her and wanted to see her once again, as soon as possible.

It was now July 1947 and I had only about 6 months left to serve in Japan then we would be together again. Time just couldn't go quickly enough for me.

Then, for two weeks there were no letters from Dawn. I was beside myself so, in desperation, I wrote to her mother. The next week I received a letter that almost destroyed me. Dawn's Mum wrote back telling me the terrible news.

On Saturday 5th July, Dawn had met with an accident when she joined a bushwalking group of nurses from Canberra Hospital to hike in the mountains around Canberra. She had always enjoyed the great outdoors and they planned to be away for two days however, Dawn and another nurse were walking along a path near the top of a cliff when both girls slipped on some mossy rocks and fell about fifty feet onto rocks below.

They were both killed instantly!

Upon reading this, I was immediately overcome with grief. I had lost a very special friend. I felt that a part of me had died with her. I would never forget that wonderful person, she would remain a part of me for all time.

I felt that I was a fortunate fellow to have met and loved her but, I had to accept that this chapter in my life was now closed. I took stock of my reality and resolved to apply my mind to work in order to dissipate the grief which I selfishly wanted to claim.

The next few days were the worst. I couldn't stop thinking about Dawn. The little things like holding hands and hearing her beautiful voice, stroking her dark hair and most of all, kissing her 'goodbye' at Central Station.

Thinking of all these things was affecting me so I threw myself into the work. This helped me during the days but, at night, when it was quiet and I had time to drift back to Sydney and her arms, it became almost unbearable for me.

I couldn't wait for 21st July to roll round when we were to leave Bofu for Shimane Prefecture on the western side of Honshu Island adjacent the Sea of Japan with Korea just across the water.

At this posting we were to be attached to an RAF Base at Miho for an air-to-ground gunnery course of one month. I assumed that the change would be good for me to clear my mind. However, it became more exciting than we had expected.

CHAPTER FORTY ONE.

Before we left for Miho we were ordered to lock away our Lee Enfield .303 rifles. This occurred to me to be most odd as we had always been ordered to carry our arms with us in Japan. However, this we did although, to me, it seemed like leaving behind your faithful hound chained to a tree. As we boarded the C47 transport I kept thinking I had left something important behind.

I also made the mistake of thinking that, as we were Aussies going to join a British unit, we would be made welcome. After all, didn't we help them in their hour of need???

Upon landing and disembarking from the aircraft we were marched to our billets. As it was a hot day with a bit of time before dinner, I thought we could take a shower beforehand so, I asked one of the Pommy airmen where were the showers.

His answer made all our men burst into peals of laughter when he said,"What showers, mate? I have no idea. I've only been here 8 days!"

The other Brits were not at all amused at our glee. Their dark faces said it all.

Something else struck us as curious at this base. Although it was a British Airforce Base and it operated 2 squadrons of Spitfires — No.11 and No.14, there was also a squadron of Royal Indian Airforce flying Spitfires — No.4 Squadron yet the two groups never mixed. The Poms kept to themselves on one side of the airstrip and shunned the Indians across the other side.

It was clear that there was an element of animosity alive and well here. On the other hand, we were here to do a job and we tried to ignore the gap and get on with the task. Not possible!

We were given 2 days in which to prepare for the arrival of our P51 D aircraft at Miho and we set about securing space in the hangars to service any which had damage or other requirements. We also had parking space allocated outside the hangar next to the Spitfires.

During our time exploring the layout of the base we wandered into the shower block and were surprised to find the space stacked to the roof with small tin tubs. This curiosity puzzled us until we found out how they were used.

When day 2 arrived I was out of bed early to leave fetid air of the room I shared with 5 Poms. Our officers had also run into another snag with the security of our aircraft where they would sit near the Spitfires on the tarmac. They had requested the British to oblige with a guard at night as we had been told not to bring our rifles.

The response from the Brits was a firm "No! Mount your own guards. Rifles are available from stores but, they are still packed in heavy grease. They will be issued and inspected this afternoon before you all go on duty tonight."

As luck would have it, I landed guard duty the first night and spent a couple of very messy hours stripping the .303 rifle and cleaning out all the grease which, for years, had kept it free of rust.

Yet another irritation surfaced at this Base when it came time to march with the Brits. Their training regime had them halting on the command on the left foot whereas, when we heard the word 'Halt!', we took another two paces to end on the right foot. This meant that when they halted, we kept marching for two steps and trod all over their heels, much to the dismay of the Sergeants in charge.

Our P51 D aircraft arrived and parked near the Spitfires. Immediately the comparisons began with comments coming thick and fast from the Poms about how beautiful and sleek the Spitfires looked against the 'fat, ugliness of the pregnant ducks from USA' with their radiators hanging down below the fuselage like 'the guts of a wounded chook'.

We tried to ignore these remarks and got on with servicing the Mustangs, realising that we had to live with this nonsense for some time so best let it go over the top.

On Friday night the truth about the little tin baths came to light when, after a hot day's working on oil changes and other minor chores, we decided to step into the shower block and wash away the day's troubles. We walked in to find all the tin baths on the floor under the running water from the showers. Inside each tub was a British airman having a lovely time with the soap and wasting water sitting down instead of standing up under the spray.

We burst into peals of laughter at this. We stood there fascinated as each man rose from the tub, another man waiting in line stepped into the same foul water, sat and began to cleanse his body.

The next day we had an even bigger problem with the hospitality of the Royal Air Force personnel. The wet mess was open to all ranks and we were allocated 2 bottles of beer each per day. Beyond that we could pay for more however, when we entered the mess, we noticed that the Poms sat at one end of the room and the Indian airmen sat away from them. We had no inhibitions about joining the Indian guys for a drink so, in an atmosphere of comaraderie, we sat with some Indian airmen to pass the time.

It didn't take long for 3 RAF types to approach the bar where we sat and insult the group.

"Look over here,... all colonial bastards drinking from the same trough with the black bastards!"

"You don't want to repeat that do you, matey?" said the Aussie.

Foolishly he did so and — WHAM! — the big Aussie fist slammed into the Pommy jaw, sending the unfortunate man to the floor. A couple of our men stepped forward to help him from the boards but this gesture was taken as a show of reinforcement by the British contingent.

Immediately, several more Poms flew off their seats and took on the group of Indian and Australian airmen. Needless to say, the room soon exploded into complete bedlam as fists, feet and chairs flew in all directions. The Red Cap British Military Police must have been tipped off about this as they were very quickly in the door and wielding heavy batons at one and all to restore peace.

A number of combatants were duly marched away and locked up, me being one. The cell in which we were incarcerated was too small to fit everyone comfortably and it became necessary for everyone to spend the night standing up. During my incarceration I had time to reflect upon the reasons that I so willingly joined the melee and concluded that it had a lot to do with blowing away some pent-up emotional baggage over the loss of my love, Dawn. It may even have gone back further than that but I was satisfied with that explanation at the time.

In the morning we were let out into the exercise yard. I looked around at a very sad and sorry lot however, it occurred to me that not one British airman had been taken prisoner with us. This struck everyone as rather selective on the part of the Red Caps.

The Base Commander then came to address us on our behaviour and suitable punishment. After referring to us as 'rabble and colonial scum' etc out came the punitive measures.

First of all, the Indian fellows were prevented from having their beer ration for 2 weeks and banishment from the wet mess. The Australian contingent received the same treatment with the added sting that we were to leave the British barracks and join the Indians at their barracks for the duration of our stay.

"A bit like Brer Rabbit and the Tar Baby," I commented as we were dismissed.

We packed up our gear and trouped over to the Indian barracks where we were welcomed with open arms and much jolly laughter. Later we got together with the Indian guys to discuss our predicament over the beer rations. We then came up with an answer;

Most unusually on this base was a Corporals' Mess which served beer to Corporals only. Among our number were 4 Corporals who had two shirts each, bearing the two chevrons of rank. By putting our Corporal's shirts on 8 men at a time, we could bring 16 bottles of beer back to the Indian/Aussie barracks per day. At the end of the week we had accumulated 160 bottles which served us well for the weekend party we threw to the exclusion of the Poms.

Hooray for justice!

CHAPTER FORTY TWO.

Following the 'Battle of the Beer Hall' I came to the conclusion that my life seemed to be plagued with a succession of dramatic moments.

I had reported for duty as usual to the airstrip as we had a big day ahead of us with many aircraft movements. On the agenda were ground strafing, bombing practice and air-to-ground rocket firing. I had four daily inspections to carry out on the airframes of our Mustangs to ensure they were serviceable for flight.

Many other airmen technicians were busy carrying out similar inspections — engines, electrical, radio, instruments and armaments. I had just completed two aircraft inspections and was walking in front of the starboard wing of a third Mustang to be inspected. I stopped right in front of the three machine gun ports which lined the leading edge of the wing. As I flipped through the papers on my clipboard my eye caught sight of the tyre on the wheel under the wing and, thinking that it looked a bit flat, I instinctively bobbed down to take a closer look.

At that precise moment the three guns began to spit hot lead into the air from both wings making a shockingly loud racket and causing me to dive forward, hitting my head against the wheel rim. Coming into contact at speed with a solid object like that resulted in a deep cut above my right eyebrow and concussion which put out my lights for an hour.

I awoke in hospital with an immense headache but otherwise, intact.

A later investigation into the incident found that a total of 18 rounds had been fired from the 6 machine guns! The culprit was evidently another tech who was innocently going about his work in the cockpit attending to instrument checks and accidentally touched the electric trigger mechanism.

Boom! Boom! as they say in the classics,...

The technician was cleared of any charges and more stringent regulations were put in place for future safety procedures. I stayed in hospital for three days for observation then released on light duties only.

Life on this British Base had become more bearable for us Aussies after we had been 'banished' to the same quarters as the Indian contingent however, that, too was about to come to a halt on the Wednesday before the last weekend we were to remain here.

The news came through that India had gained independence from Britain after hunderds of years of colonialism and subjugation. This caused all kinds of jubilation to break out in our barracks and the Indian airmen found that they were consequently going home. The joy expressed by these fellows was overwhelming. We were hugged and kissed as though we were part of their own families.

Very early on the Friday morning, every Aussie airman found himself being unceremoniously tossed into the air by Indian airmen who were about to depart the base at Miho. This was their farewell celebration for us. We were informed that Australian service personnel would be most welcome at any time into the newly independent India.

As the trucks carrying the Indians away off the base passed the British barracks the air was thick with language that their mothers would never have taught them. It was beautiful to watch. The Brits could only stand and gape.

Since we were due to depart on the following Sunday, we had to put our heads together and plan a fitting departing gesture as well. Our 'conspiracy committee' was under pressure. We needed a plan that would really rile the Poms and leave them with something to remember us by. Many suggestions came forth but were rejected for reasons of either impracticality or complication.

Eventually we found a plan that suited everyone.

Very early on Sunday morning, before the sun had risen, 30 Australian airmen left the barracks dressed in shorts and light shirts and made their way to the eastern boundary of the base to where lay Lake Yonargo. That was where we intended to commandeer all 15 of their 2-man sailing boats and make off across the bay before the Poms could take them out for the day.

We knew, from earlier reconnaisance, that the little boats were always left fully rigged on the sand at the clubhouse ready for the British airmen to make use at their leisure. This day would be their disappointment.

We found the boats as we expected and pushed them into the salty water to begin our adventure, sailing across the huge lake to the other side for as long as we wanted. At that early hour there was no wind so we had to paddle along the canal leading to the lake but, once there, we caught a very light morning breeze and got under way.

The trail of sailing dinghies stretched back half a mile as we made for the far shore. Back at the clubhouse we could vaguely make out some people jumping up and down waving their fists in the air and shouting obsceneties after the fast disappearing craft.

It did seem a shame to spoil such a fine day with foul language so we pressed onward. It took us about 3 hours of brisk sailing to reach the southern shore where we found a small village which seemed to be desserted. We beached our craft and stepped ashore.

I led a procession of sailing airmen along the only street between some charmingly rustic wooden houses. Apart from some folk working the terrced rice fields high up the mountains in the distance, not a soul was to be seen. Then I spotted a sliding screen being opened slightly so I waved in greeting to the face behind the screen.

Children started to emerge from the houses and approach us along the dusty street, giggling shyly and staring at the strange, tall white men. They seemed fascinated by the fact of our prominent noses and kept feeling their own in comparison.

Soon, adults began to join the children in the street and crowd around us curiously chatting among themselves. Then something happened which I'll never forget; three little girls dressed in Mompei pants and light blue shirts shyly approached and offered us bunches of wild flowers, very pretty and of all colours. I decided to speak with them in Japanese.

At first very nervous I began with,"Mina san, ohayoo gozaimasu" which I hoped translated into "Good morning everybody."

It worked wonders as the adults paused and bowed as one.

This gave me a boost of confidence at having been accepted. Then I felt a slight touch to my hand. Looking down I beheld one of the little girls who'd presented the flowers. It took me all my self-control not to bend down and scoop her into my arms. She looked so much like my tiny Miyoko I wanted to kiss her.

That would have been a great faux pas. A young woman emerged from a house and walked very fast toward me. It made me think I'd done something untoward. She stopped in front of me and pointed to herself and said,"Watashi Akito. (My name is Akito.) Dozo kimasu watashi no uchi e Ikimashoo. (Please come, let us go to my house.)"

She gently took my other hand and, with two young ladies leading me, we walked across the street and into her house. Phil Cadd, who had sailed with me across the lake, came with me into the house.

When inside the small residence, an older woman approached us. I gathered that she was the Mama-san or matriarch of the household. She bowed and said,"Kangei,(welcome)" to which I replied, "Go shinsetsu desu (You are very kind). Domo arigato gozaimasu. (Thank you very much.)"

She then led us further into the house and we walked into a rather large room in the centre of which was a long, low table. Seated around the table was a family of six. I bowed and said,"Mina san konnichi wa. (Good afternoon, everybody.) Doozo yoroshiku. (I am pleased to meet you.)

One of the men sitting cross-legged at the table spoke. "Anata no na wa nanto ii masu ka? (What is your name?)"

I replied,"Namae wa Gerry desu. (My name is Gerry.)"

Somebody else asked, "Dokoni osumai desu ka? (Where do you live?)

To this I answered,"Gorsu or Oosutoraria. (I live in Australia.)"

Thereafter, more questions came at me too fast for me to think how to translate so, in desperation, I threw my hands in the air and said,"Doozo warkari masen.(Please, I don't understand.)Doozo gomen kudasai. (Please excuse me.)" They all understood my problem. From then on we used gestures and the odd word to get along.

We were invited to join them at the table for a meal which we did as best we could, not being as nimble as the Japanese. We needed to half-lie down rather than sit cross legged as they did.

I noted the table setting — a beautiful white teiburu kate (table cloth) covered the table with many pieces of shokki (table ware) on the table. Food was already prepared and laid out; sakana (fish), kashi (cake), gohan (rice) and yasai (vegetables).

The meal passed in very pleasant company. Not much conversation but, toward the end, we were offered tiny handle-less cups of green tea. This is a particularly bitter drop and not at all to my taste but, to refuse, would be a great insult. We drank several cups.

Phil and I rose stiffly from our squat positions on the floor and thanked the family many times over. Then we walked outside and gathered the other men about us. I looked at the sky and noted a gathering of dark clouds to the south. This was ominous weather and

200

we determined to get going as fast as possible. We ran to the boats and got them launched, raising the mainsails as we went.

Five minutes out on the lake it began to rain and fifteen minutes later the wind picked up and the skies really opened up on us. Visibility was down to about a quarter of a mile and the waves were starting to break over the gunwales. We took a reef in the mainsail to reduce the power of the rising wind against the mast as we were in danger of going right over, far from home.

We lost sight of the other 14 craft from time to time but pressed onward, hoping to see the other shore soon. Thunder began to echo all round us and bolts of white-hot lightning flashed across the sky. We now knew we were in trouble. As the wind grew in strength I decided to drop the main altogether and just rely on the jib as the hull of our dinghy was surfing rather than sailing.

After about one and a half hours of bailing water from the boat and fighting against the forces of nature we sighted the canal and calmer waters where we gladly drew our water-logged boat up onto the sand.

One by one we counted the other craft into the beach. Only 14 came back.

"Has anybody seen the last boat?" I yelled above the rattle of the storm.

"Somebody should go and look " came a suggestion.

"OK, Phil, let's go!"

We re-launched the tiny vessel and headed out along the canal once more. We had gone about half a mile from the canal entrance when we spotted the other sail flapping furiously over the up-turned boat. Two sad sailors were still clinging to the hull.

We reached them and helped to right the boat then we both made it back to the beach in front of the sailing club. Never had I been so glad to be on dry-ish land.

It was difficult to imagine how lucky we were and how foolish we had been to steal the boats in the first place. The outcome might have been entirely different and tragic.

After we had dragged the boats high up the beach we all marched contritely back to base. Along the way I tried to remember what it was that I'd thought of that morning that now I realised I hadn't done. It was like losing the keys to a door...

Later that evening, after taking a hot shower, a meal and a few beers, we sat around at the beer hall discussing the day's events. Jokes were tossed back and forth about our lucky escape and so on but my mind was still missing the piece of the puzzle.

Then it occurred to me!

In all our meticulous planning for this great insult to the British contingent in stealing the boats that we knew they would wish to sail, we had overlooked the absolute basic tool for astute sailors — the weather forecast. Had we sought that information before setting out, we might have commenced our return trip earlier or not gone so far afield.

The outcome was not tragic, thanks only to our good luck and determination to survive the storm. It may well have been a huge mistake and embarrassment to the British Commonwealth Occupation Forces in Japan.

CHAPTER FORTY THREE.

Our posting at Miho Base was coming quickly to a close but we were kept very busy as there were air-to-ground gunnery courses to complete before we left. The competition between the British Spitfire aircraft and our P51 D Mustangs had been hotly contested however, the Poms had been left in our point-score dust so to speak and they had very little chance of making up the difference.

To prove our point and also to rub their collective noses in their own sarcastic dirt, whenever we passed British groundcrew or airmen we would tuck our hands under the arms and quack like ducks to let them know we remembered their crack about the appearance of the Mustangs — 'pregnant ducks' they called them.

A quick look at the score-board would confirm the gap in scores.

There were still some unfortunate 'thorns in the side' between our two groups and one was the snobbish attitude of the British officers. One fellow in particular who irked most Aussies was the chap who gave us guard duty the first day we arrived at Miho and ordered that, since we had to borrow rifles from their stores, those rifles had to be cleansed free of packing grease and spotless for inspection before guard duty.

It occurred to me that the same fellow was Orderly Officer of the Guard the same night that I took my turn at guard duty. The British rifles we were issued were entirely different in manufacture as were the bayonets — more like a small ice pick than the 18 inch short sword that we normally carried.

That Tuesday night I pulled the shift from 10:00pm to midnight. It was unusually warm that evening and, after patrolling on foot for an hour I decided to rest my bones sitting on the wheel of a P51 D for a moment. Presently, along came a jeep with the Orderly Officer of the Guard standing up and calling loudly "Guard, stand to, Orderly Officer!"

I positioned myself under the wing of the Mustang and waited until the jeep was close, then, with torch gripped in one hand and rifle at the ready, stepped forward and rested the pig-sticker bayonet against the Officer's throat with the challenge, "Halt! Who goes there?"

The vehicle stopped immediately, thanks to the quick thinking of the alert driver. I could see by the light of the torch that the officer's face had turned vivid white. He tried to speak but nothing came forth.

The driver, spoke for him.

"Orderly Officer here, guard!"

"Pass, friend." I responded. The officer sank to his seat and waved the driver to proceed, and they left.

Having recognised the British officer as the same haughty fellow we first encountered at Miho, I felt that the score had, more or less, been settled.

Upon termination of our duty as guards we were also obliged to return the British rifles to stores as we had received them. This required that we pack them in waterproof grease and seal them inside a calico bag which had to be sealed as well. The rifles were then received back into store and we signed them off and returned to barracks to rest before luncheon.

After lunch we were taken to our transport out of Miho, our favorite C47 transport sitting patiently on the apron near the tower. We boarded the aircraft and, when settled, I removed my greatcoat from the kitbag and wrapped it about my knees.

The other fellows looked curiously at my antics however, they would follow suit when we climbed to cruising altitude later, remembering that the month was November 1947. Winter in Japan can be bitterly cold.

The exit trip from Miho to Bofu was cold but uneventful except for the aerial view of the countryside. As we approached Bofu airstrip I glanced out the window and remarked that the seawall which held back the Inland Sea from the plain on which the airstrip was situated was at best, a grand gesture of human achievement against the forces of nature.

Should a ship become uncontrollable and breach the seawall, a disaster of gigantic proportions would ensue with water up to 8 feet deep flooding over the farms and the airstrip.

Life at Bofu continued a-pace with aircraft movements being maintained and training sorties being flown almost daily. We had occasion to worry on one day when two Mustangs, out on patrol over Yamaguchi Prefecture failed to return.

Search aircraft were sent aloft but to no avail. Two days later both Mustangs returned, having spent the ensuing time at Kochi airstrip rather than risk flying into foul weather.

On another accasion an aircraft flown by Flight Lieutenant C H Nissen landed badly and ran off the end of the runway, into a rice paddy where its wheels dug into the soft earth and the aircraft overturned, smashing the perspex canopy where the unfortunate pilot drowned in 2 feet of sludge and human excrement, still strapped into the harness of his cockpit.

This was a particularly bitter loss to the squadron as Nissen had been a hero to the rest of the 'erks' due to his fine wartime record. We called him 'Pop' as he was much older than the groundcrew. He was 27 years old!

We were, therefore, obliged to mount guard over the inverted aircraft until we could rescue it in the morning. With the body gone, we were given a roster for the night. My shift ran from 6:00pm until 8:00pm. I was driven to the edge of the runway in the truck dressed in gumboots and raincoat with rifle, torch and two clips of .303 bullets. I then had to wade out to the Mustang through the slush of many 'honey-carts' to perch somewhere out of the stinking morass.

I chose to climb up on a wing and rest against one of the undercarriage legs.

Time passes very slowly when one is placed in such an unpleasant and uncomfortable position. Every tiny movement and sound becomes a dramatic invasion of one's thoughts. I began to hear what sounded like the 'sploshes' of somebody approaching across the rice paddy. It became unbearably distinct and close so, out of curiosity and in panic, I switched on my torch.

I was horrified to see coming at me from all directions, the most monstrous, ugly, warty toads in history. Something straight out of the worst B Grade Hollywood scary movie.

I made sure none came to close to me on the wing however, I didn't let on to any of my pals when we changed guard at the end of the shift. I wanted them to share my horror too!

On Monday 16th November 1947 we were informed at a formal parade that a ceremony would be staged in Tokyo to celebrate the marriage of Princess Elizabeth to Prince Phillip on Friday 20th and that men from Bofu would be part of the Australian contingent to represent our country at that ceremony.

I had experienced some exchanges of opinion with our Sergeant leading up to this and was not expecting to be selected for the tour however, it turned out that I was and, for that, I was really chuffed.

In order to reach Tokyo we had to board a steam train at Mitajiri Station at 10:00am. We each were issued with a lunchbox containing 4 sandwiches, an apple and 2 water bottles. This seemed at lot at the time however, the entire ration was meant to feed us lunch, dinner and breakfast as we would not reach Tokyo until the following day.

Fortunately, we rode the green-and-gold BCOF Train which had steam heaters in every carriage. Thus we were not terribly uncomfortable and we found the snow-covered landscape fascinating as we passed. I think the highlight of the journey was probably the sight we had of Mount Fuji when it came into view. The words of travel writers do not seem to be adequate to describe the loveliness and exquisite beauty of this panorama.

The train pulled into the railway station at 8:30am. It was peak hour in Tokyo and the platforms were very busy. Everyone of our group was fascinated at the antics of the train packers as they pushed and shoved passengers into the carriages with their boots.

The Americans had laid on buses to meet us at the train station and we climbed aboard for the trip to the USAAF baracks for our billets. As we passed the burned-out shells of public buildings in Tokyo the evidence of the fury of the Allies' incendiary bombs was most powerful. Even the Parliament building — The Diet — was a blackened shell.

Our accommodation at the American Base was almost luxurious with clean linen sheets and woollen blankets. We dumped our kitbags and decided to take a stroll about the base to inspect their aircraft.

Apart from the line-up of B52 Superfortresses, DC 6B transports, Mitchell and Boston bombers, P51 F Mustangs we came upon a sleek, silvery single seater with no apparent means of propulsion.

There was no propeller!

I found an American airman close by and stopped him to ask,"What kind of aircraft is that without a prop?"

He smiled broadly and patted me on the shoulder.

"Buddy, let me tell ya, you're lookin' at the future of aviation there. That there's a jet engined F80 Shootin' Star."

I was still puzzled. "How does it fly?"

"Like a Goddam vacuum cleaner, my friend. Sucks air in one end, mixes fuel and fires it out the tail. Hot and fast! 500 miles an hour or more!"

"Holy cow! I don't believe it," I said, completely aghast at the prospect.

We mulled over his words as we returned to the barracks. There we saw we had been invited to the 'Rocker Club' that night to meet some American men and their wives. We looked forward to that.

The term 'Rocker' came from the fact that, in American service units the Sergeants wear their three stripes inverted to how we hang our 'hooks'. When a Sergeant reaches Senior Sergeant rank, he is given a 'rocker' to wear below the three stripes; not unlike the rocker on a rocking chair. Thus the mess is the domain of Sergeants and above where we were invited to spend the evening.

The night went well with no carping by British service personnel. It was at this time that the American Services had decided to change from their khaki uniforms for the USAAF to blue serge uniforms when they became the US Air Force and, as we were wearing our blue uniforms, we were treated as some kind of advance party in the new American uniforms.

This was all cleared up when a notice was posted declaring the difference in uniforms between RAAF, NZAF and RAF who were all present in Tokyo at the time.

Conversations at the Rocker Club also got round to the way the Yanks referred to the Brits as 'limeys'. "You guys don't like to be labelled the same, do you?"

"No, matey," I answered."To call an Aussie a limey is about as insulting as to have a Pom call us 'colonials'. You see, we became a Commonwealth in 1901 and have managed our own affairs ever since. A bit like you blokes when you tipped George's tea into Boston Harbour. We still speak the same language — more or less — but, there's no love lost between us."

"Good for you, Mitey!" the poor chap declared, trying to emulate the Aussie accent.

We danced with the American wives and drank the American beer and whiskey. We swapped uniform jackets and had photos taken hanging over each other's shoulders like the best of friends. During all this cross-Pacific confirmation of brotherhood, we noticed the Poms sitting sullenly at the far end of the room seething with jealousy, not joining in.

The next morning brought its own retribution to those who'd over-indulged in revellry. Hangovers were the order of the day and it was a painful sight to behold otherwise healthy and fit airmen creeping about the hangars and apron holding heads and wearing dark glasses. However, as ever, we got the preparatory work done for the Mustangs to be ready for the fly-past on Friday.

The line-up was rather a spectacular sight with the British Spitfires in their drab camouflage beside the Kiwi's black Corsairs next our P51 D Mustangs all brightly shining in silver. We were very proud of our flight.

Friday dawned cold but clear making perfect flying weather. The collective aircraft of the British Commonwealth were made ready for the fly-past over Tokyo Bay. The British Spitfires took off first in formations of three followed by our gleaming Mustangs and then came the New Zealand Corsairs. The vision of these fine aircraft over the Japanese capital was certainly a stirring sight. It brought a tear to many an eye. After the event, the aircraft flew back to base and were all washed down, tied down and covered against snowstorm and we were told to make ready for the evening's celebrations.

This was something we had all looked forward to for some time, to be invited to the British Embassy to be presented to the Ambassador and his wife and to form part of the Commonwealth Honour Guard. Our transport American buses drew up at the red carpet in front of the main building and we marched into a foyer where we were made to listen to the protocol for the day. This involved lining up in two's to be introduced to the vice-regal duo and then to be shunted to a designated table to enjoy a repast of nibbles and soft drinks, toast the good health of the newly-wed Princess Elizabeth and Prince Phillip.

The chap making all this declaration wore a uniform with which I was not personally familiar however, suffice to say his hat had a red ribbon round it, his lapels were decorated with red patches and the gold braid was enough to ransom a Duke or at least a Lord.

We duly lined up. My partner in this was a little fellow called Jimmy Smallhorn, another Leading Aircraftsmen like me. We nick-named him 'shorty' for obvious reasons. Our turn came to move forward to the dais and we walked with due solemnity and stopped at the top of the steps where the Equerry asked our names.

"LAC Walshe" I said.

"LAC Smallhorn," said Jim.

Turning to the Ambassador the Flight Lieutenant equerry said, "Sir, on the left is LAC Walshe and on the right is LAC Horn."

Jimmy's face went bright red. "Sir," he hissed, "My name is Smallhorn!"

The equerry smiled disdainfully and corrected himself," Beg pardon, sir, On the the right is LAC Smallhorn."

We shook the black-gloved hand of the British Ambassador and the white-gloved hand of his wife. The lady very graciously smiled and said to me, "Welcome, LAC Wlashe."

"Thank you Ma'am," I replied.

We left the dais and were shown to our seats at the long tables. When we were seated I turned to Jimmy and said, "Well mate, when this night's over, nobody will remember any of our names except yours. This story will be told round the world. You'll be famous. You'll become known as the Colonial Airman who had the audacity to correct the Equerry in front of the King's representative in Japan — the bloody Ambassador!"

We had a jolly good laugh about that for the rest of the evening.

CHAPTER FORTY FOUR.

The following day, being a Saturday, meant that we had no formal work schedule which was most fortunate as we mostly had throbbing heads and dusty mouths from the alcohol consumed the previous evening.

But it was worth it!

In such salubrious surrounds, in elegant, esteemed company and faced with free beer and wine, how could we poor 'colonials' resist? It was a truly wonderful and most memorable evening — made all the more memorable by the looks on the Poms when they saw us having such a great time.

So, as a result, the whole contingent walked very slowly about their business, feeling fragile and smiling a lot. It was decided, however, not to waste the day and we would take a trip into Tokyo city to see the sights, such as they were.

Enquiries at the Transport Office showed that there was a truck going to town to deliver USAAF mail from The States to the Yanks at Yokahama. This proved to be another bonus as we had seen nothing of the damage in Tokyo or Yokahama and the truck took us close to some of the worst fire damage in both places.

One of the most spectacular sights, however, was a huge hole close to the rail station in Tokyo which was like a large lake. An enormous 'earthquake' bomb had created the vacancy and the melted snow had quickly filled it.

With the mail delivered to the US troops, we rode the truck back through the harbour region of Yokahama where several Allied warships were at anchor or docked — mainly American, some British and one Australian destroyer. It took a long time to finally arrive at the centre of Tokyo however, on arrival, we were surprised to see that the Occupation Forces had gone to a lot of trouble to put up street signs in both Japanese and English and even re-name some streets in typical American fashion; Avenue 'A', 1st Street etc.

We found our way to the Ginza area and strolled about gaping at the buildings which remained standing. Of course the Americans had snaffled some important buildings to use as their HQ's especially the Emperor's Palace where General Douglas MacArthur had ensconced his entourage and himself. He also had taken over the Dai-Ichi Insurance Building on the corner of Avenue 'A' and Avenue 'Z' as his Operations HQ.

Eventually we found the place we sought, the Ginza Star Room where all Australian servicemen met for a cold beer in Tokyo. We sat and had a few very pleasant drinks there and then decided that we should explore more of the Ginza district. Off we went again, weaving through the heavy crowds which bustled back and forth along the pavements, lined with itinerant merchants trying to flog various souvenir junk to the Occupation Forces who were ever present and had the cash to buy.

As we walked along, it gradually occurred to me that we might have been followed so, at one place I stopped and looked back at a group of western-looking people who smiled vaguely back at me. The man was dressed in American Army uniform and had two ladies with him. The wings on his uniform indicated that he was a US pilot. One lady was his wife and the other his daughter.

"Excuse me, sir," I began, "I don't wish to be rude but it would seem to me that you have been following us for some time now."

"Quite right too, young man. Let me explain, please. Firstly, I was taken by your blue uniforms. We thought you were Americans showing off the new uniform of the USAF which will be in vogue next year. We have heard that it'll be dark blue.

"Then, as we got closer, we saw the shoulder flashes which read 'Australia' and this intrigued us." He stopped abruptly and looked a bit embarrassed. "Let me introduce myself and family, I am Major John Waldron, USAAF and this is my wife, Mary and my daughter Sarah."

I shook his hand saying, "I am LAC Walshe, Royal Australian Air Force, sir, and these are my comrades..." The other men shook the Major's hand and met the ladies.

"Now tell me, Airman Walshe, we also had another problem with your appearance. We have been taught from childhod that the Aussie people are all black. You sure ain't black."

I shuffled my feet self-consciously at this remark but chose to overlook the obvious response. Instead I said, "Major, please call me Gerry and I'll call you John. Now, to put you all right in the picture. We are descendants of British stock who landed in Australia in 1788 to set up a convict settlement. Yes, we do have a population of native peoples who were the original inhabitants of the country and are are black. But, as you can see, we are fairly pale, like you are. Since then, we have multiplied and grown into a population of about 8 million people"

"But you speak English so well." queried Mary. "And such a fascinating accent, too."

"Well, yes, Mary," I replied. "A lot of people find it difficult to emulate the fair dinkum Aussie accent. Many try but we are unique in that department. We can pick up other accents very quickly and we can tell just as quickly when a person is trying to copy the Aussie accent."

My companions were showing signs of getting impatient as I was doing all the talking so I decided to end the conversation. "So, it's been very nice to meet you. Now we must be off and see the rest of Tokyo."

"Hold on a minute, Gerry." The Major turned to the ladies and had a quick conversation, then turned back to us and said,'We would like very much to continue this conversation. Would you and one of your friends like to come to our house tomorrow, Sunday for dinner? I can pick you up at the Base about 2:00pm if you like. Which barracks are you in there?"

"No.4 west," I replied, "Thank you John, we'll be waiting."

The next day we were up early as two American airmen had invited us to look over their aircraft, the highlight of which was the inspection of the massive B52 Super Fortress. With a tail that stood over three storeys high and a cavernous interior, it certainly was most impressive. The seating 'up-front' gave the two pilots all the elbow room they could wish for, sitting on air-sprung seats and looking at rows of dials which stretched from one side of the front panel to the other both above and below the windscreens

I was also permitted to climb into the cockpit of the F80 Shooting Star. It fitted me like a glove; the seat wrapped around the torso like a very expensive sports car with everything required for comfortable control well within reach. The front panel was also intriguing in that each group of instruments was colour-coded — flying units were white, armament red, navigation blue and communication green. Everything fell easily to hand to make the stressful job of flying at least comfortable.

The engine bay also held my interest when we discovered that the jet propulsion unit was not bolted into place but rather held in place by a series of lock-over cam levers which were secured in place by safety wires.

By the time we'd seen all this it was almost time for Major Waldron to pick us up. We thanked the Yanks and made our way to the apron in front of Barracks No.4 west. True to his word, John Waldron turned up in a jeep and we piled into the seats, my companion for this outing being 'Nippy' Fisher.

The house the Waldrons occupied was a very normal, western style of bungalow. We were welcomed by the Waldron ladies and escorted into the lounge room where we sat and chatted a while. The aroma of feminine perfume almost made us swoon since we had not sampled any such smell for a long time. It was wonderful to be in their company.

Dinner of roast lamb and vegies went down a treat with wine to accompany the meal. The conversation sparkled all round the table; some about America, some about Australia. The ladies admitted making us speak just to hear the accent again. With a few drinks to lubricate my vocal cords, I could have gone on all evening however, we made our getaway about midnight.

On the way back to barracks, Major Waldron suggested that we might like to take a look at Tokyo from on high. We agreed to join him on a flight the next day to see the layout of the city and get a whole perspective of the damage.

"I'll have some inspections to perform tomorrow, John, but, if I can wangle permission, we'd be happy to go."

"Gerry, as I have told you, I am the Commanding General's pilot. My aircraft is that Mitchell bomber painted white you see sitting in front of the tower. At 1:00pm I have to fly that plane to air-test the new radio they fitted last Friday. That should take about an hour and that should give you a chance to see the city from the air. Get your senior officer's agreement in writing and away we go!"

At 12:30pm the next day I called into the orderly room and voiced my request to the Flight Officer.

"Good idea, Walshe," he said, "But there has to be a valid reason for this junket. Let's make it a Public Relations exercise. That way we can get away with the flight and also get some mileage out of the relationship between America and Australia in Japan. If we can get such a spread into the 'Stars & Stripes' newspaper that the Yanks put out, you might become world famous!

"Just make sure you wear your best battle dress uniform. It will show the Yanks that their Aussie friends are grateful for their help here and we have a strong bond with them."

I was a bit taken aback. "Sir, I don't think I'll know what to say to a newspaper interview."

He looked at me and frowned. "LAC Walshe, I have known you for some time now. You're never short of words. You'll think of something appropriate to say, I'm sure."

I thanked him for his vote of confidence. "I will do my best, sir."

John Waldron picked me up near the Mitchell bomber at 1:00pm.

"So, Gerry, you got permission OK?"

"Yes, John, with a condition attached." I told him about the P R angle.

"Oh boy! You Aussies are great guys. The General will be pleased to turn a simple test flight into a Public Relations exercise. That's just pure magic, a wonderful idea!"

We stepped up into the Mitchell 'bomber' to find that the floor was covered in light brown carpet and the seating consisted of two plush lounge chairs with seatbelts. The two pilots went forward to the flight deck and the load master and I settled down into the deep cushions of the lounge chairs.

The engines started up and the aircraft taxied onto the runway, lined up and began the take-off run. Soon we were airborne and banking left over Tokyo to take a run out to sea and over Mount Fuji for a sight-seeing trip.

CHAPTER FORTY FIVE.

Take-off from the airstrip at Tokyo was as smooth as silk. The luxuriously appointed Mitchell bomber in which we now sat climbed away in the afternoon sunlight giving me the feeling of immense power and elation. This contrasted greatly with the scenes of devastation which we could clearly see below us.

Small colonies of humpies and makeshift dwellings huddled together amid the wreckage of the docks, wharves and warehouses which had been knocked out of existence by the American onslaught of high explosive bombs and incendiary bombs. It was ugly and distasteful to see. How the people stayed alive down there was a miracle.

The aircraft turned toward Mount Fuji, its white cap shining like a beacon in the distance. At the foot of Fuji we could see steam rising from Lake Ashi which contrasted with the snow-covered fields all round and a complete divergence from the scenes around Yokahama and Tokyo.

Along the edges of the lake we saw the famous shapes of Torii gates in red and black and Shinto shrines dotted here and there with meandering pathways between. I had a very good view of this as I was standing between the two pilots looking forward through the winscreens. Ahead we saw Mount Fuji approaching. I assumed we would fly around the crater but, as we drew level, the aircraft turned and flew over the rim then dived into the vast maw of the opening. At this point the rim of the crater was above us all round. I clearly saw vents in the rim spewing steam from all sides.

That was enough excitement for me!

As we rose from the volcanic mouth of Fuji our pilot, Major John Waldron turned and said to me," Gerry, you have just seen inside the sacred mouth of this mountain. What we have just done is a big 'No-no'. If word got out about this I could be in serious trouble. Promise me

215

you'll not mention it to anybody while you're in Japan."

"Of course, John. My word on that!" I kept my promise although it was quite difficult.

The Mitchell bomber then turned and flew back toward Tokyo, passing over a mosaic of fields of many colours on the Kanto Plain below. The scenes of destruction again became evident as we flew over industrial areas where factories stood roof-less, steel bridges repaired with timber beams and planks. We turned back toward the harbour of Yokahama where several ships lay at dockside; cargo vessels as well as warships could be seen.

On to Johnson Field where we joined the circuit area and landed. John taxied the Mitchell off the airstrip to a parking position near the tower where we could see a gaggle of reporters and officials waiting for the aircraft to come to a halt.

Being the senior officer, Major John Waldron was first out the door and onto the tarmac. There we were met by six US Army officers plus two reporters and two photographers and other US Army personnel. Fortunately, John spoke first and smoothed the path for me to follow with a brief dissertation touching on the great co-operation between the USAAF and the RAAF in Japan.

Next followed a series of photographs taken from several angles and in many combinations of people, mostly with 'yours-truly' in there somewhere showing off the deep blue uniform I was so proud to display. It was a fine example of Public Relations for the Yanks as they anticipated their new uniforms to be about the same shade of blue next year.

It was all over in a short space of time and I turned to Major Waldron to bid farewell and thank him for the exciting flight over 'you-know-where'.

"We'll be leaving tomorrow, John. Will you and your lovely ladies be at our send-off tonight?" I asked.

"Be there with bells on, Gerry." was the brief answer.

As with most phases in my life, there was a planning problem. It stemmed from getting access for all our mates to the Rocker Club which was meant for Sergeants and above ranks only. After a few moments thought we came up with a plan to permit entry for a Canadian chap called Dinny Baker — a medical orderly but only a Corporal.

The way we skirted the problem of 'Sergeants only' law was to dress Dinny Baker in one of my own battle dress jackets as though he was an Aussie guest of honour too.

The evening proceeded smoothly enough until Flight Sergeant Rocky Morrison took me aside and, pointing at Dinny, asked me, "Who's that fellow there? I don't recognise him."

Quick as a flash and charged with courage that comes from a few ales, I replied, "That's our Corporal Reg Black!. He looks a bit different tonight 'cos he had a haircut at the American barber shop. Nah, forget about him. Let's have another drink, matey!"

"Good idea," he answered and we walked to the bar together.

Finally the night came to an end and we all staggered home to our barracks with Dinny. "I think I've had a bit too much to 'rink,..." slurred the inebriated corporal Dinny. With that he flopped onto my bed and began to snore.

It took some time to get him out of my uniform and into his own. Then his Canadian mates had to take him home.

The next morning we were a sad and sorry bunch of airmen with throbbing heads all round. Our Mustangs had to be inspected ready to fly back to Bofu. Their estimated time of departure was 11:00 hours so, without too much fuss, we set about our chores.

That done we watched them take off and form up over Tokyo Bay and fly back over the base in Vee formation, a lovely sight to behold.

We went back to the barracks to pack up for the final time in preparation for the 30 hour train ride back to Bofu, hundreds of miles to the south.

The buses took us to Yokahama railway station where we boarded another luxuriously appointed carriage which featured reclining seats. Next door to our carriage were 3 carriages for US Army troops; one buffet and two sleepers. We eyed off their accommodation with envy.

It was 2:30pm and the lights on the train were turned on as we had to travel through various tunnels along the way. I also noted that there was work being carried on erecting steel poles designed to carry electric wires for the new electric trains.

The train started off and we ran through country littered with the rubble of bombing again until we passed through a few tunnels and out into the plain below Mount Fuji. With the seafront on one side, the trip was fairly picturesque if we overlooked the bomb craters and the suffering of rural families tending the rice paddies. Orchards and forests swept past our windows in a procession of colourful vistas with Fujiama as a backdrop, snow capped and with a foreground of greens, blues and reds.

The steam train needed to refill the water tank and had specific places where this could be done. One was at Atami where we pulled into the station and I needed also to refill my water bottle so I stepped off the train and went to the next carriage back to enquire from an American about finding potable, safe drinking water.

"Come on in here, guy!" I stepped into Heaven on Wheels.

No sooner had they poured me a glass of water from their bulk water container than the train lurched and we were off again. I leapt to my feet and went for the door only to be stopped by another Yank.

"Relax, pal. Don't worry about getting back to your carriage. The train's going to make a few more stops. Sit down and join us here a while." I stayed a while.

Outside the snow was falling. The temperature was well below zero but, inside the carriage, the warmth of the steam heater kept us at a very nice 22 degrees. Next thing, I was served an American meat pie with vegetables and flapjacks with maple syrup to follow and finished off with coffee.

The conversation never stopped, being surrounded by US troops who had to hear about life in that place 'down-under'. Questions such as; Do you find it difficult to learn English? How many kangaroos do you own? Do you guys have motor cars in Sydney? Completely, blissfully ignorant questions to be sure but not surprising given the fact of America's rather narrow view of the world.

The fact of their troops in Korea came into the conversation and they told me of some of the tactics used by the North Korean troops to try to humiliate prisoners they captured and dragged across the 38th. parallel for questioning. I could sense there was the beginings of another conflict in what they said.

The train was slowing down for another station and I rose from my seat to go and join my comrades in our carriage but was stopped by the Sergeant.

"Gerry, do you have a mate there who could join you in here with us?"

"Why, yes. Nip Fisher. Should I go and find him?"

"Yeah, do that. Then we can hear more about that Australia of yours."

Nip Fisher and I spent the rest of that night talking with the Yanks and drinking their coffee until we couldn't stay awake. They then gave us a couple of their bunks to sleep in and left us to it. In retrospect, we assessed the love of their country by the US troops as more than just patriotism — it was their whole lives. The reason that they wear their American hearts on their sleeves.

We awoke next morning as the train pulled in to Kure rail station. Pulling back the curtain I looked out on a world covered in snow. I was glad to be in a nice warm bunk on a train with steam-heated carriages. When the train finally pulled up, we were surprised to see hundreds of people lying on the platform trying to keep warm by huddling together. Obviously, they were homeless.

It was some hours later that we arrived at Mitajiri station where we left the train and our new American friends. Nip Fisher and I stepped onto the platform feeling very pleased with ourselves after a most enjoyable trip. Our joy was to be short-lived as we then learned that we had been reported 'absent without leave' from our carriage. We had to look forward to facing some sort of punishment.

Our trucks picked us up from the rail station and drove us back to 81 Fighter Wing. I knew we would be in for a good 'carpeting' in the morning but, at the time, all I wanted was a hot shower and dinner then my own bed.

CHAPTER FORTY SIX.

My meeting with the Commanding Officer went well. He didn't actually pull out a pistol and shoot me. Rather he read me the 'riot act' as it applied to leaving a post without permission and causing the officer in charge to needlessly worry. Oh dear!

Fined two day's pay and loss of leave entitlement for two days. I wore that with glee and a memory of happy hours I spent with the cordial Yanks.

As the weather still continued to provide snow and prevent aircraft movements, we were at a bit of a loss for productive activities. I chose to walk to our 'bludge hut' which was a small single-room building constructed by all personnel from the C.O. down and made from salvaged timbers etc. It was kind of a 'boys own club house' away from the official buildings of the Base.

It was even well heated by a cut-down 44 gallon drum and smoke stack which went straight out through the roof. This is where a lot of idle moments were spent and games of cards were played.

To break up our boredom, somebody had organised a group tour of the stately home and estate of Prince Motomichi Mori. This was situated on the outskirts of Bofu City and surrounded by a 12 foot high stone wall capped with green tiles. We arrived in trucks and stopped outside the main entrance where stood two massive wooden gates under a tiled roof. Looking most impressive from the outside, we wondered what it was like on the inside.

The gates were swung open by two uniformed servants and we stood at the gateway admiring the white-pebbled driveway which led up to a tiled entrance porch. Ten massive columns supported a green tiled, gabled roof and the entrance door opened into a single-storey building which then led to a two-floor residence at the rear.

Ancient pine trees, gnarled with age, stood amid beautiful green grassed areas with neatly clipped hedges forming rooms for gardens around maple trees, cherry trees and apricot trees.

A small clear stream meandered through the park-like setting to a large ornamental lake filled with water lillies and carp of all colours. A profusion of azaleas of many hues stood about the garden edges with stone lanterns in the shallows, reflected in the still water.

Arched stone bridges crossed the waterways at many points adding to the magical panorama and beauty of the gardens. I felt that I was in a small picture book part of Japan, something hidden from public gaze.

When it came for us to leave I stood on the white pebble drive and absorbed as much of the scene as I could, determined to take with me this perfect vision. It remained with me for all time. As we left the estate the massive timber gates closed behind us with a hefty 'thud!' and we found ourselves back in the reality of rural Mitajiri with its gloomy shops and narrow, stinking streets.

The following day, Sunday, we spent visiting the Tenjin Shinto Shrine built on a hillside overlooking the city of Mitajiri. The temple is approached from a unique gateway called Torii, frequently painted red. The Japanese word translates as 'sitting bird' which is supposed to represent the perch where a bird might sit.

This ancient building has walls made of natural timber and a double roof of green tiles with up-turned eaves. It is surrounded by a garden planted with a profusion of flowering shrubs and flowers of all colours. There are many miniature stone bridges, pine trees and stone lanterns which are lit at night. Statues of Buddha are many and a large bronze bell is housed on its own near the temple. I never found out what it is used for.

I remember when I first arrived in Japan I read somewhere that the Shinto religion has beliefs similar the Aboriginal tribes of Australia in that they hold sacred all natural things; wind, sea, trees, rocks, sun, moon, stars, thunder, lightning, rain, hail and snow.

This, to me, seemed very close to my belief in Baiame, the Aboriginal supreme being.

In Hiroshima Bay is an island, Miyajima which houses many Shinto shrines, the most famous being Itsukushima Shrine also known as the 'floating shrine'. It has been built on stilts out on the water and accessed via a huge red painted Torii 500 yards from the shore. At low tide one may walk to the shrine under the Torii.

When the tide comes in the shrine appears to float on the water. Its greatest illusion is at night when the stone lanterns are lit, something akin to an Oriental Fairyland, no doubt.

Despite the cold weather which we were experiencing in December, the next days leading up to Christmas would not allow any let up of activity. The BCOF were to conduct new and more intensive patrols of the Inland Sea and the Sea of Japan between Honshu and Korea to prevent the influx of illegal migrants.

The greatest danger from these people was the diseases they tended to carry such as cholera, typhoid and small pox, any of which brought into Japan could cause mayhem. Besides the medical risks involved, the aircraft were to spot boats which might be trying to smuggle contraband, drugs and weapons across the border.

Suspect watercraft would be reported to the high-powered Navy launches who would then intercept the smugglers, some of whom had been drafted into the Japanese army in Korea during the conflict.

Over the ensuing days many hundreds of intercepts were carried out and arrests made of illegal refugees. The goods seized during the raids ranged from penicillin, sulphadiazine and saccharin to 80 tons of sugar which would have been snapped up on the black market.

Although we were run ragged by all the high pressure of this activity, at the end of the week we were told that the assignment had gone so well that we were to be stood down for four days which brought us up to Christmas. That suited me just fine.

On Saturday after Christmas I determined to finish a personal venture that I'd begun some time before. It involved going back to Hiroshima so, I arose early on the day and caught a bus to Mitajiri station to get a train to Hiroshima. There, I intended to seek the real story of the Chinese Marble Lions which I'd seen some time previously.

I was aware that the Japanese never carved lions as monumental animals; their preference was for fantastic dogs or Kuma-Inu to guard their portals and gates. It must have been during the Japanese invasion and conflict in China that the lions I saw in Hiroshima had been stolen and brought back to Japan.

When I arrived in Hiroshima I made my way to the part of town where there stood a large light coloured building in which Japanese soldiers were being repatriated and demobilized. The sign over the doorway translated as "Welcome Home — Thank you for all you have done for your country." The looks on the faces of the Japanese ex-soldiers reflected none of this gratitude. To a man, they were dejected and worn out.

I found it most curious that these fighters who had marched so proudly past the stolen lions to go to war, now had to pass them again to leave their country's service and return to their families.

Years later back in Australia, I wrote to the Chinese Ambassador in Canberra to air my concern and wrote him a very long letter of explanation in regard to the Chinese Marble Lions of Hiroshima. The Ambassador received the letter and was quickly on the phone to me, offering to send a reporter from the China Peoples' Daily newspaper to interview me at home. I agreed.

I was interviewed by the Chinese press and the story did appear in the Chinese newspaper complete with a photo of myself on the front page. Of course it was all written in a language I don't understand but I was pleased to have brought the story to the attention of the Chinese people. I have heard nothing since.

Back at the docks of Hiroshima there were ships of many nations unloading goods of all descriptions. To transport the goods to waiting rail trucks some distance away, men with 3 wheeled motor bikes would carry about a ton at a time from the wharf to the rail truck and back for another load.

Near the centre of the city I discovered something I never expected to find amid the rubble that once was Hiroshima. The remains of a Christian Church — The Church of Christ, a Catholic church which was still standing although the roof had gone and the interior blown to pieces.

There are several visions that will always remain with me from my walk around Hiroshima, one of them being the Catholic church which was being rebuilt by volunteers from the congregation. Other images are the Chinese Marble Lions at the Hall of Victorious Return and the Shinto Shrine with its Torii painted white with two Kuma-Inu guardian dogs.

I left Hiroshima that afternoon to return to Bofu with a strong feeling that I would never see the place again. I tried to forget, looking forward to a happier New Year 1948 experience. Every Christmas time, however, my mind wanders back to Hiroshima and reminds me of the conflict which was resolved with devastating results which ultimately only went to prove what I have always held, that warfare is a huge waste of resources, both in human terms as well as material.

We are, after all, part of the same human family on this planet.

CHAPTER FORTY SEVEN.

After Christmas 1947, the whole station had been stood down for four days which meant no flying and therefore, no aircraft requiring servicing or maintenance. We were free to do as we pleased within the bounds of daily orders. For most of us it was a round of showers, breakfast, 'spine-bashing', book reading and lunch etc.

Life went along very nicely, thank you, when, on Sunday 28th I was again doing my fair share of spine bashing. Suddenly the air was shattered by the sound of fast approaching Packard Merlin engines. This could only mean one thing; American Mustangs were in the air!

I swung my legs off the bed and raced to the outside balcony carrying my trusty field glasses. In retrospect, I thought this was peculiar as I would normally reach for my camera however, I stood on the balcony and watched as the two Mustangs flew overhead at about 100 feet altitude.

Both pilots seemed to be enjoying the thrill of low-level beat-up of our station, flying wing to wing and very fast. The Mustangs climbed away over the little village of Naganoseki and banked to the left, sweeping back over our airstrip.

As they approached they changed their formation to line astern with the second aircraft slightly above the tail of the leader but very close. Then, for some inexplicable reason, the propellor of the second Mustang chopped into the tail of the lead aircraft.

Immediately the lead Mustang began to lose height and headed for a low hill where we heard the distinct sound of impact.

The second Mustang pitched upward on contact, perhaps the pilot was attempting to gain height sufficient to bail out but, it too went over the same hill toward the sea and disappeared. The dread sound of the second impact was heard around the station.

I heard somebody yell, "Let's see if we can help the pilots! They may have survived."

Several men set off at a run toward the last sighting of the doomed aircraft, not realising that it was about five miles from our barracks. We just kept on running with one thought in mind — to attempt a rescue.

We found one Mustang at the end of a deep groove in the earth which commenced near the top of the hill and finished some 400 yards at the bottom. The canopy was missing which indicated that the pilot had, in fact bailed out. We scrambled down to the wreckage and saw the cockpit was empty.

About 200 yards further away we then spotted the white silk of the parachute canopy. We ran toward this hoping that we would find the pilot at least alive. Luck had run out for the poor fellow. His body was very badly damaged, there was no pulse. We drew the silk canopy over his body and looked for the other plane.

"In the drink!" someone muttered.

We looked toward the sea where a long oil slick could be seen winding its way back from a point half a mile away. No sign of the aircraft. We knew he would not have survived.

This event put a dampener on our resumption of relaxed living however, walking back toward the base, I remembered seeing something out of character with the terrain as we had run down the slope toward the crash site.

I didn't realise what it was until I actually found the evidence I sought. There, shining like a fatal beacon in the freshly turned soil of the first contact was the clear glass fragment of what turned out to be a quart bottle of whisky, its label still partly intact.

"Holy cow, fellers. Look at this." I called to my mates. "If the crash investigators hear about this, these blokes will have their reputations shot to Hell."

"Yeah, but their wives will get bugger-all from the USAAF!" called someone else.

"Good God, we'd better find the rest of the damn bottle and hide it before the team from Hiroshima gets wind of it."

For several minutes we scoured the region and managed to find most pieces of the damning evidence which we squirrelled away from official sight. This would, hopefully, keep the pilots' records above reproach and give their widows their full pension and other benefits. A sad ending to what probably started off as a day of boyish fun.

To make matters even worse, we discovered when we returned to the station that the wives of the men had been watching the fly-past as the pilots were the Commanding Officer of a USAAF Fighter Squadron and his 2IC. They had been invited over to 81 Fighter Wing, Bofu for seasonal celebrations. That day must have been the most dreadful experience of their time in Japan for the wives, now widows.

At the subsequent inquest into this tragedy we were asked to provide written statements which we all did. Nobody ever mentioned the deadly whisky bottle and a finding of accidental death was duly passed down. This suited us just fine.

We returned to work on Monday 29th December but we still had a couple of problems to solve which had been plaguing the proper servicing of aircraft at Bofu, namely sufficient hard-stands both inside the hangars and outside. It was particularly difficult to work in winter with snow, ice, rain and chilly winds almost every day. Working in those conditions was no fun at all!

Some fellows who had volunteered for service in Japan were finding the conditions too much to bear and were opting for transfer back to Australia, leaving the whole contingent short of staff.

To make things even more interesting especially for the officers was the fact that I was due to return to Australia in January 1948 which would have left a deficit in the supervisory staff. With ground staff leaving in droves, the workload for those remaining was, needless to say, increased tenfold.

Another factor which made our position less tenable and increased our workload was the reduction of the Royal Air Force presence in Japan. This was due to the poor state of the British economy of the day forcing a withdrawl of their groundstaff and aircraft.

They were scheduled to join a combined fly-past of BCOF aircraft on 26th January to mark the end of the British force however, when they withdrew their Spitfires from the pattern of the fly-past, it was up to 81 Fighter Wing to provide extra Mustangs to form the aerial letters of the B-C-O-F which was the order of the day.

My movement orders had come through which made me very happy to know that it was just a matter of time before I was sitting on a transport aircraft heading out of Bofu for Melbourne again. The date I was given was 30th January 1948.

This news also brought with it mixed emotions; happy to be going home on a 3 day trip in a Lancaster bomber converted to civil livery by QANTAS but sad to be leaving some very good mates and the only home I'd known for the past 2 years or so.

I sat on my bed and reflected on my life in service so far. Four years from the age of 17, I had seen things a teenager should not have had to witness. The destruction of Hiroshima, death to some friends and others, it had certainly had an effect on my psyche.

And the question still posed in my head; what will I do when I return to 'civvy street' as it's known in the RAAF? This remained to be seen although I couldn't help feeling a bit apprehensive.

As it turned out, I was given more time than I bargained for to consider my future as, every time I went to board the aircraft taking men back to Australia from Japan, another man was placed on board in my stead. It happened that these fellows had been prisoners of the Japs in Japan. I had absolutely no regrets giving up my seat to them as I knew well how they had been mistreated during their incarceration.

At every chance I had to board the Lancaster transport I took a good look around at the interior of this giant of the skies. Unlike the C47's in which I'd previously flown, the Lancastrian as it was now called, being in civilian livery, was a lot more comfy-looking than the Dakota. No more seats of steel tubing with canvas sling-over running the length of the sides. This time we got to sit in real lounge chairs although the port holes were too high to see through being above head height when seated. To see the view, one had to stand up.

The big bonus with travelling in this aircraft was the fact of the folding bunks which had been installed above the seats against the outer skin. These would prove to be very welcome on the longer legs of the trip.

Heating was standard — non-existent and sound-proofing the same. Thus passengers were given two woollen blankets to wrap up in and a pair of headphones which acted as earmuffs to block out the drone of the four supercharged Rolls Royce Merlins out there driving the aircraft along at 260 plus miles an hour.

After several false starts, I was enjoying a quiet 'bludge' at the 'bludge hut' when my good friend, Sergeant Potter put his head in the door and said, "Gerry, good news and bad. Which one first?"

"OK, Pottsy, give me the bad news, please, and make it good."

"You've drawn guard duty tomorrow night. 5 o'clock at the guard room. Now, the good news is, you've got a confirmed seat going out on the 'Lanc' Friday 20th. Report to Dispatch Movement Office with your gear on Thursday. OK?" He grinned warmly at my startled look.

"Wow! Thanks Pottsy. Guard duty — a doddle! Going home even better but, I'll believe that when I'm at 10,000 feet watching Kyushu disappear below."

On the evening of 17th I reported to the guard room and was kitted up warmly for my 2 hour shift. Winter uniform over which I layered a scarf and woollen balaclava with two peepholes for eyes plus the heavy greatcoat. On the hands, silk gloves plus woolen gloves with the trigger finger showing through a slot in both. Two pairs of socks and gumboots on the feet and I was ready to face the dark.

I was issued with five rounds of .303 ammunition which I loaded into the magazine plus a 6 battery hand torch which shone a ferocious beam up to 50 yards. My beat was to be the transport section where fuel might be pilfered, the laundry where we expected the locals might access the soaps we used for their own enterprises and the wood pile where building materials had been going missing.

My first shift from 8:00pm to 10:00pm went without incident. I returned to the guardroom and had a cup of tea and lay down to sleep until I had my next round to do from 2:00am to 4:00am.

At 1:30am I was woken and dressed again like a fat wombat to go out into the snow. Thus attired, I walked out again into temperatures well below zero. Snow was coming down heavily and the going was pretty tough in gumboots as the frozen slush built up underfoot.

Moving between the transport office and the wood pile I stopped a couple of times when I thought I heard a scraping sound. I took my rifle off the shoulder and loaded a round into the breech. I called out "Halt, who goes there?"

There was no reply so I called out in Japanese, "Oyake ni yare!" Still there was no response. Again I heard the noise.

"Halt or I'll fire!" These were the only warnings necessary. I then spoke in Japanese again adding more warning — "Oyake ni yare, Yuyo ni nasai!"

This was — Come out in the open, do as I say!

Again there was no response so I fired toward the source of the scraping noise. Five rounds one after the other went left and right, cutting the air like a very sharp knife. When the echoes died away I listened again. Nothing!

Now I was without ammunition so I backed up to the fence, drew my bayonet and fixed it to the rifle in the approved manner for close combat.

In one minute flat, the guardroom jeep was coming around the corner of the laundry at speed. The Corporal of the Guard leapt from the vehicle and enquired what was going on. I told him of my concern so he gave me another 5 bullets which I loaded. He used his own flashlight to shine around the wood pile but saw nothing untoward.

"See me in the morning, Walshe."

After finishing my shift at 4:00am I went back to the barracks but didn't go to sleep. I kept worrying about what I might have shot. At first light I returned to the wood pile with the Corporal and together we scoured the area for signs.

There was no body but we did see a pool of fresh blood and a trail of red spots leading away from the scene. We followed the trail to the bridge over the creek where it stopped.

"Cold water could have stemmed the flow," offered the Corporal. I agreed. We never found a victim with bullet holes in the village.

I made out my report and the case was closed. On the other hand, it was a most disturbing episode in my life in Japan. I kept thinking it may have been just a young boy or a girl that I'd shot. I thought of Miyoko and shuddered.

When I returned to work that morning I made the mistake of mentioning the incident to some workmates. Their response seemed quite cold and callous.

"Don't you worry about that, Gerry," they said. "It's probably just another 'Nip', one of many. They won't be missed!"

That worried me even more; their cynical attitude to the defeated foe. This was not what I wished to hear. I needed to speak with someone about my own feelings but, alas, there was nobody I could turn to.

I kept wondering — just how much of this life can I take before I go nuts? I seem to have had my fair share of dramas in my 20 years. Perhaps I am just feeling sorry for myself. This could be the first sign.

I tried to put the incident out of my mind. On Thursday I reported to the Transport Movements Office and picked up my papers, dropped off my worldly possessions in two kitbags and fronted up to the Salvation Army canteen for a hot cuppa. There I met three other airmen with whom I'd be travelling back to Australia.

The subject arose between them of the issue of 2 blankets per passenger. I did the right thing and explained to them the reason, that at 10,000 feet the air is damned cold and two blankets might just be enough to keep a person warm.

"Even flying in the tropics, at that height the air is quite chilly." I said.

I returned to my barracks. There was a standing invitation to a farewell drinking session at the beer hall which I declined, as I knew well how it would end and I could do without another throbber for tomorrow's flight out.

I awoke early and ate breakfast, my last in Japan, then back to the barracks hut where I picked up my travel bag and headed for the Movements Office. As I stepped out the main door of the barracks I almost tripped over the slumbering form of 'Cordite' the Base mascot dog of 76 Squadron.

He had been at the beer hall the night before and had had a few beers as was his wont. That morning he looked a bit worse for wear which is exactly what I was trying to avoid by not attending the drinking session.

I arrived at the departure point feeling excited and ready to go. All who were going were there; seven airmen and four army types plus four flight crew. We boarded the bus which took us to the Lancastrian out on the apron.

As we went, I took a last, nostalgic look around the base; past the squash courts where I learned to play the game I'd never heard of, over the moat and up the gravel road to the airstrip. As we passed all the buildings it seemed to me that I was seeing them for the first time as I'd previously taken it all for granted.

We drove through snow drifts and along rows of Mustangs parked left and right of the track. I fondly gazed at A68-703 and A68-720, two Mustangs I'd worked on recently. I said farewell to them under my breath. Both these aircraft were destined to fly in the Korean war some years later.

The little bus came to a stop near the door on the 'Lanc' and the loadmaster stepped out with a notebook in hand. He read from a list of names and, as names were called, passengers boarded the aircraft. Being the fourth person called, I was shown to seat 4 which was close to the door. This suited me in case we had to ditch in the drink. I would be first out!

The flight crew did their preflight checks while the ground crew cleaned the snow from the wings and tailplanes. With all this done, the crew hopped aboard and went forward to the flight deck. The passengers wrapped up in blankets and the engines began their start-up routine.

Presently, with all engines purring nicely, the brakes were released and the big 'Lanc' began to roll forward to the edge of the strip where the engines were run up to full revs.

We turned onto the strip and waited for the green Aldis lamp from the tower. There she went! The pilot opened up the 'taps' and the aircraft commenced rolling down the strip, gathering speed, lifting the tail and suddenly, the ground was falling away.

We were on our way back to Australia via Okinawa, Philippines, Darwin. Oh, what a feeling!

CHAPTER FORTY EIGHT.

Once we were airborne the aircraft turned left and headed out over the Inland Sea where countless small fishing families made a good living catching the inhabitants of those waters.

I rose from my seat to view the last piece of the Japanese mainland slip away below. The southern tip of Kyushu Island disappeared without so much as a whimper. I felt I was really on my way, now.

I had been introduced to the navigator before leaving Bofu and I had made mention of my interest in learning navigation when I applied to join the RAAF. He gave me a map to follow as we completed various legs of the trip.

I was, therefore, able to identify certain points of interest as we over-flew them. Before we left Kyushu I gazed down on the area where I had found the young mother and her baby strapped to her back after the typhoon. The memory of this event brought tears to my eyes.

Cruising at 8,000 feet we had settled onto our flight level and the navigator, Eric Richards came back to ask the passengers if we would like a cup of tea. All agreed and he obliged with several steaming cups from the tiny galley just behind the flight deck. At that altitude it was most welcome.

Eric also invited me to see the layout of the navigator's table which sat on the port side of the aircraft just behind the pilot. He gave me a few pointers in basic navigation and referred me to his charts, pointing out several places of interest as we flew.

Flying over a series of tiny islands he mentioned that the spots visible above the surface of the East China Sea were actually the peaks of submarine mountains in a chain which extended from Japan to Indonesia. The mountain chain was named by the Japanese Ryuku Retto or 'arch'.

To enhance our communication while taking a navigation lesson from Eric, we both wore headsets of earphones and microphone so that shouting at each other was unnecessary. I also discovered that, in order not to be encumbered with blankets and stuff, the aircrew had small heaters installed at their feet.

I did learn a lot during the hour or so I spent at the navigator's table. Use of the sextant, slide rule and compass headings, all part of the game in this part of the aircraft.

"Look out the right side of the aircraft, Gerry. That smudge you see on the horizon is Formosa Island, just off the coast of China. Now, in 10 minutes time, I will have to report our position to Radio Naha, USAAF Airbase at Okinawa.

"If you go and look straight out the front windows, you'll see Okinawa dead ahead." Our Lancastrian was right on track.

Eric called up the tower at Naha and requested permission to over-fly the island. The tower came back with permission granted. It took us about ten minutes to fly from one end to the other of this most important Pacific Ocean island. I made note of the many atolls sprinkled around the main island and the numerous airfields which could be easily seen from our position.

We reported leaving the Naha control zone as we flew past the ten mile position south and the tower wished us 'good flying'. The vista became nothing but water so I decided to retire to my bunk and get a bit of 'shut-eye'. When I opened the capsule containing the bunk I was pleasantly surprised to find another two blankets which would ensure I was warm enough.

I awoke about 3 hours later having slept soundly and warmly. I climbed down from my nest and peeked out the porthole. All I could see was sky, sun, sea and a few grey scattered clouds plus a great expanse of the 'drink'. I listened carefully to the syncopation of the engines but found nothing in their tune to worry about.

I noticed that the air seemed colder now. The reason was we were at 12,000 feet in order to clear the razor sharp mountains of Luzon Island which rose to over 8,000 feet just north of our destination at Clark Field. Eric pointed out that we would cross the northern coast of Luzon in 10 minutes at Escarparda Point. That would be one hour from touch down at Clark Field.

I looked out the porthole again ten minutes later to see we were flying into rain. I hoped that this was not going to herald a typhoon as it was now the season. We crossed the coast as predicted and I gazed down on the watery plain of northern Luzon with the Cayayan River running through it. This watercourse was also known as the Amazon of Luzon.

The scenery below was fascinating to see all the rice paddies flooded and various shades of green beginning to show as the crop grew. There was no sign visible of housing although I knew the farmers would be close by somewhere.

We presently ran into some turbulence as we had reached the mountains north of Clark Field. My mind could only think of three topics now; one, that it was damned cold where we were, two, that when we landed it would be steamy and hot and three, we had not eaten since leaving Japan apart from bread and butter sandwiches and coffee or tea and biscuits.

I was snapped back from my reverie when I detected a change in the tone of the engines as we were now descending to join the circuit at Clark Field. I looked through the porthole and saw the airfield coming up fast. I sat back in my seat and applied the seatbelt. I even imagined I could smell hamburgers cooking!

We joined the right hand circuit and, although it was raining, we made a gentle landing and rolled to a stop near the tower where we would be found V.I.P. accommodation. The engines shut down and the door swung open. Immediately I wanted to strip off most of my clothing as the atmosphere of Clark Field rushed in, hot and humid.

I managed to rip off my battle jacket and jumper but was stuck with my long-johns and two pairs of woolly socks. Best to get to our digs and get changed into something summery.

Before my mind could jump back to the subject of food, a truck pulled up with two white-helmeted Military Policemen who asked us to join them at the Sergeants' mess for afternoon tea. We agreed readily and were taken to a spacious room where we indulged in a fantasy of waffles and honey topped with fried crisp bacon washed down with buckets of real coffee and cream — real cream!

We ate our fill. The whole afternoon's parade of food was most memorable. In fact I still drool at the thought.

As it was getting late in the day we were then invited to join the rest of the personnel on the parade ground to witness the Sunset Gun ceremony, a most solemn part of the American way of Military life.

We got back into the truck to be driven to the parade ground as we were not permitted to walk anywhere on account of the Huk Communist guerillas still taking the odd pot-shot through the fence at people here.

The parade ground had three squadrons of USAAF troops on

parade duty for the ceremony. They marched past and halted next to the flagpole where the field gun was also situated. A Military Policeman stood beside the gun watching the sun as it sank behind the horizon, ready to fire the shot.

BAM! The sun had disappeared and the flag was now lowered with due care to be folded and taken away for safe keeping until 'reveille' the next day. The band struck up and the troops marched off leaving us standing there. Then the rain came down again sending us back to the truck.

The M.P's took us back to our billet and said they would take us to dinner later. That gave us time to have a shower and shave. We were informed that a dance was to be held as it was Friday night and some girls were being brought into the camp from town. I declined on that offer but said that I would rather visit their P.X. Canteen where I knew there were items which I really wanted to buy.

One special item was a furlined bomber jacket which, when I was passing through here previously, were selling for only $30.00 U.S. Since I didn't have U.S. dollars beforehand, I had managed to scrounge about $40.00 during my term in Japan. So, now I had enough to make that purchase which would serve me well during the rest of my flight home.

Besides the jacket I also bought a slab of Red Hen Beer. This was the first time I'd seen beer in steel cans rather than brown 'long-neck' glass bottles. To go with the beer I bought some salty crackers which would go round the Lancastrian for all.

After a light breakfast of flap-jacks, maple syrup and ice cream washed down with strong black coffee, we thanked our hosts for their hospitality and boarded the aircraft. It was raining again and I was wearing my new fleecy jacket. The sweat was streaming out of every pore but, Gee Whiz, I looked great and felt great!

The aircrew had done their ground checks and the engines kicked over amid clouds of blue smoke. The door was slammed shut and the brakes released. We rolled slowly to a position near the end of the runway while the engines were run up to peak revs. Then, all checks finished, we got the green Aldis lamp from the tower and we rolled onto the runway, gathering speed. The tail lifted and soon we were again winging our way through the low cloud.

At 2,000 feet the aircraft levelled out and this gave us a good view of the ground. It looked a bit like a huge duck pond with water everywhere. In the distance I could see the city of Manila with the

River Pasig wandering through the crowded buildings where millions of people went about their daily lives.

Further out toward the foothills lay the villas of the wealthy landowners partly hidden among lush gardens and trees. The indescriminating rain fell everywhere.

The aircraft began a turn to the left and Manila Bay came into view. With another turn to the right, we got a better view of one of the best anchorages in the world with the island of Corrigidor smack in the middle of the entrance. It shocked me to see the number of rusting hulks drawn up on the beaches and in the deeper water. This, however, didn't deter the locals from using them as fishing platforms.

The cabin temperature began to drop and I realised that we were on our way to 10,000 feet again. Time to rug-up!

We broke through the cloud cover and the sun looked quite out of place after the gloom of ground level weather. I decided to break the expected monotony of the long flight ahead and I asked our navigator if I could join him at the chart table again. He said he would be glad of the company.

Together we checked the altimeter, airspeed indicator and plotted our course on the relevant chart. I was amazed at the way in which all this was achieved as all I could see outside was cloud. Eric assured me it was by deduced reckoning, something that all aviators had to practice to be sure of their position.

We broke cover and I was able to see for miles ahead; Mindoro Island passed by and we were approaching Mindanao with Panay on the starboard side. Dead ahead was Cebu and Bohol Islands with Leyte Island on the port side then beyond that Mindanao Sea.

As we passed over Cebu Island with Cebu town in view, Eric offered a piece of history that I had not heard before concerning the explorer Magellan.

"You must have heard of Ferdinand Magellan, Gerry?"

"Oh yes," I agreed, "But not a lot beyond the straits named in his honour."

"True, but he did a lot more than discover the route past Cape Horn. He found the way to the East Indies by sailing west which Christopher Columbus missed and, in so-doing, he named the Pacific Ocean. By right of discovery, the islands that comprise the Philippines remained in Spanish hands until 1898. It was at the town of Cebu that Magellan raised the cross of Jesus Christ, the first one in East Asia, 24 years before Francis Xavier arrived here."

I was intrigued.

"In fact, it was the 'Vittoria', Magellan's ship which was the first to actually circumnavigate the globe, proving that the world was round — not flat! However, he didn't live to enjoy the accolades and rewards. He was killed by the natives of Mactan Island near Cebu in 1521. Today, a monument stands in Cebu town to mark his passing. It's just a simple stone cross."

I was amazed. Having never heard the full story before it made me rethink what I knew about history.

Long after we'd passed the last of the Philippine Islands, Eric worked his magic again at the tea making and brought everyone a nice cup of tea. As the only foodstuff aboard was bread and butter, we fell upon it like starving children knowing well that the next stop would be Darwin, a few hours away.

One of the highlights of this trip was the skipper who came back from the flight deck bearing certificates which declared that each one had crossed the Equator. This was received with great good cheer from all aboard. I thought that this would be a good excuse to break out the Red Hen Beer which was roundly applauded by all.

With a couple of beers under my belt I felt a bit sleepy and decided to curl up and pass the time in Slumberland. I was woken some time later with the aircraft being shaken by turbulence as we crossed the northern shore of Dutch New Guinea. Looking out the porthole, I could see storm clouds massing in the distance. The day was fading fast and we were still miles from Darwin. I just hoped that Eric's skill at navigation was as good as his history.

My fears were totally unfounded. The revs of the engines soon indicated that we had begun descent into Darwin and soon we had joined the circuit area. The big plane touched down and we taxied toward the Customs building.

Having been caught once before by the 'Great Aussie Surprise', I covered my head with a blanket before the door opened and a cannister of smoking gas was flung unceremoniously into the cabin. The novices to this practice coughed and spluttered for a few moments until the door was re-opened and they fell out onto the pavement.

"OK, youse blokes. You can come out now!" called a voice through the fog of disinfectant haze. "Welcome to Darwin!"

CHAPTER FORTY NINE.

Arriving at Darwin at 7:30pm reminded me that I was now quite hungry having eaten breakfast at 7:00am with only cups of tea or coffee plus bread and butter sandwiches en route from Clark Field, Philippine Islands. After we cleared Customs we were taken to the RAAF mess for tea. For me it was a large T-bone steak and vegies followed by fruit and custard with as much bread and butter as one could manage. All this was helped along with a huge enamel mug of strong Aussie tea. Just wonderful!

Before we left the mess we were issued with a 'poncho' each. This is the ground sheet which doubles as a 2 man tent when teamed with another 'poncho'. It also can be worn as a raincoat which was its purpose here as the tropic skies were pelting down at us as we walked to our small bus. The bus drove us back toward our Lancaster which was parked near a line-up of aircraft of many types and from various airlines.

I decided to take a stroll along the line. The aircraft included C47's, a C54 Skymaster with 4 engines and tri-cycle undercarriage and a De Havilland D86 pre-war 8 passenger fabric-covered aeroplane which did the run to Singapore and Malaya. QANTAS aircraft were in evidence with two Lancs and a new sleek silvery item which had the look of a greyhound ready to race. We learned that this was the new Lockheed Constellation which carried an enormous number of 59 passengers! Unbelievable! Where will it end?

Now, I was feeling replete and relaxed and looking forward to a good night's rest. I walked back into the main reception building and was met by the flight crew coming out with their bags.

"Back on board, Gerry! We're off to Sydney." The skipper smiled and ruffled my hair as he passed.

"But we just got here, skipper!" I protested.

237

My protestations met with nil response so, all who were going south climbed back aboard the Lancaster for immediate take-off. It was midnight Saturday/Sunday 7th — 8th February 1948 and we had already been flying for some 12 or 13 hours from the Philippines.

'At least we'll get some sleep on board' I thought to myself.

The engines started up one after the other, belching blue smoke and spitting flames out the 6 exhaust ports either side of each nacelle, easily seen in the dark. The chocks were removed, brakes released and we rolled forward toward the runway.

The engines were run up to full revs and the magnetos checked individually while the entire aircraft shook like a spaniel out of the water. Then the noise died down and we turned onto the 10,000 yard runway to line up between the lights which seemed to stretch into infinity.

The pilot got the green flash of the Aldis lamp from the tower and opened the 'taps' causing the huge aeroplane to leap toward the end of the runway. The tail came up and again we were airborne, turning southward into the night sky.

We climbed to about 8,000 feet and I made my way forward to sit with my friend Eric the nav. Together we pored over charts of the Australian landscape where he had already drawn his track. Above the drone of the four Merlin engines I could hear somebody snoring. Looking around, I discovered it was the relief pilot Rodney McAlpine already spine-bashing his way to Sydney, oblivious to the noise surrounding him but, in spite of that, his snoring could be heard above it all. I had to giggle.

Flying over the Katherine River aerodrome construction site, Eric pointed out the flashing yellow lights of the machinery working below, a truly fascinating vision from that altitude. He was pleased to announce that we were right on track for Sydney.

My eyes were getting quite bleary at that stage of the night and I excused myself from Eric and returned to my seat, wrapped the blankets round myself and went to sleep, lulled by the monotony of the old reliable Rolls Royce engines, churning away just outside the skin of this retired warbird.

By the time I awoke, we had passed the Diamantina country, the Barkly Tablelands and the Great Australian Basin. I took a peek out the nearest porthole only to be greeted with a vista of brown, flat, sunburnt country. Looking back over the tailplane I could just make out a large town which, I was informed, was Bourke.

I looked at my watch. It was 8:00am on Sunday morning. It would take us another 2 hours to reach Sydney. The trip from Japan had seen me encased inside this machine for a total of 32 hours flying time. I would not be unhappy to step out onto terra firma in Sydney.

Coming over the Blue Mountains west of Sydney the tone of the four engines was reduced to a low hum as we began our slow descent toward Mascot Aerodrome. Sydney Harbour shone brightly before us and, after a circuit of this fabulous spectacle and passing low over the old 'coat-hanger', we turned out to sea for an approach to Sydney's airport at Mascot.

We joined the circuit pattern over the suburbs and prepared to touchdown on one of the sealed runways. As we let down the undercarriage, I was surprised to see a rail line cutting across the runway which we were headed for. This was the old line which took coal to Bunerong Power Station. Luckily, the train didn't run on Sundays.

The aircraft touched down quite lightly and rolled off the runway to the apron in front of QANTAS terminal building. The door opened and out we stepped into the blazing summer sunlight of a Sydney Sunday. The metal exhaust ports of the big Merlins crackled and popped as they cooled down after their long run from Darwin which reminded me of the great technology we had relied on to get here.

Everybody was out of the Lancaster and we said a round of 'good-byes' to each other. The other two airmen with me decided to get a lift into the city with an Air Force truck to get a bed for the night at Air Force House in Liverpool Street. We would get the train to Melbourne the next day.

There wasn't much sleep that night at Air Force House as it was dance night being a Sunday. The trams rattling past in George Street also added to our discomfort. Having spent the past 2 years in a rural setting in Japan, I wasn't used to the buzz of big city life.

The next day was a lovely sunny day and we decided to take a stroll around the city. Soon after setting out it became clear to me that this was a huge mistake as, everywhere I went, there were reminders of Dawn, my late-departed love. I hastened to Central Station to the R.T.O. to pick up our travel passes for the night train to Melbourne. Even this was traumatic as I had to pass the very platform where I had last kissed my Dawn goodbye.

At 8:00pm I found myself sitting in a 'dog-box' carriage on a train to Albury and then, on to Melbourne to the prospect of starting my life again as a 'civvy'. A frightening thought.

After an uncomfortable journey in both the NSW train to Albury and VicRail train to Melbourne, we got out at Spencer Street where the other chaps had friends and relatives to meet them. My 'rels' were nowhere to be seen!

We rode in a RAAF truck to Laverton Base where we were given a leave pass for 6 weeks. After that we would return to Laverton for formal discharge from the Service.

From Laverton I made my way back to Black Rock where I hoped to be united with my loving family. I was certainly looking forward to the money which had been sent back for safe-keeping to Verna, my white mother. The amount in the bank account would be sufficient to either launch me into my own business with a garage like the one in which I'd done my apprenticeship or even to buy a house in the suburbs and settle down. This was an exciting thought.

I expected the money, held by Mum in trust for me, would amount to about 540 pounds; in today's money, about $100,000.

It was late in the day when I finally arrived at the house at Black Rock. I walked to the back door rather than knock on the front door and I found Verna in the kitchen preparing a meal. She looked up and dropped her wooden spoon on the floor in shock.

"Oh, goodness Gerald. We didn't expect you 'til Friday. How come you're here early. I'd arranged for someone to meet you in Melbourne on Friday."

I dropped my bag expecting to at least get a hug or a small peck. Even 'Hello!' Nothing!

"Who, Mum? Who did you arrange to meet me?" For some reason I decided to challenge her.

She looked down at the stove and smoothed her hands on the apron.

"Oh, I hadn't yet decided," she answered, "But, I would have found someone. But that doesn't matter now, does it? Now that you're here."

She stooped down to retrieve the wooden spoon, probably glad of the excuse not to eyeball me.

Just then her husband, Syd came through the door. He shook my hand.

"Hello Gerald. Did you have a good trip back?"

"Yes, I did." I answered, feeling like a lilly on a dirt can.

I ate dinner with the two of them. There was an awkward conversation of sorts but certainly nothing very warm or friendly.

After dinner we sat about in the lounge room but neither Verna or Syd seemed to be interested in hearing about my adventures overseas. I was very aware that neither of these two had smiled at me. I was obviously an inconvenience here.

However, they did speak about how well my sister Joyce was doing with her husband Melvin at the guest house they had up at Mount Macedon. They had a little girl called Irene and worked as managers for the owners.

"You must go up there and see them, Gerald," my mother urged.

"What about Bonnie?" I asked. "I hear she has a daughter too, Lorraine,..."

"Ohh, we don't talk much about them, Gerald. Gran hasn't spoken to her since she had to marry that US marine soldier. He gave her a baby out of wedlock, you know!"

"But, Mum, she is your own daughter for God's sake!"

I was irritated that my mean-spirited grandmother still ruled this family with an iron, uncompromising fist.

"Look, Gran won't speak to her and I don't dare go against Gran, Gerald."

Fortunately, the conversation didn't last long that night. I was sleepy after my long trip home and I made my way to bed. The train trip had exhausted me and I needed a good long rest. The next morning I decided I would spend the next 6 weeks of leave travelling around Victoria seeing some old mates — anywhere away from here!

Before this could happen I needed to access the funds I'd had sent home for Mum to mind in our joint bank account. Over breakfast the next day, I asked her about the bank account. She looked back at me, shocked.

"Well, you see, I don't have the book here. It's down at the bank. There was some problem which they are looking into."

I suspected that this was not right. I began to smell a very dirty rat here.

"OK, Mum, you and I can go to the bank together and get the book back this morning."

She went a deathly shade of white.

"No, Gerald honey. I can't go. I have to work today."

I shrugged. "Well, I'll go by myself. You just write a note authorising me to go alone and I can show them my papers to prove my identity."

"Well, I don't know about that either, Gerald." she replied.

My senses were now on 'red-alert'. Something was dreadfully

241

wrong here and I meant to find out what it was.

I rose from my chair at the breakfast table and stared into her eyes.

"Mum, I know now that you are lying so, stop lying to me. Where is the damn bank book? I want it now. Go and fetch it for me!"

Verna took off her apron and went to her bedroom. She returned shortly after with the bank book and handed it to me. Now it was my turn to be shocked.

When I turned to the last entry page I found, instead of the expected 540 plus pounds, a balance of just 4 pounds! It was all gone. I had to sit down. I was consumed with anger. I felt sick and close to throwing up.

How the hell could this have happened? Then I remembered something that Yurana had said to me long ago. She had held me close against her breast and said, 'Remember, Nabby, the only person you can really trust in this life is your mother.' No, Yurana, not this mother — Not Verna!

"So, what have you done with the money, Mum? How could you have spent over 500 pounds of my money and not bother to tell me?"

"Well, times were tough here during the war. We had to live, you know."

This woman didn't seem to understand that what she'd done was wrong as she attempted to justify the theft.

"Mum, that I can understand. But, what about from August 1945 to February 1948? There was no bloody war on then, was there? For God's sake, you have blown the cash that I was counting on to begin a new life back in civvy street. I really should have known better than to put the fox in charge of the bloody hen-house! I trusted you again and now you've betrayed my trust."

I could feel my blood pressure mounting so I cut the conversation and went back to pack my things, collect the stuff that I'd posted back regularly from Japan and clear off. I opened the cupboard where all my souvenirs and other items had been stored and found — NOTHING! She stood behind me whimpering, wringing her hands but never an apology for her actions.

She must have realised that what she'd done was illegal and she possibly feared that I would call the police to investigate the theft.

Verna's explanation for that was that the house had been burgled some months prior and everything in that particular cupboard had disappeared and she was too frightened to tell me.

I left the house in a dreadful rage. I had never felt so angry. After all the dramas in my short life so far, I wondered if this was going to be the one thing to actually push me over the edge. I needed to calm down and not allow this to happen as the one thing I had left was my sanity. I clung to this at all costs.

I found myself standing alone on the street with nowhere to go. It was now most important to find somewhere to stay as I could never go back there. I knew I could so easily commit murder. As I walked along the street I thought of my sister-in-law, Marge, married to David, who also lived at Black Rock.

I knocked on her door and she invited me in. We sat and had a cup of tea while I related the morning's events to her.

"Gerald, where will you stay? I have a spare room here, you know. You are most welcome to kip here with us. I could do with the company as Dave is away at present and Tricia and I are here by ourselves."

'Thank you, Marge, but I have to warn you, the rest of the family won't like you giving me somewhere to stay." I could not prevent the bitterness of my voice showing.

She smiled and patted my hand.

"Gerald, that is the least of my worries. You see, when David married me, Gran couldn't cope with a person from another Church in the family and we haven't spoken since. Of course, at the time I was also pregnant with Tricia which fact also put Gran's nose right out of joint. So, you see, helping you in this way will not affect my standing in that queer family in any way. You know, they're all mad — except you and me, naturally!" She winked and immediately put me at ease. I found that I was breathing normally again.

I could sense that here, I had a friend in my hour of need.

Later that day I went round to see another friend of mine, John Brosnan. When I arrived at his house, I was surprised to see 3 motor cycles in the driveway. I knocked at the door and his mother opened it to me.

"Hello Gerald!" she cried. "How lovely to see you home at last. Come on in." She threw her arms around my neck and kissed me in very motherly fashion, a contrast from the reception I got from Verna. I followed her into the sitting room where I found John as well as another two mates from school, Brian Angus and Peter Shaw. We spent the afternoon talking and swapping yarns as we hadn't seen each other for many years. It was just like old times again. I enjoyed their company and conversation.

Eventually I got the chat around to the motorbikes in the driveway.

"Geez, Gerry, get down to the dealer in Melbourne. They've got hundreds of ex-Army bikes there. Harley Davidsons and Indians as well as the Pom's BSA's. You must get one yourself, then there's no more transport worries. Go anywhere — any time!"

I saw a light go on in my head. Yes, that was the answer, I could be free to travel wherever I like on a bike!

"John, what are you doing tomorrow?" I asked.

"Nothing much, why?"

"I'd like to buy one of those bikes. But first I'll have to get over to Laverton to draw some cash from my paybook. How do I get a licence to ride?"

"On Friday we can go up to the Police Station and get one organised for you. It's quite easy."

The next day we did just that. I got the cash from the RAAF pay master and bought myself a 1942 WLA series Harley Davidson, ex-Military Police motor cycle. It even had a fitted windscreen, lights all over the front and crash bars back and front. What a magnificent machine!

I rode back to Marge's place to show her my new acquisition. When I arrived she had some news for me.

"Your mother rang me and told me that when she told Joyce that you were home again, Joyce said you should visit her at the guest house up at Mount Macedon for lunch on Sunday. How about that! This could be an 'olive branch' being held out."

I pondered the proposition a moment. Perhaps it was just to show me how far up the social ladder she'd come since we last met. I would go and let her gloat, if that was her game. There was no harm in that, after all, she was still family.

"Yes, Marge, I'll go, and thanks for the news."

I contacted my mates. Brian and Peter to see if they could make the trip with me on Sunday. Yes! They could. That was a bonus because Joyce would be just as surprised to see the other lads as I was to receive her invitation. I was allowing myself a moment of mischief.

Both Brian and Peter were her old boy-friends!

CHAPTER FIFTY.

Early on Sunday morning the three of us set off for Mount Macedon Guest House for lunch. As we passed through the small hamlet of Digger's Rest I had a really strange sensation overcome me. It was as though I'd been here before. I knew I hadn't so I dismissed the thought and continued on without any more consideration.

We arrived at Mount Macedon and took a good look around. The old place was built overlooking the valley below. It reminded me of some of the tranquil spots I'd visited in Asia. It was most relaxing atmosphere.

Joyce and Mel met us at the door. I shall never forget the startled look on Joyce's face when she saw the other lads with me however, she was very diplomatic and begged me to introduce them to Mel and herself.

Amused by this charade, I did so without hesitation. There was never a hint of recognition!

She showed us into the house and into the Manager's quarters which was a 2 bedroom apartment. Very nicely appointed for the era with polished wooden floors and heavy furnitures. We entered the bedroom and there, hanging on the wall behind the bed was a Japanese painting I immediately recognised as one I'd brought back from Japan in 1947.

"Oh, Gerald, I see you recognise the old painting there," she began. "Mum gave it to me some time ago. She said that you gave it to her."

I did not answer. The painting had been stolen from my cupboard by Verna. I always suspected that this was the case. Now I had proof!

We sat down to eat and, during the meal, I was to receive another monumental shock. I casually asked Joyce how they had landed such a great job, managing this magnificent guest house.

"You've never done this kind of work before, Joyce." I offered innocently.

"Oh, don't worry about that, Gerald. We had to buy the damn job. It cost us 350 pounds!"

"Gee, that's a huge sum. Where on earth did you get that kind of money from?" I asked, feeling the hair rise on the back of my neck.

"Well, Mum said she could give us the money as we only had 100 pounds at the time. I was quite surprised when Mum offered us the cash. I had no idea she had that kind of money. Did you, Gerald?"

I almost choked on my food. I swallowed hard and drank some water.

I looked directly at my sister and said, "Yes, Joyce, I did know that Verna had that kind of money. You see, it wasn't hers,... it was really mine! She was supposed to be holding it in trust for me in a joint bank account." I slammed down my knife and fork making Joyce jump.

"Oh, dear, I had no idea that was the case, Gerald. I did wonder how she came to have that amount of money. I am embarrassed. And, to make matters worse, at the moment I have no way of paying it back to you. I am sorry."

I picked up the utensils again and looked at Mel. His face was scarlet but he held his tongue. The other boys were silent.

"Joyce, don't worry about that," I said, "Mum has been lying and cheating all her damn life. I knew that, but I had to learn the hard way didn't I? Even her own family is not excluded from her ways of lying and cheating and now, stealing apparently!"

We finished the meal virtually in silence and rose from the table, eager to leave the place. My head was spinning with confused thoughts about what I could do to resolve this nasty situation.

The three of us got back on the bikes and rode off toward Black Rock again. We turned onto the Calder Highway at Digger's Rest toward Melbourne. I didn't see the Buick motor car that hit my motor cycle leaving me unconscious on the roadway. My mates told me later that the driver went off to call an ambulance but did not return to the scene of the collision.

He probably thought he had absolved himself of further involvement by such an act. We thought it quite callous.

I was taken to Melbourne Hospital by ambulance where the staff very kindly took excellent care of me. I had suffered several broken ribs, multiple cuts and bruises to my head, legs and arms. I remained unconscious for 24 hours.

When I finally awoke I could not focus my vision and I was unable to speak. I vaguely remember seeing blurred images of people in white coats moving around the bed. The effort of becoming lucid was overwhelming so I slipped back into a land of peaceful slumber.

The next time I opened my eyes it was dark and the lights in the room were on. Wonder of wonders! I could focus on the young girl standing at the foot of the bed, dressed in a starched white uniform with a dinky little white hat perched atop her head. She was writing on a clipboard, so intently that she didn't notice me staring at her at first. So, I raised my hand to wave.

"Sister! Oh,... Sister!," she called. "Our young motor cyclist is awake in bed number 3."

An older woman appeared dressed in a starched blue uniform with an enormous white veil on her head.

"Lovely to see you, Gerald." she said and took my wrist in her hand to test my pulse. "How do you feel today?"

I tried to speak. My mouth was dry and the words wouldn't form properly but eventually, I managed to mumble that I was very sore and I had a splitting headache.

"Well, that's to be expected," said the Sister, "After everything you've been through. I'm very pleased to see you back with us. Now you just lie back and rest. I shall inform the Doctor that you are awake."

I was in Melbourne Hospital for two days where the nursing staff were most kind and helpful. Of course, nobody from the family came to visit me. I wasn't surprised by this. My two mates, Brian and Peter, visited me and told me that they had taken care of the Harley bike. It was in a specialist garage awaiting repairs. Thank God for friends!

So, I was still being treated by the family as the pathetic white Aborigine!

The Doctor visited me on the second day to inform me that the injuries I'd sustained might lead to a mental condition that could affect my future.

"You had injuries to your legs and arms as well as the broken ribs but, the head injuries might result in a numbness to the right side of your face. This is because some of the nerves on that side have been damaged. That will not stop you from full recovery but be careful how you go. It's something you will have for the rest of your life."

I told the Doctor that I was a bit concerned about not having any visitors from the family.

"Have they been informed, Doctor?" I enquired.

"Oh, yes. Your friend John has let them know as they are your next of kin." He smiled down on me like a caring father. "We are going to discharge you from here tomorrow but, you won't be going home. We'll have you transferred to Laverton RAAF Hospital as you are still an airman. There you can effect a total recovery and then go home."

Oh, wonderful! I thought, Six weeks of leave and I have to spend at least half of it flat on my back.

I did my time at Laverton Hospital and finally made my way back to Madge's house.

"Nobody from the family bothered to come and visit me in hospital ," I complained.

"Well, Tricia was ill with tonsilitis and I couldn't get away," Madge pleaded. That did not excuse the others.

The Harley was duly repaired and John took me to the shop to see it returned. We walked into the showroom in Collins Street and I saw it straight away. I sat on the saddle and gripped the familiar handle-bars. It was at that moment that the words of the Doctor at Melbourne Hospital came flooding back to me.

"Your mind may have closed off this episode but small things will remind your brain of what has happened. The shock of remembrance may make you break out in a cold sweat. If your body begins to shake, leave whatever you are doing and sit down quietly somewhere."

I knew exactly what he meant.

The bike shop owner came over to me and asked if I was OK.

"I'm sorry," I said, "I cannot get my legs to move. I have to get off the bike. I was warned about this."

John and the shop owner helped me from the machine and we went into his waiting room to have a cup of tea together.

"What the hell can I do about this?" I asked. "I love the Harley but if that's going to happen everytime I get on it, I won't be able to ride it."

The shop owner looked at me and said, sympathetically, "How about selling it to a friend?"

"Like who?"

"I can put your Harley into the showroom and sell it for you. I would want a percentage of the money out of the sale."

"OK," I said. "Then what?"

"I also have an ex-Army as-new 500cc Indian motorcycle which I've just finished respraying a nice shade of maroon. All the great features of the Harley with saddlebags and, only done 1500 miles! There are about as many Indians as Harley Davidsons in the US Army but, the big difference is, they are better used with a sidecar as they have reverse gear and a bigger tank."

He smiled and sipped his cup of tea.

"Now then, Mr Walshe, I've told you all this not to convince you but, to give you an alternative. Here comes the 'punch-line'. I am prepared to take your machine as a trade-in and clean swap it for my beautiful Indian over there." He pointed through the glass partition at the gleaming motor bike waiting my inspection. It certainly appealed to me.

"What do you say to that?"

I considered his words carefully.

"I am interested but, I'll have to be sure that I won't have the same reaction when I sit on the Indian." I answered.

He placed his cup on the small table and stood up.

"Please, let me show you around it."

We walked into the showroom and I stood beside the Indian. I felt fine.

"Sit on it." he suggested.

I threw my right leg across the polished leather saddle and gripped the handlebars. I sat, feeling exalted and comfortable.

We shook hands and I became the proud owner of the beautiful maroon painted Indian motorbike.

About 2 hours later I rode the machine back to Madge's place with John in close attendance all the way. When we sat down inside the house the thought came to me of something my father, Ken Carr had said to me a long time ago about falling off a horse.

'When you get thrown from a horse, you have to get up and get back on, otherwise you will never have the nerve to ride again'

He was right of course and that wisdom applied equally to my situation here.

Later that night we went back to John's house where my other mates Brian and Peter were also. We had a few drinks and in the course of conversation I mentioned that I would have my discharge from the RAAF very soon. After that, I intended to travel north to New South Wales to find employment. Victoria held nothing but bad memories for me and, since the family had virtually disowned me, I had no reason to stay here.

The memory of my early years with Yurana was the happiest of my life and that was all up north. So it was decided, I would go north and live a happier life.

On St.Patrick's Day 1948 I received my discharge papers. I was now officially an adult and a civilian. I didn't have much money but I did have 4 petrol coupons. I had no idea what I would find as employment in Sydney but, this was to be my life's second adventure.

I decided to leave Melbourne on Friday. As it was now Tuesday, I began to collect my belongings for the trip north. My school friend, Peter Shaw told me since being discharged from the Army, he wanted to travel round Australia. As a civilian he'd been unable to settle down and asked to come with me on the first leg of the trip.

"Of course, Pete," I said. "I'd be glad of the company. Be here on Friday morning and — bring your petrol coupons!" He laughed loudly.

Over the next few days I made a point of visiting many of the places I wished to remember in Melbourne. One of them was the Navy League Training Depot where I had learned all kinds of marine skills and tried to become the man who, unfortunately, the family had no time for. Upon visiting the depot hall I found that a plaque had been installed with the names of past cadets who had served in the recent war. Those who were killed had 'K.I.A.' after the name and those who survived had 'S.' after the name.

I was stunned to see that my own name was up there, listed with an 'S' after it. Most surprising of all was the fact that, of all the boys who went to serve, I was the only one who'd joined the RAAF.

Back at Madge's place I sat on my bed and contemplated my life so far. The past 10 years had been spent with people I didn't like and who despised me — my own family. I had been wanting to get away from them for a long time. Tomorrow, I would achieve that break.

Although the thought made me extremely nervous and apprehensive, I also felt confident of the outcome.

The hardest thing for me to deal with now was becoming a civilian. Having been part of a huge team for so long it was going to be difficult to be just me, Gerry Walshe against the world.

In the morning I went outside and looked over my Indian bike. I took a rag and wiped the dew from the saddle and handlebars and began to load my belongings into the saddlebags and tied my kitbag onto the pillion seat. The fact that I was still wearing my blue uniform didn't worry me at all as it was woollen and would keep me warm on the Indian.

Besides that, I had my US bomber jacket from the PX canteen at Clark Field — fleecy lined leather and designed to eliminate the wind.

I said 'goodbye' to Marge and Patricia and thanked them for their kindness in my hour of need. I said I would write to let her know of my new life up north. I kicked over the big motor and pulled my Army surplus goggles down over my eyes.

Peter and I rode through the streets of Melbourne and out onto the Hume Highway going north. It was a beautiful, warm day and we rode at modest speed, not wishing to break any speed laws. Heading for a new life, we didn't look back. We had no regrets.

I felt at last like a dog off the leash for the first time. I was free to plan my life as I wanted it to be. I breathed in the sweet, fresh air and reflected upon how lucky I was at the age of 21 years to be able to begin a new life. I had been given a second chance and, by God, I would make a success of it.

I had no doubt of this.

ACKNOWLEDGEMENTS.

I finished writing this book back in 1985. I have to admit, not really being a trained author nor academic, I just wrote what came to mind from years of experience. It wasn't until 2010 that I answered an advertisement published by Goldman Manuscript Services that I got a positive response to my request for somebody to at least read my 'ramblings' and give me an honest assessment of the chances of having it turned into a book.

Mike and Glenys Smith read my raw writings and decided that there was a story in there that needed to be aired. For this I am eternally grateful. For anyone else who has a personal story which they think merits consideration for publication, I can wholeheartedly recommend you contact Mike and Glenys. (See the fly-leaf for information.)

Having dodged live ammunition on three occasions, been slammed by a Buick car at speed and survived all manner of health hazards, I reckon I'm doing OK for an old bloke of 84. I still get a thrill from wandering around Air Museums and talking 'shop' to other odd fellows connected with flying.

I trust that you, the reader, have enjoyed the story so far. There could even be a sequel. I'm working on that right now.

Gerald K. Walshe
Malua Bay.   2010.